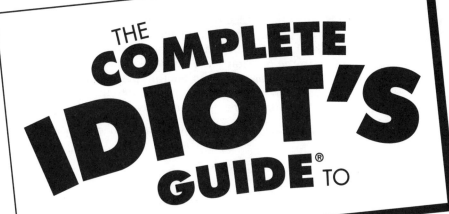

THE COMPLETE IDIOT'S GUIDE® TO

Improving Your IQ

by Richard Pellegrino and Michael Politis

alpha books

A Pearson Education Company

Copyright © 1999 by Richard Pellegrino and Michael Politis

THE COMPLETE IDIOT'S GUIDE TO & Design are registered trademarks of Pearson Education, Inc.

International Standard Book Number: 0-02-862724-5
Library of Congress Catalog Card Number: 98-88701

03 02   8 7 6 5 4 3

Interpretation of the printing code: the rightmost number of the first series of numbers is the year of the book's printing; the rightmost number of the second series of numbers is the number of the book's printing. For example, a printing code of 99-1 shows that the first printing occurred in 1999.

Printed in the United States of America

Note: This publication contains the opinions and ideas of its authors. It is intended to provide helpful and informative material on the subject matter covered. It is sold with the understanding that the author and publisher are not engaged in rendering professional services in the book. If the reader requires personal assistance or advice, a competent professional should be consulted.

The authors and publisher specifically disclaim any responsibility for any liability, loss or risk, personal or otherwise, which is incurred as a consequence, directly or indirectly, of the use and application of any of the contents of this book.

Contents at a Glance

Part 6: Behave Yourself   **231**

Contents

Foreword

What's the most powerful muscle in the body? The one between the ears—the brain, an organ of enormous complexity, which we use so little of. The world needs the very best thinking possible from every person on the planet. It's critical that we all learn to think more effectively: The world is changing too rapidly and the challenges ahead of us are too huge to leave our collective brain power unused. Yet little is being done to help people learn to be effective thinkers. Of the thousands of hours spent in schools, almost none are spent learning how to think better.

Realizing this, I'm delighted to see this *Complete Idiot's Guide to Improving Your IQ* because it provides a practical guide to understanding more about how your brain works and how you can use it to accomplish your life goals and help build a better world.

If we could tap into the powers of the mind, we would not only be smarter, but also more effective, wiser, and happier. The difference between "normal people" and "geniuses" is not in the genes, but in ourselves: It is the degree to which we effectively use our brain's abilities to accomplish what we need to get done.

So, how do you learn to use your brain effectively? Tools. This book provides you with a working knowledge of how your brain works so you can use it for your *own* purposes. Biomedical research has moved neuroscience ahead at a pace that would amaze Einstein himself! Do you have to be a brain surgeon to understand how the brain works or to radically improve your ability to use it? The good news—no. The other news—it takes more than inherited smarts or good intentions to understand your brain and to tap its enormous potential.

The Complete Idiot's Guide to Improving Your IQ provides the cutting edge of neuroscience and psychological research. The authors show, in language that respects the brain *and* the reader, how the brain works. Beyond this, it is a body, mind, *and* spirit "training" manual, offering practical methods to help you develop your senses about the world around you, the people who inhabit it, and yourself. The authors show how you can be maximally effective within the context of your desired goals—in part by learning to "think your way" into a more effective, actualizable vision of the world.

I encourage you to try the exercises in this book, and my wish for you is that they will open up the wonderful world of your mind and positively change your life. The authors cannot guarantee that one read of this book will up your IQ by 200 points. But they *do* promise that you will become more intelligent in ways that matter to *you*. It's hard work, but it will seem like play; and when work and play are indistinguishable, magic happens. Read on, and see what kind of magic can happen for *you*.

Joyce Wycoff

Joyce Wycoff is an author, speaker, and founder of the Innovation Network, **www.thinksmart.com**. Her publications include *Mindmapping: Your Personal Guide to Exploring Creativity and Problem-Solving* (1991) and *Transformation Thinking, Tools, and Techniques that Open the Door to Powerful New Thinking for Every Member of Your Organization* (1995). She has co-authored *To Do... Doing... Done! A Creative Approach to Managing Projects and Effectively Finishing What Matters Most* (with G. Lynne Snead, 1997) and *Breakthrough Selling: Customer-Building Strategies from the Best in the Business* (with Barry Farber, 1992). She has been helping people learn to increase their personal effectiveness through the creative use of techniques that improve their thinking effectiveness.

Introduction

You picked up this book because you are intelligent. You want to grow, in body, mind, and spirit, and that is all the brain asks of any aspiring Pilgrim who wants to reach the Promised Land, kingdom, or dimension called "enlightenment."

This is an intense book, but it does not demand that you leave your job, spouse, or circle of friends to become one of "the chosen." We *all* are the chosen, as long as *we* chose to become the Einsteins, the ones with "da brains" who get the job done in ways that are innovative, effective, fast, and enormously enjoyable.

First, a confession from the writers. When we first took on the job of writing this book, we had no idea what we would write about. We had no idea that the application of the very ideas that we propose here would move *us* up to levels of vitality and intellectual intensity that we never imagined possible.

And another thing is worth considering very carefully. Everything in this book is proven, scientifically. In the following pages, you will not find egotistical motivational opinion, lofty untested cerebral postulates, or formulas for making a perfect life from the Wizard Publications at www.Oz.com. If there was no basis in real scientific, sociological, or medical fact, the idea in question went into the shredder.

In Part 1, we find our feet, conceptually and scientifically. We ask, "What is intelligence?" We then provide a widespread, functionally applicable definition that so many others have not thought of before—straight out of Webster's dictionary. How do we measure effective intelligence? How do "lower" animals on the evolutionary chain use analogs of our human intelligence, and what happens to the circuitry of *our* brains when we become learners and doers rather than spectators? We'll start off with road maps of the nervous system as seen with the eye, the light microscope, and the electron microscope. We'll also show how we can learn faster from mistakes, and recover faster from disease or trauma-inflicted deficits in brain circuitry. The brain is sort of like a computer. And, directly and indirectly, we are the best repairmen and programmers available.

In Part 2, we consider the input that our brain uses for raw data. An army is as effective as the intelligence service that feeds it information, and the Central Intelligence Agency field workers in our possession are biologically superior to anything built by NASA. How does the eye convert strange electromagnetic waves into the wondrous sensations that we call light? How do the ears on the side of our heads allow us to hear virtually every kind of sound made, from frequencies as low as 20 cycles per sec to as high as 20,000, and to determine where that sound is coming from, to one degree arc? How do we feel the other sensations: touch, vibration, taste, smell, and "electrical vibrations" (which are very, very real)? What is the sensation of pain and why is it the opposite side of pleasure?

Our sensors are highly specialized and the processing centers on the way up to the cerebral cortex are complex. But, amazingly enough, we can understand them with contemporary neuroscience, and we can modify those senses in ways we all already use. That's the good news. The *better* news—we can become supersensory machines, so that we are ultra-highly informed about our environment (in terms of things *and* people), and a better informed mind is *always* a smarter and more effective one.

In Part 3, we take up processing. What happens when information reaches the cerebral cortex, the place where we do our "thunkin'?" Sight, sound, touch, vibration, position sense, taste, and smell all combine to give us a multimedia "movie in the mind" that changes every second. It is also a movie that we pre-write in our heads and modify for the needs at hand.

Special skills are needed to become superprocessors. One is the art of listening, which is more than just shutting your mouth and letting the other guy yap away. Then there is memory, which involves how the lessons learned and associative connections made are stored. Learning strategies and sites of memory storage will be discussed.

We will provide you with some very powerful ways to improve your memory skills so that you can use your brain for the higher functions of learning. And speaking of action…how does a mental plan become action? How does the brain make a muscle move so a limb moves ahead or pulls back in accord with the desired plan? It's not just about one brain cell, one muscle, and one action. We also anticipate actions, whether we think we do or not. Training ourselves to anticipate actions and results DOES make things happen the way we want them to. This is not motivational propaganda; it is biological fact.

What we do when we "talk back" to the world is the subject at hand in Part 4. As any athlete knows, there is an intelligence to muscular action. Driving a fast ball in for the third strike isn't just about tossing the ball into the catcher's glove, it has to be planned and executed. Talking back is also about communication because life is a constant, interpersonal give-and-take between people.

And there is the autonomic nervous system, the "involuntary" part of the nervous system (autonomic nervous system), which controls blood pressure, sweat glands, pupil size, and visual perception. If you think you can hide what you are really thinking, think again. Knowledge of the autonomic nervous system can tell you if the noble desperado who wants you to ride with him is a liar or if you are a liar yourself. "If you live outside the law, you have to be honest," is the credo that reminds every rugged individualist that the "what-goes-around-comes-around" theory is a rule. Knowing what you and others really mean can save you much unnecessary pain and free up brain space for intelligence development.

Emotion and thinking are not exclusive processes; they are very integrated. As will be shown in Part 5, a passionless person cannot be an intelligent one, and neither can somebody possessed by an emotional extreme. It is a matter of balance *and* intensity. There are specific parts of the brain that deal with the intelligence of emotion. They are found in the "limbic" system, which used to be considered a primitive part of our brain left behind by evolution and is thought to be scheduled for the genetic shredder in a few hundred years.

But research in the last decade has proven that these limbic areas are extremely important in helping us learn, motivating us to learn, and remembering what we have learned. We also talk about "the Zone," a condition of "state" in which body, mind, and spirit are all working together at maximal speed. "The Zone" is a real place—the place from which we are maximally intelligent. It creates a situation in which we get everything we want and need, with maximal efficiency. There are very real biological correlates that can be measured and can tell us that we are in "the Zone."

In Part 6, we tackle consciousness. The "conscious" brain is what we identify as the part with which we think, feel, and act. The "unconscious" mind creates images, programs, and circuits that never rest and are "beyond our control." Or are they? In the last five years, the innovative research in cognitive neurobiology tells us, with hard facts, that we can identify, watch, and modify the unconscious mind; and we can make it our servant rather than our silent master. And, oh, what a powerful servant it can be.

This book cannot be read in one night, but give it an evening and we think you will continue. Your comments and suggestions, good or bad, are welcomed. "The truth shall set you free," and we invite you to share our freedom with us.

Extras

Throughout the text, you'll find helpful nuggets of information offered to help you in your quest to improve your IQ. Here's what to look for:

Mind This!

Warnings and cautionary tips that help you avoid common pitfalls or misunderstandings about how the brain and intelligence works.

What Does It All Mean?

Definitions of technical or frequently misunderstood terms and concepts.

Brain Food

Factoids and anecdotes that clarify a point, provide a special insight, or point you to further ways that you can improve your IQ.

Use Your Head

Tips and common-sense advice to incorporate into your day-to-day life—they'll help you become an Einstein in no time.

Part 1
What's So Smart About Being Intelligent?

Intelligence—what does this word really mean? Conventional wisdom equates intelligence with scoring high on tests, maybe even being a little nerdy. But being intelligent is something much more complex—it's not just about what you know. Instead, it's about what you do with what you know. Sure, you need to gather information as you go through life. But the real trick of intelligence is how you use that information to achieve your personal goals.

In Part 1, you'll learn about the building blocks of intelligence—the toolkits you need as you go about your decision-making life. And you'll learn how to maximize that toolkit, so you can take charge of your life and your learning process. Along the way, you'll discover why the IQ test is a very misleading measure of your intelligence.

Most importantly, you'll learn the basics of your brain's intellectual "wiring"—the mechanics of how your brain gathers and processes information, and how to stream-line and improve that wiring to maximize your learning potential. Finally, you'll be introduced to the concept of "effective intelligence"—a way to take your natural brain power and harness it to achieve whatever goals you choose to set for yourself and your life.

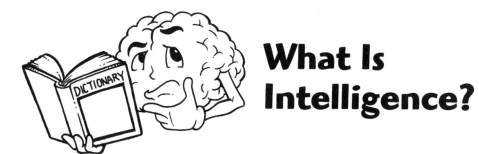

Chapter 1

What Is Intelligence?

In This Chapter

➤ Intelligence is really effectiveness

➤ Be your own Einstein

➤ The importance of being intelligent in many ways

You have a brother who is smarter than you; a friend who does better on the mid-term exam; a job that feels like it's over your head; or a vision that needs some cranial power before you can blast it up to the stars. You find yourself identifying with the Scarecrow in *The Wizard of Oz*, and you'd like to find the "great and glorious" wizard to give you a brain.

No need to go searching for the Yellow Brick Road. As the scarecrow discovered, you really don't need a brand new brain. You can increase IQ—your *intelligence quotient*—with methods that stop short of full-scale neurosurgery. All it takes is a little time and effort on your part.

Defining Intelligence

Intelligence is more than being able to recite Shakespeare after one read or to do calculus in your head. Webster defines intelligence as, "the ability to apprehend interrelationships of the perceived facts (and situations) in order to appropriately guide actions toward desired goals." In other words, the intelligent person is able to identify a problem and find its optimum solution. Hence, intelligence is *effectiveness*.

Mind This!

Intelligence is more than just book learning or the ability to score well on tests. It's no use at all unless you can harness it in your quest to achieve real-life goals.

For example, a *smart* businessman can add figures quickly in his head. A *clever* businessman can flatter you with praise while stealing your ideas. An *intelligent* businessman knows that if he can create a win-win situation with you, he can establish a money-making relationship that will extend far beyond this one sale or deal. This way of understanding intelligence democratizes it and makes it accessible to all.

Nature or Nurture?

But, you say, some people are born smart or raised smart. You have to have parents who met at a MENSA meeting and who raised you on Mozart and Shakespeare instead of Reba McEntyre and the cartoon channel; or intelligence depends on inheriting the right karma from a past lifetime. Well, could be...but probably not.

Human effort in the face of adversity has shown that the brain can, in effect, rewire itself: Even after nerve injury and degeneration, well-motivated patients almost always improve. Ask Heidi Von Belz, a Hollywood stunt double who was completely paralyzed by a neck injury in 1980 and found herself breathing through a respirator. Today, she is walking on her own two feet, living her own life again, her way. Or talk to Christopher Reeve, who broke his neck in a fall from a horse. His comeback has been astonishing. These people, and countless others in the annals of medicine, demonstrate conclusively that the ability to maintain—even regain—function has as much to do with strong motivation as with the number of nerve cells that survive a spinal cord injury.

Want more hard proof from the lab? There are two kinds of fibers in our muscles, red and white. Red muscle fibers enable us to maintain long-term, low stress activity. White muscle fibers are specialized for fast, rapid movements. When an athlete trains for long-distance running, he or she builds more red muscle fibers than white muscle fibers in his calf muscles. A sprinter has more white muscles. If you retrain a marathon runner to be a sprinter, most of the muscle fibers will convert to white muscles. A sprinter's muscles will convert to red muscle if he has a desire to impress his new girlfriend with an Olympic Gold medal in the 30-km event and follows through with it. If either stays at home and watches figure-skating, the calf muscles will degenerate into flab.

"That which does not kill me makes me stronger," wrote Nietsche, and the theme song from *Rosanne* repeats the point. It holds true, particularly when it comes to the most powerful muscle of them all—the brain.

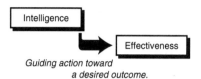

Figure 1.1: The route to effective intelligence.

The Many Facets of Intelligence

Okay, so now you realize that effective intelligence, or E.I., is about more than just thinking fast—it has to do with thinking deeply and creatively. It is commonly measured by something called the IQ (or *intelligence quotient*).

Different Types of Einsteins

But "intelligence" is still a pretty tricky concept—there's more than one kind, after all. There are mathematical Einsteins who can add figures in their heads faster than a calculator; Einsteins who can do theoretical calculus about the origins of the Earth with ease; and more pragmatic Einsteins, who use their skills and intelligence to draw up building plans and build skyscrapers to the sky.

In the field of medicine, a diagnostic Einstein uses the clues of your symptoms to identify your disease; a surgical Einstein wields his scalpel with the skill of a virtuoso; and the research Einstein plays detective in the lab, searching in the world of microbes and viruses to find their nemeses.

What Does It All Mean?

Effective intelligence is our ability to use our minds to creatively answer questions or solve practical problems. If we expand our definition of intelligence to include our ability to be effective, its measure, the IQ, can be replaced by EQ (or *effectiveness quotient*). But EQ is not a number; it's more of a state of mind.

Similarly, in the world of music, there are the brilliant composers who pluck beautiful melodies from the thin air, and extraordinary instrumentalists who take plain notes on a page and convert them to universally powerful emotional experiences. The fact that some of them can't add up a hotel bill or read the reviews of their performances doesn't change their genius, any more than the mathematical Einstein is any less intelligent, simply because he or she can't play the piano. Again, all of these people have one thing in common: they are very effective in what they do.

Mind This!

Single men are baffled by the way a working mom can keep track of the kids, the TV, that monthly report she brought back from the office, and a conversation with her husband—all at the same time. (Married men just thank God they can). And let's not forget the ever-present *woman's intuition*.

Clearly, intelligence covers a lot of conceptual territory, and not everyone starts out with a big dose of every available kind. But all of us have at least a little of each to begin with—it's up to us to develop one, some, or all of the different kinds of intelligence to the best of our abilities.

The EI Hall of Fame

The term *Renaissance Man* has long been used to describe a jack-of-all-trades who is maximally competent in each one. In these politically correct times, it would probably be more appropriate to use the phrase *Renaissance Person.* You could call Woody Allen a Renaissance Person: He's an accomplished comedian and comedy writer; film producer, director, and actor; published author; and jazz clarinet player. In other words, a Renaissance Person makes important contributions in many different areas of endeavor, and is proficient in using many different *kinds* of intelligence.

As we all know, Albert Einstein was a physicist who revolutionized our view of the world. However, he was also a political activist who helped start the League of Nations and championed the war against Nazism in Europe; a human-rights activist who fought racism and bigotry during the McCarthy years; and a musician who played tear-wrenching Mozart and wicked Bach from the bow of his fiddle. But for all his brilliance in these many fields, as a sailor, he kept getting lost and needed the Coast Guard to get him home. Not everyone can make major contributions to so many important fields of endeavor, but all of us have a few areas in which we can excel. All we need to do is to learn how to tap those abilities.

Brain Food

Ben Franklin, the scientist who discovered electricity, was also a folksy satirist who broke into the established English press by using a pen name; engineer of one of the most successful political experiments in history (the United States); a diplomat; and a scholar—as well a homely man who could nonetheless steal the heart of every woman in Philadelphia.

Measuring *Effective* Intelligence

The standard measure of intelligence is calculated by the *IQ test*, which really only measures certain skills, and has been accused of cultural and economic bias (more on that in Chapter 2). In addition to these flaws, the IQ test is a relatively static measure—although it measures specific skills, it doesn't register your ability to *use* those skills. EI, however, is a more dynamic concept. It takes into account your success in achieving goals. Remember, the ability to guide action toward desired goals is a key part of the definition of intelligence. Your EI quotient is constantly evolving as you define and redefine the goals you choose to pursue.

To Be Maximally Effective, Keep an Open Mind...

In school, you're trained to incorporate information according to reflex—to pigeonhole it into general categories. And people tend to carry this habit over into daily life. When you hear Michael Bolton, you think soft, easy-listening. When you hear Willie Nelson, you think "classic country," while Shania Twain makes you think of the category "new country." What about the Grateful Dead? If you remember their phenomenally successful 1967 "American Beauty" album, you know that the musical styles on it range from hillbilly country to blues to rock to a cappella folk to riffs that could be called classical. And how about the Beatles? Would you put the entire "Abbey Road" album into one musical genre?

Similarly, we label politicians as being on the right or the left, but ignore the fact that most of the time a politician will take a conservative position on one issue, but a more liberal stance on others. *No* politician is a staunch Democrat or Republican on *all* the issues. But we pigeonhole them—and all the other information we encounter in our daily lives—because it is a convenient way of organizing tremendous amounts of information from our external environment.

When you are *thinking creatively*, you open the door between these individual pigeon holes that you customarily use and allow your acquired information to intermix freely. Only by doing this can you begin to see new connections between discrete bodies of knowledge and come up with whole new ways of looking at the world.

Everything relates to everything else, in some way. Although compartmentalizing information, people, and ideas is often useful when you're trying to organize the information that floods into your life from TV, books, conversations, and observations, it nevertheless tends to limit your perspective and possibilities. Breaking down those compartment walls opens up those possibilities, and lets you see the world in whole new ways, as in Example 1.1:

What Does It All Mean?

Thinking creatively means being willing and able to consider information without pigeonholing it. It's a way of thinking that forces you to look for new relationships between perceived facts, without relying upon preconceived assumptions.

Example 1.1:

Question: The kidney is part of what system?

    A. Urinary

    B. Cardiovascular

    C. Skeletal

    D. Central Nervous System

    E. All of the above

Answer: E

    But keep in mind:

    A is correct *anatomically*—because the kidney is connected to the ureter, which drains into the bladder.

    B is correct *hormonally*—because if blood flow to the kidney is low, a hormone called renin is released, which causes an increase in blood volume and a constriction of blood vessels.

    C is correct *biochemically*—because vitamin D is converted to its active form in the kidney, and kidney problems cause osteoporosis (bone breakdown).

    D is correct for *alternative medicine*—because in Chinese medicine, the kidney and its acupuncture meridian system controls fluids, and the brain is part of the fluid system.

When physiology students are asked the question in our example, they all answer A on the first day in class. By the end of the six-week course, however, they have acquired much more data about the human body, as well as new ways of organizing that information; and find it necessary to answer "all of the above."

An open mind means more than just breaking down the compartment walls between information categories, however. It also means that your mind is open to *receive* information from as many sources as possible.

...and Gain Control of Your Communication Skills

So, a big part of intelligence is the aquisition of information. And another major contributor is the creative synthesis of the information you've acquired. But once you've done *that*, what next? How do you get from just *having* knowledge, to using it to get to your desired goal? The answer is communication. Obviously, ideas that stay trapped in your brain are not particularly useful. Brain output has to be expressed, and you can do that both verbally and non-verbally. Most people think of communication in terms of words, but actually our body language often speaks the loudest.

Alan Alda used a little of Groucho's comic genius in his characterization of Hawkeye Pierce in the hit TV show, "MASH." See how a bit of dialogue from that show illustrates how shifting the context of a piece of information brings the humor to life. In this scene, Hawkeye is given an arterial graft to be implanted into a patient with an open chest by Nurse Kelly, a Polynesian woman. The artery is the wrong size; too small.

> Hawkeye: "Kelly, I wanted Rigatoni. This is spaghetti."
>
> Kelly: "Doctor, I'm half Hawaiian and half Chinese. Could you put that in ethnic terms I understand?"
>
> Hawkeye: "A small eggroll."
>
> Kelly: "Thank you…we don't have one."

Brain Food

"Last night I shot an elephant in my pajamas…what he was doing in my pajamas, I'll never know." Groucho knew how to use a context-shift in a joke to make it transcend the merely funny and make it immortal. But you can't focus only on his talent with words—you have to consider the grease-paint, cigar, and great backup music from Harpo, as well. All of these elements were a necessary part of his classic comic delivery.

The message gets across with much more clarity and vitality than "I need a one centimeter graft and this one is 80 percent too small." As for how important this is in the real, non-TV world: Ask any clinician who is trying to relate important medical information to a patient who can't spell *biology*.

The point is, the more flexible and creative you can be in your communication techniques, the more effective you will be in attaining your goals, no matter what they are.

The Least You Need to Know

➤ Intelligence is the ability to apprehend interrelations among facts and to use it to guide action toward the achievement of your desired goals.

➤ Although there are many different kinds of intelligence and genius, all intelligent people and geniuses have one thing in common: they are effective at attaining goals.

➤ Intelligence is not just something you're born with—your education and experiences also contribute to your intelligence.

➤ Open-mindedness to new information and to new ways of understanding that information is key to increasing your effective intelligence.

➤ Knowledge alone is not enough—*effective* intelligence requires effective communication as well.

How Should We Measure Intelligence?

In This Chapter

➤ Why the IQ test was developed

➤ Some limitations of the test

➤ An explanation of what an IQ test is

➤ The qualities that are measured

➤ Having the tools isn't enough

"How smart or dumb you are depends on where you're standing," country speedster Burt Reynolds said to New York actress Sally Field in "Smokey and the Bandit." In other words, intelligence is *context-sensitive*. Sally did not recognize Hank Williams, a sure sign of stupidity out in the "sticks," but of little consequence in the city. In the context of Sally Field's life, Hank was just not very significant.

With people living in so many different circumstances and facing so many different challenges, is there one consistent way to measure intelligence that is independent of circumstance? Is there a single common denominator? Let's take a closer look.

IQ, a Test Taken Out of Context

"It doesn't take a genius to figure that out!" is something we say all the time. But what is a genius, anyway? How do we measure genius? The knee-jerk answer—the IQ test: a pencil and paper exam that gives us a number at the end, our *intelligence quotient*. But the IQ test ranks us against each other instead of measuring our ability to handle the tasks at hand.

It sounds so clean, so mathematical, so *scientific*. Everyone takes the same test, no one cheats, and you can show how smart or dumb people are with a single number. But this composite number does not tell the whole story. There are other things to consider.

The original IQ test was developed by psychologist Alfred Binet and psychiatrist Theophile Simon in 1904. It was intended for use by the French Ministry of Education to distinguish between mentally retarded and normal school children so that kids in need of special care could be identified early. Later, in 1912, the German psychologist, W. Stern, argued successfully that the test score should be divided by the chronological age of the test subject, and the Intelligence Quotient was born. It was a test to see if someone had the mental *tools* for what we call "effective intelligence."

The original test, with its original intention, made sense: Why send a deaf kid to music school if he can't hear the notes? But as the results came in, someone got the idea of using the new standardized test to identify the *smart* kids, the children who thought faster than most of the others in particular subjects such as identification of forms, similes, differences, word identification, vocabulary, calculating numbers, and so on. And the results came to be used to "fast-track" the students who scored highest on the test.

Suddenly people began to feel that the person with the biggest and fastest tools would win. Is this valid?

Brain Food

The inventors of the original IQ test would be appalled by the way the modern version is used in schools. "We are of the opinion that the use of our scale will not be its applications to normal pupils, but rather to those of inferior grades of intelligence," said Alfred Binet in 1908.

Tool Time

A hammer is nothing but an unwieldy piece of metal and wood. It is only useful if you

    a) have one available.

    b) have a task that requires its use.

    c) know how and when to use it.

    d) pick the thing up and do the job.

A deficiency in any one of these areas can affect outcome. Take c), for example. If you're looking to comb your hair, a hammer is pretty useless to you. But sometimes, a deficiency in one area can be made up by outstanding performance in another. For example, if you don't have a hammer, you can still drive a nail: If need be, you can use a rock or the heel of your shoe. What's true about the hammer is also true about the tools measured in the IQ test. Having them doesn't get you very far if you can't, or won't, use them.

As the hammer example makes plain, if you restrict yourself to measuring the number, quality, and type of tools you own, you really don't have enough information to judge how you'll perform in a problem-solving situation. Hence, IQ alone cannot measure how you *guide action toward your desired goal*—one aspect of the definition of intelligence.

Mind This!

A resting horse has a normal heart rate of between 30 and 45 beats per minute. A well-conditioned horse has a resting heart rate a few beats lower than that. But you don't give a horse the winning trophy before the race starts because of a low resting heart rate.

A Hammer Is a Hammer Is a Hammer...Or Is It?

And, of course there are all sorts of hammers: There are ball-peen hammers, narrow head hammers, broad head hammers, magnetized hammers, smooth head hammers, serrated head hammers, hammers combined with hatchets, roofing hammers, and the list goes on.

Now, suppose you're alone with your family in the wilderness, and you need to build a shelter and gather your own fuel and building materials. If you're asked to pick the best hammer for the job at hand, you'll almost certainly choose something like the hatchet/hammer because it has multiple uses and would best serve your purposes.

On the other hand, if you're a roofing contractor, you'll probably consider the hatchet dangerous and unnecessarily clumsy. For your purposes, a magnetized roofing hammer would be the best choice. We're back to Burt Reynolds here: *How smart or dumb you are depends on where you're standing.* If you're standing in the middle of the woods, you'd be a fool if the only tool you supplied yourself with were a roofing hammer, and you'd be equally foolish to stick to a hatchet when laying roofing tile. The intelligence of your choice of tools can only be adequately measured in the context of the job to be done. But the IQ test doesn't have any way of recognizing this.

The standard IQ test has other failings as well. It doesn't take generational or gender differences in test subjects into account, for example. To show how these factors make a difference in the ways we process information, take a look at the following multiple-choice question (not from the actual IQ test):

Chris Carter is:

a) A relative of a former U.S. President

b) A football player

c) A writer

What Does It All Mean?

Intelligence is really determined by a combination of factors: Available tools + desire + ability to maximize effectiveness of the available tools = outcome.

Although the test-giver may only acknowledge one correct answer to this test, all three are actually correct. Your individual choice of answer is likely to be generational- and gender-dependent. Because ex-President Jimmy Carter has relatives named Christopher, this might be the answer chosen by baby boomers who were old enough to vote in the 1970s. The football fan (a largely male group, even in this day and age) might recognize the name of the Minnesota Vikings' wide receiver, who has been doing a great job for the team in recent years. And any twentysomething "X-Files" fan knows the name of the writer who created the show that gives his or her earthbound life meaning.

I'd Rather Be a Hammer Than a Nail...

Brain Food

Measures of intelligence have taken a wide variety of forms throughout the history of humankind. Today, some of those measures are pretty hard to believe. In ancient times, the size of your Roman nose was considered to be a sure-fire indicator of your intelligence and effectiveness. If only hook-nosed comic, Jimmy Durante, were born 1800 years earlier!

Nevertheless, people love to compare themselves to others. We live in a competitive world, after all, and we are constantly being ranked by ourselves and others. The IQ is an easy way to make such comparisons. But the problem is with the criteria that are used to *make* those comparisons—does the IQ test really give us the best way to decide if one person is better than another for the specific task at hand?

For its time, standardized IQ testing was not a bad idea, considering the other measurements of intelligence that preceded it in general use. Skull measurements, for example, were once used to *scientifically* support the claim that there were intellectual differences among the races. Phrenology (which measures the size and location of bumps on your head and relates them to certain cognitive abilities) was another technique that enjoyed a period of popularity. Hitler took these physiological measures one step further when he extended his definition of the *master race* to external features, such as blonde hair and blue eyes.

Obviously, when compared to those earlier measures, IQ testing was an improvement. But is it useful now? What does it actually measure? And does it tell us anything at all about any person's effective intelligence?

The Rest of the Toolbox

The IQ test measures a number of different elements, each of which requires a specific set of cognitive abilities—what we might call "tool sets." These are:

➤ *Information*: You're asked a series of multiple choice, largely definitional questions about a variety of words, concepts, or topics; and you are scored on the answers you give. The topics are meant to be about things that any reasonably aware person should have absorbed from the social and cultural environment.

Tool Set #1—Language comprehension; ability to store information; ability to retrieve information at will.

➤ *Comprehension*: You're asked to read passages and respond to a series of questions relating to them. These are designed to measure everything from your ability to understand the meaning of proverbs to your ability to make moral and ethical choices that are consistent with societal norms.

Tool Set #2—The ability to draw meaningful abstract generalizations from concrete phrases; the ability to draw clear, concrete behavioral responses from abstractions such as proper moral and ethical behavior.

➤ *Arithmetic*: You are presented with a series of questions requiring you to perform numerical calculations within a time period that doesn't allow for much time to work out the answers on paper.

Tool Set #3—The ability to rapidly manipulate numbers in your head; the ability to intuitively determine whether your answers make sense.

➤ *Similarities*: You're asked to judge 13 paired items and to explain how they are alike.

Tool Set #4—The ability to look at all facets of an object or concept, and find relationships that are not obvious at first.

Use Your Head

Information, comprehension, and vocabulary questions on the IQ test are the areas that are the most susceptible to gender, cultural, and generational biases.

➤ *Digit Span*: You're asked to repeat two series of numbers or digits, one forward and one backward. The series consists of a maximum of nine going forward and eight going backward.

Tool Set #5—Skill at immediate auditory recall, attentiveness, and the ability to weed out unnecessary inputs to concentrate on the task at hand.

➤ *Vocabulary*: You're asked about the meaning of certain words.

Tool Set #6—A broad vocabulary that allows you to pick just the right word for the job.

➤ *Digit Symbol*: This is a timed test. You're given a set of nine symbols; each associated with the numbers 1 to 9. You then see a long list of numbers and are asked to write the matching symbol next to each one.

Tool Set #7—The ability to rapidly assimilate information and perform a new task.

➤ *Picture Completion*: You're shown 21 different pictures, in each of which a significant element is omitted.

Tool Set #8—Attentiveness; the ability to compare an actual picture or situation with a mental image, and then to discern subtle differences.

➤ *Block Design*: You're presented with 10 designs in a booklet. You must then reconstruct these designs by using a set of multicolor blocks in a prescribed period of time.

Brain Food

All the tool kits that the IQ test measures are important, but they are only a small part of the intelligence story. And they can only measure generalized knowledge. That's the trouble with standardized tests of any sort—they assume that we all share certain basic facts and assumptions about the world. This is where the bias creeps in. Some efforts have been made to remove the bias from IQ testing, but they've met with little success so far.

Tool Set #9—The ability to reason and judge through mental and physical trial-and-error; to judge how best to assemble various elements to achieve your goals.

➤ *Picture Arrangement*: You're given eight groups of three pictures each. Each group of three depicts a sequence of events, and you are expected to put them in the right sequential order within a designated period of time.

Tool Set #10—The ability to sequence.

➤ *Object Assembly*: You're given four jigsaw puzzles to assemble.

Tool Set #11—The ability to analyze a task visually and coordinate it with simple assembly skills.

As you can see, the test does not measure effective intelligence per se, but it does measure *some* of the tools you need.

The Least You Need to Know

➤ How smart or dumb you are depends on where you're standing.

➤ The IQ test was developed to measure abnormally *low* intelligence.

➤ Effective intelligence requires the ability to *use* a wide variety of tools.

➤ The IQ test measures some, but not all, of the tools necessary for effective intelligence.

Chapter 3

Tools Don't Do the Job, People Do the Job

In This Chapter

➤ Complexities of building your life

➤ Knowing what you want

➤ Interacting with others

➤ Some simple ways to make life easier

Having bigger and better tools is great, but it doesn't necessarily mean that you can do the job they're designed to handle. Remember, being able to get the job done is half the definition of intelligence.

Imagine that you live on a planet inhabited by millions of other life forms. Imagine that you learned to live side-by-side with the most powerful of this planet's species, getting fat off of its garbage. Imagine that you learned to do this so well that you never had to evolve, not even over the course of a million years. Imagine, in other words, that you are a cockroach on planet Earth.

In a world where a hundred species become extinct every day, the cockroach remains as it has always been. It comes out in the dark, can eat anything produced by humans, and has learned to crawl faster than any human can swat it.

The roach, of course, wouldn't score very high on an IQ test, but it certainly has at least a simplified form of effective intelligence: Its goal is survival, and it certainly gets *that* job done effectively. Our lives are much more complex than this, and we want to have just a tad more fun, so we need a few more higher-level learning skills than the cockroach has. This chapter will look at just a few of the higher-level skills you need if you want to live a fulfilling life.

You Can't Always Get What You Want

We've all heard the adage: "Ignorance is bliss," but it usually isn't true. In fact, ignorance is often very dangerous. So much so that it's a condition that is strictly avoided by your brain. For that particular organ, another adage is far more appropriate: "The more (information), the merrier." And for that reason, your brain is constantly sampling the environmental soup with its multiple sense organs.

The "tool sets" measured by the IQ test involve information retrieval, processing, and motor or verbal output. In other words, they measure skills our brain has at its disposal to sample and analyze that environmental soup. But we need more than these skills in our day-to-day lives. We all know of a few Brainiacs from our school days who never seemed to manage to get their lives together once they went out into the "real" world. And we all know a few who were judged *intellectually challenged,* but who went on to make a successful life for themselves. Just having (or not having) the IQ-tested tools is obviously not enough to predict your chances of having a fulfilled life. At least as important is that you can master the complex interactions that constantly occur between you and your environment.

As we've already made clear, the IQ test really only addresses one of the two aspects of intelligence—whether or not you own the tools in the tool box. And having those tools does give you something of an edge (after all, its easier to drive that nail with a hammer than with a rock). But the IQ test fails at predicting how well you can use those tools in the pursuit of your goals.

Well, that raises the question of what we mean by goals, doesn't it? We all have them—some are more difficult to attain than others; some are more basic than others. Like our buddy the cockroach at the beginning of this chapter, we certainly have survival at the top of our list. And, if you want to get Darwinian about it, we probably have "reproduction of the species" hardwired somewhere as well. But those goals only set the stage for what most of us would call really living. Simple survival, for ourselves and our species, is just not enough for a life that feels fulfilled and fulfilling.

Many people have tried to compile lists of these beyond-survival needs, but the one I like the most is one I heard from motivational guru, Tony Robbins. He says that people want certainty in their lives, a sense that they have some idea of what the future holds, and an island of security in a changing world. At the same time, people want variety—after all, too much certainty can be boring. Significance is very important, but this is balanced by the need for love and connection. And most of all, says Tony, people need to grow and contribute.

When you buy a new Jaguar, it's not the hunk of metal that you want. This particularly expensive hunk of metal is simply a vehicle (pardon the pun) that lets you satisfy your need for significance and certainty.

What Does It All Mean?

There's an important difference between your *needs* and the *vehicles* by which you attain them. You may try to meet your need for significance by buying new clothes that make you feel well-dressed or important. The clothes are the vehicle by which you satisfy your need to feel significant.

Moreover, you can satisfy your needs using any one of a variety of *strategies*. For example, your desire for significance can be satisfied by pursuing your own personal development, by being a bully, or by ridiculing others.

What About the Outside World?

So what does all of this have to do with intelligence? Well, true intelligence involves understanding what you really want or need. Without that knowledge, you can't apply yourself to solving the problem of how to get it. It also involves having an understanding of the real wants and needs of others.

Why is this understanding so important? Two reasons. First, your unconscious mind is extremely powerful, and it will always try to act to secure what it has judged to be your most important need(s)—no matter how hard your intellect denies or hides from them. Denial is simply the action of your conscious mind as it tries to thwart unacknowledged, subconscious needs. By consciously re-orienting your actions or goals to be more consistent with the needs defined by your subconscious mind, you become more effective because now you and your subconscious don't work against each other.

Second, there's the benefit of knowing the basic needs of the people around you. After all, you don't live alone in the wilderness—you often need to enlist the help of others to get what *you* want, If you understand their needs, you'll find it easier to get them to work with you in fulfilling your own.

Use Your Head

Sometimes, it is not clear exactly what your goals are. Research on *"split-brain"* patients has shown that the two hemispheres of your brain can have totally different views on things, and can even disagree. One patient, when asked what he wanted to be when he grew up, replied, *"a draftsman"* with the left hemisphere of his brain and said, *"a race car driver"* with his right hemisphere.

Mind This!

Analyze your actions in light of your needs: Are you using the best vehicle? Are you using a constructive strategy? Think about good friends and analyze their behavior in a similar way. Are you beginning to get a handle on predicting behavior?

"Every Scientist Should Know How to Be a Shoemaker"

So said Albert Einstein, the great 20th century physicist. No doubt he came up with this insight back in 1905, when he was barely making enough money to buy the paper and ink on which he worked out his theory of relativity. Or maybe he thought about it when the Nazis seized his bank assets and put an international price on his head in 1933. But these experiences served him well. They gave him perspective, and perspective is one very important intelligence-related skill that standard IQ tests don't measure well.

Putting things in their proper perspective can help us to stay balanced. Coming up with goals is easy, but getting to them takes a bit more skill, not to mention judgment. Without perspective, that judgment is hard to come by—you can't prioritize, judge your timing for best effect, or effectively channel your energy to maximize your chances of reaching your goals.

Fun with Fractions

Ordering your life effectively takes some effort. It certainly requires that you balance the demands of your life so that you can maximize your choices and your energy. It's helpful to think in terms of a *life in thirds* formula when you're organizing your day-to-day life. Here's the basic breakdown:

> 1/3—Work or activity that is expected of you, in accordance to your role or status in your world. For example, if you are a parent, you're expected to perform tasks and fulfill responsibilities related to raising your children. This is work that is assigned to you.

> 1/3—Work or activity that you have contractual obligations to perform. This would be, for example, the tasks and responsibilities related to your job. This is work in which you negotiate and accept the final terms.

> 1/3—Work or activity that you set for yourself, in accordance with your personal desires and for your own personal development. This would be what most people consider playtime or leisure time, hopefully allowing you to express yourself fully.

Every day should have some portion of each third to it. If the role-based aspect of your day's efforts is missing, you lose contact with the larger social world and your place within it. That leads to alienation. Omit the contractual element, and you lose the satisfactions (not to mention the practical utility) of a job well-done and well-compensated. Drop the element of self-expression and you're stuck in an "all-work-and-no-play-makes-Jack–a-dull-boy" syndrome—you're not living and growing, you're just enduring.

And remember, although the "fractions" talk about work, the true Einsteins of the world don't distinguish between work and play. Everything they do has the capacity for providing pleasure, growth, and enrichment.

Balancing Act

The life in thirds formula is only one way to establish a balance in the way you organize your life. Other cultures have developed different ways of accomplishing the same thing. Traditional Chinese medical practitioners, for example, divide the human experience into five basic emotions, each controlled by a different organ system, and each associated with a color. These are:

> Laughter—Heart—Red
>
> Sympathy—Spleen and Pancreas—Yellow
>
> Grief—Lung—White
>
> Fear—Kidney—Blue
>
> Anger/Depression—Liver—Green

Craving or hating one of the five colors is closely correlated with deficiencies or excesses of *chi* (energy) in the corresponding organ system. What emotion are you most often stuck in?

Emotion Can Turn the Gain Up or Down

As humans, we perceive and react to the world around us through our senses and emotions—turning them into conscious thoughts only comes later. Our judgments tend to be based on our emotional responses—to the adequacy or inadequacy of a certain vision of the world or to a particular plan of action.

Understanding and putting your emotions in perspective is one important way to increase your effectiveness in achieving your goals. Uncontrolled emotion can get in your way. Life can be thought of as a constant stream of emotion, a changing tapestry of *states* of mind. Some are positive and desirable, and some are negative and self-destructive. All, however, are powerful. But you have more control over your emotional responses to the world than you might think.

This control is good because the greatest determinant of outcome is your emotional state. With or without a high score on an IQ test, your emotional balance (or lack thereof) can make or break your chances at effectively achieving your goals.

Brain Food

Imagine this. You're taking the children for a Sunday ride in town when a freight train rumbles by, blocking traffic. The kids are fascinated. You study each car as it goes by, and tell stories about all of those nights Woody Guthrie spent riding the rails and writing songs. Now consider this. It's Monday. You're fifteen minutes late for a meeting with your boss on why you're always late. Do you think you're going to look at this freight train in the same way?

For All This, People Still Have the Unquenchable Desire to Build

Coach Bill Parcels brought the 1989 New York Giants to the Super Bowl—a blue-collar, hard-won victory for a team and coach that exemplified the values of the working class. The Giants won many games along the way, and Parcels had ten barrels of Gatorade dumped on his head by his victorious players in the closing moments of the fourth quarter. You would think that Bill would be a happy camper. But no.... according to his wife, Coach Parcels did celebrate after winning the Super Bowl—for a whole 15 minutes. Then he started worrying about how he would win next year's game.

Bill Parcels was suffering one of the unexpected consequences of attaining a goal. Dreams are great things to have, but sometimes—especially if you've been working towards that dream or that goal for a long time, actually achieving it can be something of a letdown. What you should know about flying to the star of your choice is that you will enjoy the ride more than reaching the destination. You're faced with an empty *"So what do I do next?"* feeling the next day.

The Good News

Neurological research explains why we get that sense of "let-down" after achieving success. There are real chemical and structural changes in the brain that happen when we achieve something after hard effort. The levels of certain brain substances increase dramatically, and it is this increase that sets off the rush. Every athlete knows about the endorphin rush of victorious competition. Every student has experienced the post-finals rush of energy that energizes him or her into a blow-out party after the exams are done. The rush comes during the build up to, and the immediate realization of, the success. And when the circumstances that made the rush occur are changed—because you've finally successfully achieved your goal—all those chemicals drop back to normal levels. Coming down off this "natural high" can be difficult.

Due to complex chemical actions in the brain, the endorphin rush is experienced as a privately enjoyed blissful state. Drugs have been used to mimic this response, but they are unsatisfactory replacements for the real thing. In other words, there's no real replacement for the naturally induced "thrill of victory."

What Does It All Mean?

Endorphins are naturally made substances that activate at least three classes of receptors in the brain. During a rush, they and other neurotransmitters (including *noradrenaline* and *serotonin*) increase in the central nervous system (CNS). This activates pleasure centers in the brain.

The Better News

Each time you succeed against or within your environment, you not only experience the thrill of victory, you also learn how to repeat your successful performance. Your brain increases in complexity. More brain cells connect with other brain cells. More circuits are made. More receptors are stimulated. More underused circuits are opened for business. (This will be taken up in greater detail in Chapter 5.) Success has a great effect on your perception of the world—it makes you feel better about yourself and your environment, and it makes you more confident about your ability to succeed in other areas, as well.

Something to Try

Remember a time when you had an enormous success. Close your eyes and try to vividly relive the moment. Reconstructing the sensations is one way to increase your ability to duplicate the moment in your pursuit of future goals. When visualizing, it may help to think about the following questions:

Did you feel light or heavy?

Where in your body was the *center* of your biological mass?

Did you feel like mass or energy?

Did time go by more slowly, faster, or did it exist at all?

Did you find yourself grounded to the earth or the sky?

Were you scared?

Were you more powerful physically, emotionally, and/or socially?

What in your life was most important at that time?

Did you know more than you thought you did?

Did you feel *drained* physically, but lifted spirituality?

Did people feel drawn to your presence?

Identifying the emotional sensations that accompany your successes is as much a tool to be used to increase your effectiveness in attaining goals as any that might be measured by an IQ test. So is understanding just exactly how your body (not just your brain) goes about accumulating and processing information from your environment. Chapter 4 will give you some insights about how the nuts and bolts of your nervous system get into the act.

The Least You Need to Know

➤ Bigger and better tools do not necessarily mean more effective intelligence.

➤ People set their goals according to their perceived needs.

➤ Because effective intelligence involves guiding your action toward a desired goal, you must first know what you want.

➤ Understanding the role of your emotions in guiding your behavior is key to becoming effectively intelligent.

➤ Success is a great incentive to increasing your effective intelligence.

Chapter 4

Slugging It Out— How Even a Snail Can Learn

> **In This Chapter**
>
> ➤ A basic orientation to the building blocks of any nervous system
>
> ➤ How the human nervous system is very much like the snail
>
> ➤ How snails learn
>
> ➤ What happens to the snail nervous system when it learns
>
> ➤ How snails get smarter, and stay that way

Life is complicated. To understand how we handle these complications, we must understand something about the nervous system. But the human nervous system is highly complex, while the mechanics of its operations are more simply described. The nuts and bolts of our neurological processes can be more easily understood if we start out with a description of a simple brain (I'm sure you are aware of a few), and look at how it learns about and adapts to its environment.

Meet Andy, from the species of aquatic snail called *Aplysia.* Andy Aplysia can become a genius among his fellow snails in much the same way that we do. His nerve cells look like ours, release the same kind of chemicals as ours do, and reorganize themselves to adapt to environmental challenges like human nerve cells.

The next three chapters address the nervous system in more detail. It's important for you to understand how the brain works in order to understand the various ways in which you can increase your intelligence. You can read these chapters in any way you wish. If the amount of detail scares you, skim it, and then proceed to Chapter 7, where we look at more practical issues.

So let's begin by taking a closer look at Andy's nervous system.

The Generic No-Name Nervous System: Andy's Inner Workings

A road map of the circuits in the human brain would be pretty hard to read. It would have to take into account the tens of billions of neurons that make up the human brain, the number of connections per neuron (averaging several thousands per neuron), and the quickness of a nerve impulse (60 to 100 meters per second). Add in the approximately 100 *spectator* cells per neuron (they influence neuron-impulse conduction and conduct impulses themselves) and you can see that the human brain's hard drive is megaBIG. But the basic architecture of Andy's much simpler nerve cells is close to our own. Studying Andy will tell us a lot about ourselves.

Although snail nerve cells are not exactly the same as our own, there are enough similarities to make certain generalizations. For example, any nervous system—Andy's or ours—is divided into two general categories, the *peripheral nervous system* and the *central nervous system*. Both contain nerve cells, most of which are similar in structure and function.

What Does It All Mean?

The *central nervous system* consists of the nervous tissue within the brain, spinal cord, and back of the eye. The *peripheral nervous system* consists of the nervous tissue found everywhere else (skin, muscle, ear, and so on).

The Microscopic Players—Underpaid and Underrated

The basic snail and human nerve cell are charged with conveying information from one place to another. In the course of doing this, they will receive input, customize information, and pass it on to the next cells. Consider one of Andy's nerve cells, diagrammed in Figure 4.1.

Figure 4.1: Diagram of a nerve cell.

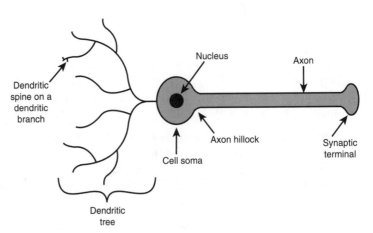

How the Information Is Gathered

Information is retrieved by structures called *dendrites*. The *dendritic tree* contains branches and buds (spines) that have receptors for various *neurotransmitters* (chemical substances that carry messages from one part of the nervous system to another). Some, called *stimulatory neurotransmitters*, change the electrical charge of the dendrite, causing it to send a mini-signal to the axon. Others, called *inhibitory transmitters*, neutralize this charge and effectively turn the signal off. Dendrites receive information from one or the other type of neurotransmitter.

Dendrites are connected to the cell's *soma*. (Soma means "body" in Greek.) This is where the nucleus, or control center, is located, and it's the part of the nerve that feeds the rest of the cell by sending building blocks, neurotransmitters, and essential nutrients out to the dendrites and the axons. The soma also plays a role in gathering information and passing along messages from the dendrites and the axon.

What Does It All Mean?

Neurotransmitters are chemicals released by one nerve cell in a chain, which then diffuse and are picked up by receptors in the next nerve cell. Therefore, the chemical carries information and transfers it from one cell to the next.

Go or No Go

The *axon* is the part of the cell that conducts large-scale electrical signals, called *action potentials*, to the next neuron along the chain. Not all signals received by the axon are passed on, however—it has a decision-making structure (called the *axon hillock*) that determines whether the signal will be allowed to make the trip.

Our friend Andy has a pretty basic nervous system—nowhere near as complex as that found in the average human. For you and me, a single motor neuron (one that goes to the muscles) gets input from about 10,000 other nerve cells. Some of these are *stimulatory* (they have a positive electrical charge), and some are *inhibitory* (they cancel the charge). The decision about which of these signals to send along is made in the axon—on the basis of "majority rule," so to speak. If there are more stimulatory inputs than there are inhibitory ones, you get the action potential. If the inhibitory inputs are in the majority, no action potential is formed.

What Does It All Mean?

An *action potential* is a wave of depolarizing electrical charge that reverses the normal negative charge on the inside of the membrane. This is a fancy way of describing the electrical signal, which passes information from your spinal cord, for example, to the muscles in your arm.

Moving on Down the Line

Once it makes its decision to transmit a signal, the axon conducts the impulse to the next cell in line. That next cell receives the signal in its *synaptic terminal*, which is the end of the line for any individual signal. Inside the terminal are little packages of neurotransmitters called *vesicles*. When the signal (the action potential) arrives, the synaptic terminal releases a neurotransmitter, which it sends along to the dendrites or soma of the next cell in the chain. This is picked up as information by the next cell, which sets up a new signal, passes it along to the soma, and so on down the line.

Before we go on, here are some rules about neurons:

➤ They don't divide. What's there at birth is all there is. Then they start dying.

➤ Usually only one neurotransmitter at a time is released through the axon terminal.

➤ The axon is very fragile. If crushed, it can grow back, but very slowly (1 to 4mm per day).

➤ If a neuron stops being used as an active part of the circuit, it dies.

➤ Dendritic trees can change shape and form; axon terminals can sprout collateral branches.

What a Charge!

As you can see, information is encoded both electrically and chemically by the nerve cells. But where does the electricity come from? The electrical charge comes from *ions* (charged particles) carried in the atomic structure of such elements as potassium, sodium, and calcium. These ions are always passing back and forth through the membrane of the axon, and their movement is determined by whether or not there is an action potential to respond to.

In a *resting* axon—one that doesn't have any action potentials—there is a specific balance in the number of sodium ions (with a positive charge) on the outside of the membrane and potassium ions (also positive) on the inside. The inside of the cell itself carries a natural negative charge, giving the axon a negative charge in relation to the environment outside its membrane. But once an action potential occurs, sodium ions move into the cell, changing the balance of ions and *depolarizing* the cell, so that the charges inside and outside of it are approximately equal.

Depolarization is not a stable condition for the axon, however. Once a certain amount of sodium ions make it into the cell, the border closes down and no more can get in. Shortly after that, potassium ions start feeling crowded, what with all these sodium ion interlopers, and they start streaming out across the cell's membrane until the original ratio of ions inside and outside the cell has been restored. This ongoing shift of positive to negative charges and back again is the source of the electricity used to encode messages.

Once a message is encoded electrically, it can be transmitted to the next nerve cell in the chain by the process described earlier in this chapter. Each message is a discrete unit and is made distinctive by its frequency and its intensity.

The Supporting Cast

You may have noticed that the description of the chain of nerve cells sounds something like the biological equivalent of an electrical wire—it's what electrical impulses travel along to get from one part of your body to another. The analogy isn't far from the truth. And, as with electrical wire, your nervous system needs insulation to keep those sparks from flying off where they don't belong. That insulation is provided by a substance called *myelin*. Although not all nerve cells are myelinated, the myelinated ones are much more secure—the electrical charges they carry move much more speedily and are much less likely to spark or short out.

Therefore, nerves (which are just a large bundle of nerve cells) are divided into *unmyelinated axons* (that is, nerve cells that act like uninsulated wires) and *myelinated axons* (that behave like insulated wires).

What Does It All Mean?

Myelin is a fat-rich substance that insulates the nerve cell and is produced by two different types of cells. In the peripheral nervous system, it is produced by *Schwann* cells, with one cell producing one myelin sheath. In the central nervous system, it is produced by *oligoden-drocytes* (one oligodendrocyte can produce up to forty myelin sheaths).

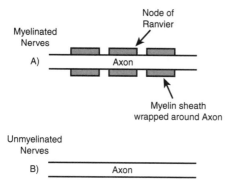

Figure 4.2: Myleniated and unmyleniated nerves.

These myelin sheaths are organized with spaces in-between called the *nodes of Ranvier*. The electrical impulse will jump from space to space, traveling under the myelin in-between. These impulses can travel at speeds of up to 60 to 100 meters per second. If, however, these myelin sheaths are damaged in some way, the conduction of information along these nerves will be slowed down and eventually may even stop.

Mind This!

Multiple sclerosis is a disease of the central nervous system that results in the disappearance of myelin. As a result, information transfer within the brain is disrupted and people can have many different symptoms. In the peripheral nervous sytem, this can happen as well. One disease is called Guillain–Barré syndrome, in which the myelin will suddenly be attacked and begin to disappear. People can be fine when they go to bed and paralyzed when they wake up. Luckily, people almost always recover.

Physical and Chemical Support

Use Your Head

Be careful! Your brain may be only your second favorite organ, as it was for Woody Allen in "Sleeper," but it is certainly your most fragile organ. Any type of brain or spinal cord damage (from trauma, stroke, etc.) will result in irreparable damage to the brain. Brain nerve cells do not grow back, but many scientists are actively working on changing this.

An *astrocyte* is another type of cell in the brain that provides physical support—it has been called the *skeleton* of the brain. In addition, astrocytes maintain a specific environment around synaptic terminals so that excess neurotransmitters are mopped up and ionic concentrations are maintained at the right levels. Astrocytes surround all the blood vessels in the brain, carefully determining which of the blood's chemicals enter the brain. When the brain is damaged, these cells will also form a *scar* in the brain and may inhibit nerve regrowth after brain injury.

If you are confused by all this, don't worry. Move on. We wanted to provide a road map so you could see where we are taking you and why. If you want to know everything about your cerebral instrument (brain), you can start with the bibliography. If you are nauseated from digesting too much information too quickly, we'll gear back into something more dynamic with our host, Andy (Soon-to-be-Amadeus) Aplysia. So strap on your seatbelts as we take a road trip around the nervous system of the snail.

Don't Blame Him, He Was Born a Slug. What's Your Excuse?

The players—20,000 neurons. Their locations—four ganglia (a collection of nerve cell somas) centered around the esophagus.

Andy Aplysia has a tough life. Crawl around underwater, mate with yourself (snails are hermaphrodites), and be sure that your gills are protected and irrigated.

Even though the Aplysia has a very simple nervous system, it still has to learn. It lives in an environment that changes constantly. Dr. Eric Kendell and his colleagues spent the last twenty years examining how snails learn in an effort to see whether we would get any clues about how people learn.

Classically, psychologists have identified several different types of learning and many of these can be found in the snail. Because its nervous system is so simple, Dr. Kendell and colleagues were able to correlate changes within its nervous system to these types of learning. The types of learning we are going to discuss here are sensitization, habituation, and conditioning. In addition, we will talk about short-term learning and long-term learning (lessons that one learns and retains for more than one hour).

Before we begin to look at these in the snail, you need to know a little bit about the snail anatomy.

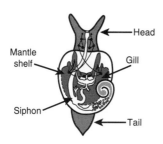

Figure 4.3: Anatomy of a snail: Andy Aplysia

Andy Aplysia's Nervous System

As you can see from the figure, the snail has a head, a tail, and a *gill*. The gill must be kept in moving water in order for the snail to breathe. Next to the gill is a hole called the *siphon*, where the snail expels seawater and waste, and above the siphon is the *mantle shelf*. In the following examples, Dr. Kendell and colleagues examined the gill withdrawal reflex. That is, when you touch the gill or the siphon with a noxious stimulus (a stimulus that the snail finds threatening), the snail will immediately withdraw its gill and siphon to prevent them from being injured. This reflex can be desensitized, habituated, and conditioned, as discussed in the following sections.

33

Sensitization

Imagine you are walking point for Dorothy and the gang on the way to Oz. The Wicked Witch of the West has placed danger everywhere. Your survival depends on your being keenly aware of changes in the environment around you. Every noise may be important and the slightest change will make you jump. Under other circumstances, you may not have heard any of these noises. This awareness is *sensitization*.

How does this sensitization occur? Well, let's take a similar situation for Andy Aplysia.

Andy Aplysia Problem #1: Andy finds himself in a strong current in turbulent waters. Many pieces of debris are floating in this current and Andy has been hit by a few in the siphon. Remember, when the siphon is stimulated, the snail pulls in its gills. Because of the increased debris, he must be particularly sensitive to any disturbance in the current that might signal an impending collision. How does he do this?

Solution: Andy will strengthen the reflexes that are already there. It's not important for you to understand the exact processes that are involved, but you should know the general types of changes that occur in the nervous system. What happens is called *presynaptic potentiation*. Accompanying neurons, called *facilitatory interneurons*, change the amount of chemical released from the sensory neuron (coming from the siphon) in response to a stimulus. More neurotransmitter is released (a stronger signal is sent), prompting a stronger response in the motor neurons that go to the gill, and there is more rapid gill reflex withdrawal.

Figure 4.4: The gill withdrawal reflex.

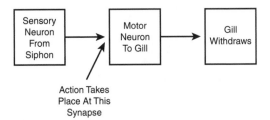

This sensitization can occur extremely rapidly but, as described, it does not last for more than an hour.

Habituation

Have you ever watched satellite or cable television, and forgot to take a flashing icon off of the screen? Suddenly your spouse walks in and gets rid of it. You didn't even notice it. You didn't even know you were married! That is *habituation*. This process happens with smells as well. I am sure you have walked into a room and noticed an unusual odor that is not noticed by the inhabitants because they have habituated to that smell. Habituation is extremely important and is a way for the brain to ignore intrusive stimuli that have become a permanent part of the environment and would otherwise be very distracting.

Andy Aplysia Problem #2: Andy still finds himself in a turbulent environment and is being hit by small pieces of debris so that frequently he is withdrawing his gill too much and not getting enough oxygen. If he continues to respond to every single small piece of debris, he may asphyxiate himself.

Solution: Habituation. On a cellular level, habituation is the exact opposite of sensitization: less neurotransmitter is released from the sensory nerve in response to the stimulus. Eventually, so little neurotransmitter is released that it doesn't cause an action potential in the motor nerve to cause gill withdrawal.

In the laboratory, these experiments are done by stimulating the snail's siphon. Stimulation of the siphon by ten repetitive pokes is considered a training session. Even this brief lesson decreases the strength of gill withdrawal. Andy has learned something instantly, but it only lasts for a few minutes. This memory is short-term. If Andy is subjected to four sessions, however, he becomes an Amadeus for three weeks. Short-term memory becomes long-term memory.

What happens to the snail brain when it gets smarter? Adapting to the environment is a front-line reflex that takes instincts but not smarts. Retaining the lesson is the hard part. What happens when Andy becomes Amadeus? Two things: change in neuron chemistry and then change in neuron architecture.

Thanks for the Memories

Short-termlearning in habituation and sensitization occurs at the level of the synapse, the space between two communicating nerve cells. This results in either more or less neurotransmitter being secreted from the synapse, which either turns up the response or turns it down. This sort of change appears to last for only up to one hour. If Andy is subjected to four sessions of ten pokes in the siphon, the habituation will last for three weeks.

This is really a memory of sorts, and it is extremely important for Andy's (and our) survival. It enables us to learn lessons and apply them to new situations. This requires more than just chemical change at the synapse; it actually involves changes in the structure of the brain itself.

So for sensitization, we see the following changes:

➤ Increased numbers of axons from sensory to motor neurons, so the motor neurons can *hear* more. (Andy snails have 50 percent of the number found in Amadeus Aplysia.)

➤ Axonal sprouting of sensory neurons (tips near axonal terminals can bud off another branch or two), often into areas they normally don't go.

➤ Extension of the dendritic trees of the motor and sensory neurons along with increased numbers of dendritic spines (buds on the tree).

➤ Increase in the number of active synapses (connections) between sensory and motor neurons. (When Aplysia is not in training, only 10% of the synapses are active, whereas 65% of the synaptic terminals in snails-in-training are actively releasing neurotransmitters.)

In habituation, long-term memory is accomplished by reversing the process. Basically, dendritic trees that are not used become pruned down. Fewer connections are made between sensory and motor neurons, and those that are present become less chemically active.

Everything that happens in the snail neuron when the Aplysia adapts to its environment and learns how to make long-term adjustments occurs in our neurons. We have developed a few new tricks, however.

The Science of Drooling

Conditioning is an old behavior that was first described in dogs by Ivan Pavlov in the last century. Offer Lassie a piece of filet mignon and watch her mouth water in anticipation. This is a normal biological response. Then, for a few days, ring a bell every time you show her the steak she is about to devour. Then take away the steak and just ring the bell. End result—bell alone gets watery mouth. You have conditioned the salivation response to a new stimulus, that is, the ringing of the bell.

This happens in humans as well. As children, many of us would associate our mother's call to dinner with food and immediately get very excited, salivate, and run to the table. We didn't know there was food there, but we knew that that stimulus of our mother calling us was associated with the presence of food on the table.

Andy can be conditioned as well. We have seen how Andy can withdraw his gills when his siphon is moved. This makes sense. But can you make him withdraw his gills when an irrelevant part of him is touched, like his mantle shelf (back) that does not even have an active neural connection to the motor neurons that fire off the gill muscles? Answer—yes.

You repeatedly stimulate the siphon and the mantle shelf at the same time. Andy withdraws his gills in rhythm with your poker. After several sessions, you just stroke the mantle shelf. Andy pulls in his gills in tempo with your beat. Andy activates unused (inactive) pathways or forms new ones to accommodate this. Again, the structure and function of the brain change with learned behaviors.

Conditioning can be positive and negative, and can be paired with almost anything. Think of the kid who won't stay with a male, bearded baby-sitter because one of her mother's boyfriends, who happens to be bearded, was mean to him two years earlier. Think about why you hate broccoli now—your mother forced it down your throat when you were five.

There are other aspects to conditioning that make learning faster, more long-lasting, and more appropriate to the challenges at hand. Pain and pleasure.

No one has yet to identify pain or pleasure centers in Andy's brain. But he most assuredly has them. We certainly do. Many pain and pleasure centers have been identified in the human brain which, when stimulated, make our inner selves go "ouucchhh" or "ahhhhmmm." Many of them, particularly in an area called the hypothalamus, are located less than a centimeter apart. They are all activated by hormones from the blood or neurotransmitters released from input neurons. As you read on, we will show you how to use them to your advantage.

The Least You Need to Know

➤ Nervous systems of snails and humans contain neurons and surrounding glial cells.

➤ The snail brain can accommodate immediate changes in its environment with little effort.

➤ Snail learning for long-term adoption involves changing the chemistry and structure of the nervous system.

➤ Humans can be conditioned to respond in certain ways to certain stimuli. Many of these conditioning responses are old and may not serve you any longer.

➤ Stimuli and response can be rematched, sometimes for good and sometimes for bad.

➤ Pain and pleasure are both part of learning.

➤ The way snails learn is very similar, on a cellular level, to the way we learn.

Chapter 5

Making Connections: Synapses and Brain Circuits

In This Chapter

➤ How signals get from one nerve cell to the next one

➤ Synapses have an incredible packing density

➤ Examples of how synaptic circuits process information

➤ How the brain is built from its cellular building blocks

In the last chapter, we visited Andy Aplasia and saw that learning takes work and changes in brain wiring. We talked about how electrical impulses zoomed their way from one axon to the next through synapses and how these chains of nerve cells transmitted information from one place to another. Simple, right? Yes and no.

Remember the old "telephone game?" Person A whispers something to person B, who whispers it to person C, and so on down the alphabet. The message is transmitted only once, at a rapid speed. "Pia Matter lies under the Dura Matter in the Brain," gets heard, interpreted, then passed on to the next person. If the first person to hear the message has trouble discerning the Ps from the Bs, the message may sound like, "Be a matter lies under the dura matter in the brain." The next one in the line might hear the message slightly differently, too, so that the message says, "Be a matter fries under dura matter in the plain." The third in line might hear that message perfectly, but his brain is going to try to impose some kind of grammatical sense on it (something our brain *always* tries to do), so this person is likely to spout something like: "Be what matters, frying under duress is to blame." The last person, in a hurry to finish, declares confidently that "Bees fry under a durable flame." Well, they do, but that isn't exactly what the original message meant.

The Skull Is a Very Noisy Room

This is a good example of how even a single flaw in the chain of interpretive command can distort the original signal. You can think of the voice traveling through the air in this game as analogous to an action potential carried by the nerve cell's axon, and each player is acting like a synapse. The transfer of information between people is the point where information can get distorted, and that's true as well for your nerve cells.

But before you go for an elective decapitation because of cranial miswiring, think again. Coordinated distortion and balanced competition between neurons is what makes the nervous system work.

The skull is a very noisy room, with hundreds of billions of voices vying for attention. Our nerve cells are an argumentative bunch, and their numbers grow with every one of their disagreements, making us stronger, cerebrally speaking. Most of this cranial noise is created by the synapse, and chaos is transformed into order through the creation of new *synaptic circuits*, a phenomenon that occurs during the course of our brain cell's arguments.

Brain Food

Here's a simple example of the wiggle room that is inherent in the interpretation of data. Consider how the same letters can be broken down and reconnected. The letters "heisnowhere," when put into words, could mean "He is nowhere" or "He is now here." One break between letters puts the invisible culprit in the here and now, or away from the game entirely.

Oh, Those Spunky Synapses

To understand how a message gets from, say, a motor nerve cell to the brain, you've got to know a little about the synapse. This microscopic gap between nerve cells was intuited long before it was seen. Before the days of the electron microscope, in the early part of the 20th century, a British researcher, Dr. Sherrington, stimulated the leg nerves of cats, and noted that there was a delay before a reflex contraction of the limb or activation of reflex nerves happened. This suggested to Sherrington that there had to be synaptic decision-making *stations* in the spinal cord. These stations turned out to be synapses.

Even before Sherrington, Spanish biologist and physician, Ramon y Cajal, working out of his 19th century mountain cabin-turned-laboratory in the Pyrenees Mountains, also suggested the existence of synapses. Certain nerve cells in the brain stain black with silver. By examining these neurons with a primitive light microscope, Cajal was able to infer the existence of synapses.

With modern technology, we can now clearly see synapses under the electron microscope. This remarkable instrument shows the *typical* synapse as a space between the axon of the transmitting cell and a flattened, specialized area of the receiving cell.

The synaptic *cleft* itself is very small. This allows the brain to pack one billion synapses into one cubic millimeter of brain! There are 2,540 cubic millimeters in an inch, giving a packing density of 2,540,000,000,000 synapses per square inch. No wonder we can fit such incredible computing power in the small space between our ears.

Figure 5.1 is a simplified diagram of a typical synapse. Information in the form of an electric impulse (the action potential) arrives from the left and enters the presynaptic terminal, causing vesicles in the terminal to release neurotransmitters into the synaptic cleft. In this way, electrical information is converted to chemical information. The neurotransmitters travel across the synapse. After delivering their message, the neurotransmitters are then deactivated, picked up by the presynaptic cell, and recycled for reuse.

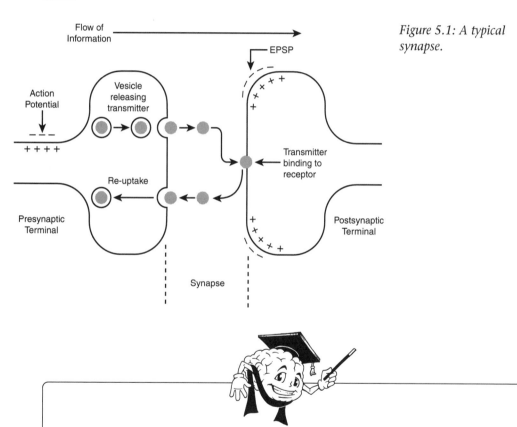

Figure 5.1: A typical synapse.

Mind This!

Even the nervous system has to take out its garbage. But agents like insecticides can mess with the recycling of neurotransmitters and have dire effects on your body. Cocaine is another recycling villain.

Let's Break It Down

The synapse, however, isn't the whole story in transmitting information. Many different structures play important roles in the process. A partial list of the actors in this enterprise includes:

➤ Neuromodulators—diffusible substances that stabilize or destabilize neurons without acting as neurotransmitters.

➤ Regulatory receptors—on the presynaptic terminal, which senses if too much neurotransmitter is being released and feeds that information back, thus slowing further release.

➤ Presynaptic enzymes—inhibit the activity of neurotransmitters if released in excessive amounts.

All this activity is powered by little power plants called the mitochondria. These little dynamos supply the energy needed for neurotransmitter release. And it is here that the rubber meets the road. Without neurotransmitters, no message can be delivered. There are between 20 and 30 identified neurotransmitters in the brain, and the list grows monthly. Examples of neurotransmitters include acetylcholine, norepinephrine, dopamine, and serotonin.

The last chapter introduced you to the two types of neurotransmitters—stimulatory and inhibitory—and gave you a rough idea of how they work. The first type sets up one kind of action potential in the nerve cell, called the *excitatory postsynaptic potential* (EPSP for short). The second one sets up an *inhibitory post-synaptic potential* (IPSP). The interaction between these two types of electric potentials is the mechanism by which your nervous system processes and transfers information. IPSPs and EPSPs gather together in the cell. The decision whether or not to fire the axon depends on which one of these charges is stronger at any given time.

There are four things to remember about the behavior of EPSPs and IPSPs:

➤ After they are produced, they spread out in all directions and their power decreases with time.

➤ Two EPSPs or two IPSPs can combine to form larger versions, but timing is very important here. If an EPSP with a power of 10 meets another with a power of 10, they *can* add up to 20. But if the first one got to the cell early and hung around for awhile before meeting up with its buddy, it will begin to lose power. By the time the second one arrives, full strength, the first may have degraded to a power of just 5, and you'll only get a total combined power of 15.

➤ If an EPSP tries to combine with an IPSP, the two together can cancel each other out. Let's take that EPSP with a power of 10 again. If, instead of meeting up with one of its pals, it runs into its opposite number, an IPSP of equal strength, then it's sort of like basic math: 10 minus 10 equals 0 power.

➤ As all these electrical impulses flow down the dendritic tree and towards the axon hillock, they form a single message, the magnitude of which determines whether the axon will be fired.

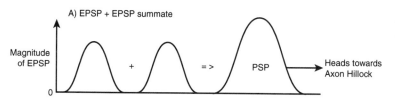

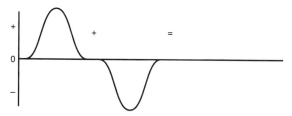

Figure 5.2: The electronic show of hands.

Mind This!

Axons work a lot like the binary code used in computers: The message can only be "on" (excitatory) or "off" (inhibitory).

Living Microchips

So, now that we've got a bunch of synapses doing their excitatory or inhibitory thing in a string of neurons, how do we get to the next stage—passing the message along to (eventually) reach the brain and be processed? This occurs according to a couple of different patterns:

➤ Fan-out—One of the simplest types of patterns seen is called *divergence*. A single neuron sends its message out to several distinct message receivers. This is called *fan-out.* In Figure 5.3, you see that a single presynaptic terminal has excitatory synapses passing a message along to several receptive dendrites.

Figure 5.3: The fan-out architecture.

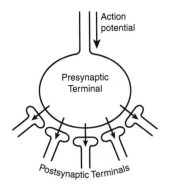

➤ Fan-in—In figure 5.4, you see that three separate neurons—labelled A, B, and C—feed their messages onto a single dendrite. If A and B are sending excitatory impulses and they both arrive at the dendrite in time, they'll combine when they meet up. If, at the same time, C is sending an inhibitory message, it will cancel some, if not all, of the excitement that A and B are carrying. (Sort of like a wet blanket at a party.)

Figure 5.4: The fan-in architecture.

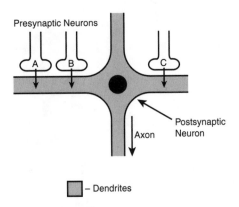

➤ Presynaptic inhibition—Figure 5.5 shows how that last situation plays out in the nerve cells. The neuron labeled (B) is inhibitory. Just not excited at all. When an excitatory potential (call it A) comes by on its way along the neural chain, (B) can cancel it out. Instead of firing off enthusiastically, potential (A) decides that maybe it would rather spend a quiet evening at home, and never makes it to the party going on over on dendrite (C).

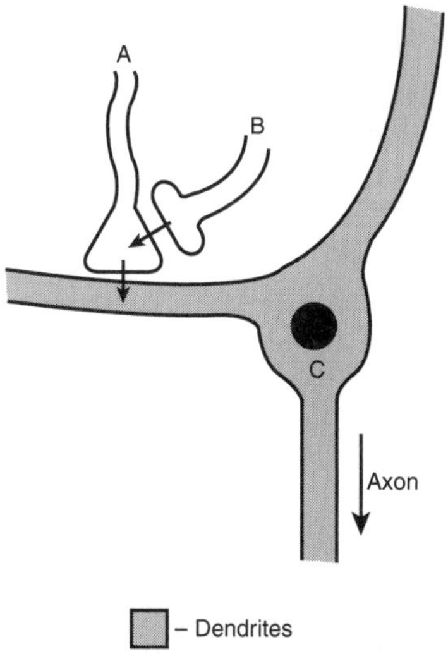

Figure 5.5: The presynaptic inhibition architecture.

☐ – Dendrites

➤ Afferent inhibition—Figure 5.6 shows a somewhat more advanced message circuit. Axon (A) has synaptic connections with the dendrites of two other neurons (let's call them B and C). When these two neurons get the nod from axon (A), they each generate those excitatory potentials, the ESPS. But (C) is *also* sending an inhibitory message to (B), so the message poor old Y gets is contradictory. Axon (A) says, "Let's party," while (C) is saying, "Why not curl up with a good book?" Neuron (B) gets excited at first (axon A is pretty persuasive) but the quiet counsel of (C) puts a stop to the fun fairly quickly.

Figure 5.6: Afferent inhibition.

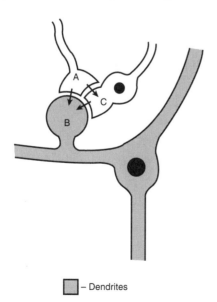

☐ – Dendrites

45

Let's Build a Brain

By this point, you can see that the system of passing messages along from neuron to neuron can become increasingly complex. We started out talking about *chains* of nerve cells, but the structure is now beginning to look more like a *web*. And the message so far is pretty basic: "yes" or "no," "on" or "off," excited or inhibited. It's like reading machine code for your computer—a string of 1s and 0s that don't really seem to mean much in themselves. How do we get to meaningful messages? How does all this basic code get processed?

Figure 5.7: A neuron with its dendrites.

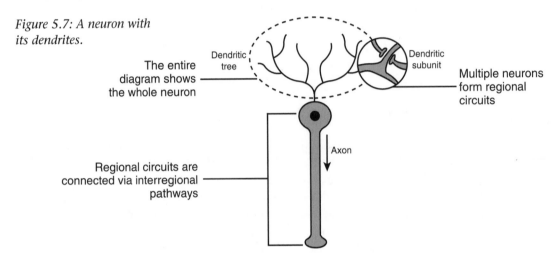

The entire diagram shows the whole neuron

Dendritic tree

Dendritic subunit

Multiple neurons form regional circuits

Axon

Regional circuits are connected via interregional pathways

Interactions between neurons of similar or different properties set up local circuits that pass information along. These local circuits have specializations: speech, for example, or motor function. But specializations generally have to be coordinated with one another. For example, the speech center messages need to coordinate with action centers in order to get your lips and tongue into the speech act. Obviously, then, it is necessary to have interregional communication between the various specialized circuits in the brain.

You've covered a lot of technical territory about how your nervous system processes information. Now that you've got a grip on the basic mechanics of the process, it's time to see how all this apparent hard wiring changes—and how you can influence that change.

The Least You Need to Know

➤ Decisions about sending transmissions on are made at every station in the brain at the synapse. It is a primary site of information-processing.

➤ Synapses are small spaces where neurotransmitters are released, converting electrical information into chemical information.

➤ The effects of the neurotransmitters depend on the architecture of the neuronal circuit.

➤ Synaptic circuits are built into dendritic subunits. Several dendritic subunits are found on each dendritic tree for each neuron.

➤ Groups of neurons form specialized local circuits that communicate with other specialized circuits.

Chapter 6

From Slug to Slugger

> **In This Chapter**
>
> ➤ Understanding the complexity of the human nervous system
>
> ➤ How the building blocks of nerve cells and synapses are assembled in the brain
>
> ➤ How information competes for access to the *great decider*, the cerebral cortex
>
> ➤ The brain as a decision-making machine

We have the most complex brains on the planet: How much greater we are than the snail. But at the same time, how much greater our challenges are than the ones Andy Aplysia faces. But we still know very little about how we handle those challenges. It may seem that you've wandered far afield from the original topic—how to increase your IQ—but, in fact, you're now just about ready to take a practical first step in achieving that goal. Because one way to increase your effective intelligence is to work on the physical architecture of your information processor—your brain.

Now that may sound like a pretty tough job. You're not a brain surgeon, after all. But it can be done—and if you understand the way your nervous system works, you can get a pretty good idea of how to go about it.

From Wiring to Wisdom

So far, you've learned about the basic building blocks of the brain, your nerve cells. And through looking at Andy's schooling, you've gotten a brief, basic sense of how they can change when you learn. In the last chapter, you learned how nerve cells are linked together in order to pass information along for processing. You can think of all this as a crash course in the way your brain is wired. Converting that wiring so that you can increase your intelligence means upgrading that wiring system: increasing its capacity and complexity. Sound tough? Well, if Andy could do it, so can you.

All Roads Lead to Rome

The one thing to remember about your nervous system in general, and your brain in particular, is that everything is connected to everything else. There *is* a sort of chain of command, but events at the furthest reaches of the system, occurring in the smallest part of a single cell, can have a major impact on how your brain works.

One way to look at this is to think of your nervous system as the neural equivalent of the old Roman highway system. The roads connected all the outposts, cities, and towns of that ancient, far-flung empire, but ultimately, every last one of them led to Rome. In our metaphor, Rome is your brain. Figure 6.1 provides you with a visual image of this central hub of your neural highway system.

Figure 6.1: The road map of the human brain.

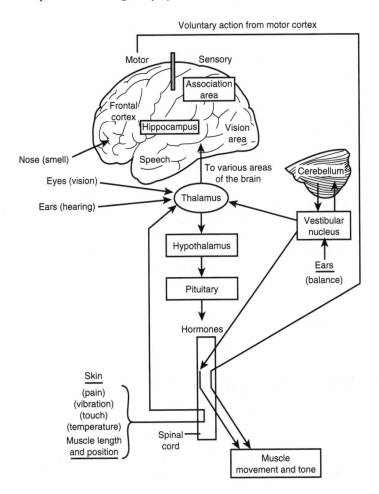

The brain is not just a single, featureless organ. It has several specialized structures, each with a particular function or set of functions. They're represented by boxes in our diagram, and a brief description of each is as follows:

➤ The cerebral cortex is the *voluntary* command center, and it is divided into two parts: a motor organ that sends out commands, and a sensory part that collects and evaluates information. Without the cerebral cortex, we would have no voluntary functions.

➤ The thalamus is the relay station that collects information from all of the senses except olfaction (smell), and sends it on to the cerebral cortex.

➤ The hypothalamus gets info from the thalamus and cerebral cortex, and translates thoughts and brain commands into actions that are carried out throughout the body by hormones.

➤ The pituitary gland is ruled by the hypothalamus. The pituitary is often called the master endocrine organ, exercising its power over most body organ systems.

➤ The cerebellum gets its informational input from the muscles, and then sends information back to the spinal cord so that muscle movements are smooth and coordinated.

➤ The spinal cord collects information from every part of the body below the neck, and sends impulses back to them from the brain.

Mind This!

In your nervous system, everything is connected to everything else. This implies more than simple intercommunication—it means interdependency as well. When one part is hurt, all parts suffer. "We're all in this together" is the watchword of your brain's various structures.

Like the branches of the government (theoretically, at least), your brain operates according to a system of checks and balances. For example, let's say that you're enjoying a business lunch with a colleague and your foot accidentally brushes against his or her leg under the table. You're aware of the contact because of input—neural messages—from the skin and muscles of your offending foot. These messages travel along your nerves, eventually arriving at the spinal cord, where they interact with one another and ultimately are dispatched to the thalamus to report the event.

In the thalamus, each individual impulse competes with the others for the chance to tell its story of contact. The thalamus sorts out what each impulse is trying to say and organizes all the messages into a coherent form that it can pass along to the big boss—the cerebral cortex. But the raw report is not enough—the boss wants more information than the simple sensory data from your foot. Emotional centers are consulted, asking such questions as, "Did I kick my companion by accident?" Once all the data is in, the boss is ready to issue a command: Move your foot. This order is issued through the corticospinal tract to the spinal cord, which dispatches the signal to your foot: Move! Now!

This is one example of a *regulatory feedback loop*. And such loops occur throughout your nervous system, whether you are consciously aware of them or not. You're probably not likely to notice if secretions from your pituitary get excessive, but you can bet that your pituitary does and it signals the hypothalamus to not stimulate it as forcefully to make hormones. Similarly, if your thalamus and cortex are getting too forceful in their commands to your hypothalamus, your hypothalamus won't wait for you to notice how beleaguered it's getting. It simply changes the hormone composition of the blood so that the cerebral cortex and thalamus calm down.

How We Listen to the World: Sensors and Sensory Circuits

Chapter 5 showed you how nerve cells are linked together to transfer information from one place to another. These linked cells can form very long chains. For example, information that originates in Michael Jordan's toe (say an opponent on the court stomps his foot) has to travel more than six feet to get to his cerebral cortex. But these long informational highways ultimately carry the information to the spinal cord and the brain, where it gets processed and customized. Then the brain, acting on the information it has received, sends what it deems to be appropriate response signals to muscles, bones, and other organs. The whole process, however, starts with perception.

What Does It All Mean?

Modality is a particular type of information from the outside world that we define according to what we perceive; for example, vision, hearing, pressure, vibration, and pain.

Perception is simply the receipt of stimuli. The brain receives information on many different types of phenomena in the natural world: visual, aural, olfactory, and physical, for example. It doesn't receive *all* the information that's out there, of course—your sense organs won't register x-rays, for example, or the sound of a dog whistle, or colors beyond a certain spectrum. Nevertheless, nerve endings from the skin convey information about a great many sensory *modalities* such as pain, vibration, touch, pressure, and temperature.

Our old friend, the neuron, sometimes clusters in bunches that are called *ganglia*. Clusters of neurons from your peripheral (that is, non-brain or spinal cord) nervous system are found next to your spinal cord.

Nerve impulses, from the skin for example, travel up to these clusters, where they are sorted out for transfer to the brain. The route they take (called a *tract*) to reach their ultimate destination in the brain is determined by their *modality*. For example, most of the fibers that convey information about vibration and pressure go up the dorsal (back) spinal tract, while most information about pain and temperature go up the lateral (side) tracts of the spinal cord.

Ultimately, all the information taken in by your skin will eventually go to the thalamus, which consists of two egg-shaped structures that sit under each of the cerebral hemispheres (cerebral cortex). But, within the overall traffic of skin information, each modality (pressure, pain, temperature, or vibration, for example) sends its impulses to a different spot in the thalamus. From these different sites (or nuclei), it is sent along to the cerebral cortex, where we *feel* the world. Figure 6.2 shows how this happens.

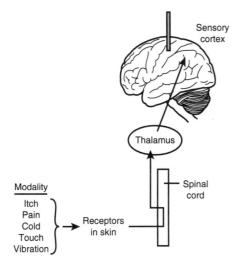

Figure 6.2: Neural wiring for the sense of touch.

Figure 6.1 shows how your eyes and ears convey information about light and sound directly to the thalamus. Visual input goes to an area called the lateral geniculate nucleus; auditory messages are dropped into the brain's voicemail, the medial geniculate nucleus, which is conveniently located next door. The next stop for both of these message types, or modalities, is the cerebral cortex, where the movie of the outside world is formed.

But your eyes and ears collect other information, not just light and sound. For example, your ear collects information about your head position. This information doesn't get packaged with the messages about sounds, but goes on its own merry way, straight to the cerebellum—bypassing the thalamus entirely.

Messages from muscles and joints about muscle length and limb position have their own route to travel. They synapse in the spinal cord or brain stem, head north to the thalamus to specific nuclei, and then travel further north to the cerebral cortex. Other

Brain Food

The brain listens to internal environmental body changes (hormonal shifts), as well as to the sensory inputs from the external environment. The hypothalamus has an open gateway to the blood, and if it picks up messages that the hormonal system is getting out of whack, it signals the pituitary gland to step in and get things back to normal.

What Does It All Mean?

There are many other modalities, and many more details about how they make themselves heard. But one sensation goes to the cerebral cortex directly without involvement of the thalamus—*olfaction*. What the nose smells goes directly to the brain. The significance of this fast-tracking of smells is unclear, but because of its direct route to the brain, olfactory information does not get distorted in the thalamus and spinal cord like the other senses do.

information generated by your muscles and joints, the ones that have to do with keeping your movements smooth and coordinated, take the express route to the cerebellum without making a thalamus pit stop.

Although we aren't getting *all* the information that is out there, the body is less concerned with giving us a *true* picture of the world than it is in giving a sufficiently detailed picture for our purposes. Anything else is just excess—and can in fact be so distracting as to work against our best interests. In other words, the body is designed to be *effective*, not perfect.

How We Talk Back!

Your brain's central area for *action* is the frontal lobe (refer to Figure 6.1), which deals very heavily with your muscles. Signals telling the muscles to contract go through the corticospinal tract (the connection between the cortex and the spinal cord), directly to motor neurons that cause muscle contraction and limb movement. Signals are also sent to ensure that the movements are smooth and timed just right. This last set of signals is sent along the *involuntary* tracts, that is, these signals govern actions that are outside of your conscious control. Another set of signals travels on a side branch that goes to the basal ganglia, which controls what the thalamus sends up to the cortex. Problems in the basal ganglia result in the involuntary tremors often seen in Parkinson's disease. Let's examine this more closely.

Because your brain operates on the feedback principle, when things get out of hand in one part of your system, other parts kick in to bring things back under control. One example of how these feedback loops work is seen in the basal ganglia, which is the system that keeps muscle tone balanced and prevents muscle tremors. If there are defects in these ganglia—if they can't quite get their job done—you get involuntary tremors.

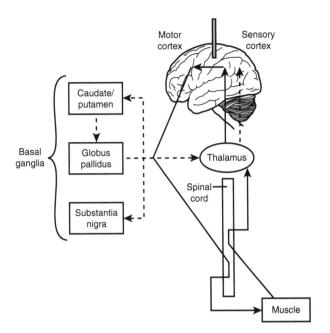

Figure 6.3: Neural feedback loops.

The feedback loops in the basal ganglia, shown in Figure 6.3, are as follows:

➤ The big loop: The muscles inform the brain of their position and the brain adjusts accordingly. Muscle-stretch receptors travel to the spinal cord, thalamus, cerebral cortex, back to the spinal cord, and finally to muscle.

➤ The middle loop: The cerebral motor cortex sends a signal through a couple of substations to eventually arrive at the thalamus. Information then goes back up to the sensory cortex, helping it see how quickly and extensively the muscles are being stretched.

➤ The inner loop: Through the release of a series of neurotransmitters, two of the substations that relay the cerebral cortex's signals (the substantia nigra and the caudate butamen) inhibit (turn off) each other.

In Parkinson's disease, the substantia nigra degenerates so it no longer affects the middle loop. The cortex is now misinformed, so it can't make appropriate decisions about muscle activity and tries to compensate. That's what the jerky movements are: the cortex's attempt to adjust to changes in muscle length that aren't really happening.

Mind This!

Remember, everything is connected to everything else. A small change somewhere can have unintended effects all over the brain.

Not all movements are subject to such potential misinterpretation, however. One such movement is the spinal *reflex*: You touch a hot stove, you withdraw your arm very fast. This is a reflex, involving neuronal circuits that are all below the neck. Sensory neurons activate spinal cord motor neurons, which cause the reflex removal of roasting arm from hot object. The knee-jerk reflex, caused by hitting the kneecap lightly with a rubber hammer, is another such reflex, as is the contraction of your pupil in response to bright light.

Figure 6.4: Wiring for reflex responses.

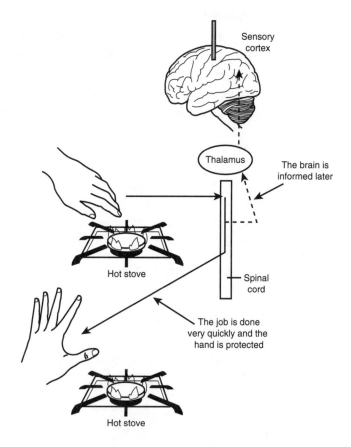

You don't have to be Einstein to have healthy reflex responses. You do them without thinking. But reflexes can be fine-tuned to meet your needs. With practice, you can train your reflexes to work faster, better, and more appropriately for your needs.

The Neuronal Road Map in Your Brain Changes with Experience

The central gateway to learning is the hippocampus (see the road map of the brain). This area of the temporal lobe in the cerebral cortex is the last to mature in early human life, and the first to lose cells in senile dementia in later life. The hippocampus is where we convert short-term exposure to information into long-term memory.

As long as you still have your hippocampus, you can learn and retain new knowledge. And, as our pal Andy showed us, *anything* you learn—not just schoolbook stuff—can be converted to long-term memory. Let's look at what he showed us once again, this time with reference to how *you* learn.

Your brain circuitry changes both as you become experienced and as you become smarter (there is a difference between the two). On a cellular level, the same things that happen to Andy Aplysia's brain as he learns about advanced gill protection happen to *your* brain circuits, too. More connections are formed where they are needed; excess unused ones are pared down; and the sensitivity of your circuits changes, according to what is needed for the environment and tasks required.

For example, let's say your arm is amputated in an accident, so the brain will no longer receive any sensory information from your arm. This would normally go to the strip of cortex just behind the Sylvian fissure. Before the injury, this part of the cortex had the face, chest, arms, and legs represented on it. Now, if the sensory information from the arm is gone, the areas represented by the legs increase. This *always* happens, and is particularly enhanced when the person is determined to use what they have left after an injury or stroke—the brain cooperates with the body's efforts to compensate.

Brain Food

Medical students learn of the case of HM when studying how the hippocampus serves as the seat of learning. HM had severe epilepsy, the result of tumors in the hippocampus. The removal of the hippocampus on both sides stopped the seizures, but HM lost all capacity for long-term memory after surgery. He could remember everything about life before the operation, but he couldn't retain anything he learned after surgery for more than a few minutes.

Translate this to modalities. We've all heard about how, if you lose one of your senses, the others get stronger. Tibetan monks use this capability all the time to heighten their senses. As a matter of fact, the state of mental *calm* during deep meditation is a self-induced sensory deprivation situation that allows you to hear, see, and feel with your inner senses—your *gut* senses.

Figure 6.5: How the brain alters its architecture in response to changes in stimuli.

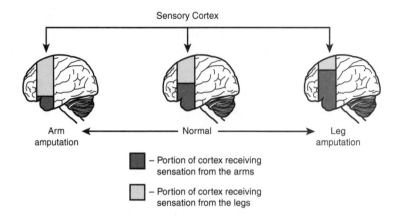

Try This at Home

Try the following to see how your circuitry works:

➤ Blindfold yourself for a day, under supervision. Take note of how much more you can hear with your ears, sense with your skin, taste with your tongue, and smell with your nose.

➤ While blindfolded, try to perform a task you know you can normally do well. You'll become much more aware of all the component movements that go into doing that task. Watch yourself improve.

➤ Put in earplugs and watch the world around you. See if you see anything more than you normally do.

These simple exercises show that your brain circuitry *can* change, and that you have some control over the process. Does that mean people can recover from devastating neurological injuries? You bet—as the real-life example of stuntwoman Heidi von Beltz illustrates.

Once again, we return to Burt Reynolds. In the early 1980s, Heidi von Beltz was making *Cannonball Run II* with Burt Reynolds and Dom DeLuise. She was sitting in the back seat of a stunt car that hit another car head-on at high speed. She woke up with a high cervical fracture, and almost died right there on the street. Instead, this remarkable woman survived and, in spite of the fact that the rest of the world thought her life was not worth living, she and her family disputed them all. She worked for ten years, until finally she was able to walk in a standing frame—a remarkable feat. She had the worst of all possible spinal cord injuries but was able, through sheer determination and hard work, to move back toward recovery by always keeping a very positive attitude and, of course, having the total support of her family.

Do Something!

Your central nervous system is where decisions are made by your brain, but the specific location of that decision-making depends on the modality or modalities that are carrying the information on which the decisions are to be based. Modalities mix at the level of the spinal cord, thalamus, and cerebral cortex. Each modality *fights* for a superior voice in the cerebral cortex, the ultimate great decider.

And so, we see that the brain is a decision-making machine. It receives input, customizes information, and takes action in a never-ending loop. In Chapter 7, we'll take one last look at that loop. We'll get down to cases about the decision-making function of your brain, and how you can work on that function to make your brain work more effectively.

The Least You Need to Know

➤ In your brain, everything is connected to everything else.

➤ Sensory systems create a *construct* of the world.

➤ This world construct is not perfect, but must be effective to allow us to flourish.

➤ Effective action relies on effective feedback, even on the cellular level.

➤ The neuronal map changes, according to what we experience and do.

➤ The brain is a decision-making machine.

Chapter 7

The Triad of Effective Intelligence

In This Chapter

➤ The brain is a decision-making machine

➤ How to evaluate a decision

➤ The triad of effective intelligence

➤ How a Russian and a slug will help you follow through

It should be clear by now that the brain's main job is to make decisions. The brain is always making choices: left or right, stop or go, up or down? In the world visible under the microscope, yes/no decisions are made at every synaptic connection. Fancy biological footwork on the part of the axons and the complexity of the system as a whole decide whether the signal goes through pathway A faster or earlier than B.

Even from where we see the world, outside the microscope, life is all about decisions. Think about how many decisions you make, even in an uneventful day. The most exciting thing about this force, this power of decision, is that you already possess it and know how to use it. Everything you do in life is the result of a decision, even something as mundane as scratching your nose. You already make thousands of decisions a day. Increasing your effective intelligence simply means taking conscious purposeful control of the process.

Decision-Making: An Ongoing Process, Whether We Like It Or Not

The brain is always making decisions because information is always being fed into it. The spinal cord relay nuclei and the thalamus don't put "out to lunch" signs on their synaptic doors, even when we think we are in "checked-out from the world" mode. When we sleep, our dreams are a series of "what-if" suggestions put together in the editing room of the unconscious brain. But decisions can be proactive or reactive. The question is whether you proactively choose among several possibilities or reactively choose after your options have been reduced for you.

Complete this exercise:

Pay attention to your activities over the next three hours and write down every decision you find yourself making—from whether or not to scratch an itch to whether you really want that second cup of coffee. Think about all the options you had available to you at the time that you made those decisions, and make a note of which ones were of your own devising, as opposed to which ones resulted from some source outside of you.

Decisions Have Consequences

Proactive decision-making is not for the faint of heart. Every decision you make has consequences—and if you make *proactive* decisions, the responsibility for those consequences falls to you. Making a true decision means committing to achieving a result and then cutting yourself off from any other possibility.

Taking responsibility can be a little unsettling, but if you're seeking to increase your effective intelligence, consequences are what you are seeking and responsibility is a positive thing. Above all, by learning to be proactive in your decision-making, you gain a measure of control—without which there can be no effectiveness in your intelligence or your actions.

What Does It All Mean?

The word *decision* comes from the Latin root *de,* which means "from," and *caedere,* which means "to cut."

Yes, it's true that you cannot control all the things that happen to you in your life, but you can control the meaning you attach to them, the lessons you learn from them, and the decisions you make as a result of them. A new, congruent, and committed decision leads to action. A series of decisions lead to a series of actions, which begin to take you in a different direction, and ultimately to a different destination. Remember, it only takes a very small change in course to lead to a very large change in destination down the road. The power of decision is your rudder.

Evaluating a Decision

We've already established that the brain is a decision-making machine. The act of making a decision is built into its structure, even at the most elementary level. So much so that, even when you decide to not decide, you have nonetheless made a decision.

But was it a "good" decision or a "bad" decision? That depends mostly on whether the results brought you closer to your desired goal at the time. That is, after all, the very essence of effective intelligence. Applied cranial power directed for a desired goal. Another important point: Nothing happens if you do not take action. Even a bad decision is usually preferable to a decision not to make a decision. Why? Because it stirs the waters. It gives the brain some feedback to work with. It's not important initially to know how you're going to create a result. If you commit to it, you'll find a way.

The *triad of effective intelligence,* then, begins with a decision. The three, taken together, are as follows:

➤ Process available information, make judgments, reassess past approaches, and make a decision.

➤ Take action.

➤ Gather sensory information about results and present this information to the brain.

If you have clear goals, keep making decisions based on results, and take action on these decisions, the intelligent brain has no choice. It simply *has* to "guide action towards the desired goal", in effect, to become more effective. And *that* is the message of this book: by increasing your effective-intelligence skills, you increase your overall intelligence, including those skills measured by the "IQ" test.

When you're trying to accomplish a specific, well-defined goal, the skill-improvement process is cumulative: The results of large-scale decisions are built from many small decisions. If, for example, you decide to explore the possibility of doing stand-up comedy, your decision opens up avenues of action: You may start reading the daily paper for material and even start roughing out a few jokes. Actions you take are more specific and give rise to new decisions. As you accumulate more material, you may begin to realize that you've got the makings of an act. Your next decision may be to explore the open-mike venues in your area, which opens new possibilities for action— deciding to go to a few places to see how other fledgling acts are doing, and maybe even signing up for a stint at the mike yourself.

Complete this exercise:

The way to make better decisions is to make more of them consciously. Practice making conscious decisions. Take note of results. Reassess and make more. For this exercise, resolve to start your day by making a list of the main goals you wish to accomplish before bedtime. Now, put the list away, but keep a log of all the little decisions you make during the day: What you bought, who you spoke to, what you spent your time reading or watching. At the end of the day, take out your initial list. Assess your moment-to-moment decisions in light of how they moved you closer to or further from accomplishing your goals. Put a red plus next to the small decisions that, at the end of the day, brought you closer to your goals. Mark a black negative mark beside the decisions that set you back or just sidetracked you. Over time, you'll find that you can improve your ratio of red to black marks—visual evidence that you've improved your effective decision-making.

Just Do It: Not Just For Sneaker Ads

Making choices is about taking risks—taking a leap of faith. Sometimes even risking it all. But we do this every day—just by walking down the street. As you'll learn in Part 2, your senses don't report "objective" reality to you—much of what you see is purely an interpretive product of your brain. And your brain can get very creative with the sensory raw material it receives. So every time you take a step, you're taking a leap of faith that there really *is* solid ground to receive your footfall. Every time you reach to put a glass on a tabletop, you're risking the possibility that the table is *not* where you thought it was—that it's even there at all.

So, since we're all born risk-takers, why not convert this into a life skill? Take a few chances by making decisions and committing to following them through. Even if they don't work out, they're great learning tools for the *next* time.

Complete this exercise:

Get up out of bed and face the big, bad world on *your* terms. Make a conscious effort to make all the little decisions meet the end goal. If you're aiming for that stand-up career, how will an apparently minor decision help you achieve the goal? Well, which would be better: to go to lunch with your co-workers (and maybe get a few funny observations to work into your act), or to eat alone in the office and use the time to rough out that joke that isn't quite working yet? I don't know, but spend a day thinking about your goals *before* you make decisions and see what a difference it makes.

To paraphrase Tony Robbins again, "Success is the result of good judgment. But you can't develop good judgment without experience—and experience is often the result of poor judgment." Don't fear mistakes—even the most negative experience is grist for the mill of developing judgment. After all, at the very least, you learn not to make *that* mistake again.

It's All In the Follow-Through

The risk of making decisions involves more than the risk of mistakes—there is also the risk that decision-making will lead to change. In fact, it almost surely will. But most of us are wary of change, and so we avoid it unless there is some undeniable benefit that will come of making that change. How can Andy Aplysia help us learn how to follow through on our decisions? The answer is found in something called *conditioned response*.

A decision leads to action. If your decision involves changing something in your life, habits, or behavior, the actions that follow your decision may also be new and unfamiliar to you. This may mean changing the way you respond to normal stimuli. In other words, you may find yourself asking your nervous system to break an old stimulus-response pattern and replace it with the new one. This will take some work.

This brings us back to Andy, Pavlov, and the law of reinforcement. Any pattern of emotion or behavior that is continually reinforced will become an automatic and conditioned response. Any behavior that is *not* reinforced will eventually dissipate. This is key: If you are trying to break a pattern, it is very important that you find a replacement behavior that is at least as satisfying and convenient as your earlier one, or you will revert back to the old pattern.

What Does It All Mean?

A *stimulus* (a burning feeling at the tips of your fingers, for example) elicits a *response* (pulling your fingers from the fire). Many responses are *reflexive*—you don't think about them, you just do them. But a *conditioned response* is learned—firewalkers condition themselves to ignore their instinctive response (to jump *off* those hot coals) and to just keep on walking.

What this means is that after deciding to affect a change, you should reinforce the new behavior immediately, continually, and consistently. Remember, this new pattern requires actual physical, chemical, and electrical changes in the brain, and that takes time. It takes Andy Apylsia 30 short pokes in the gut to learn to alter his response to that particular stimulus. How many pokes do you need? The answer lies in the balance between pain and pleasure.

Nothing changes unless we change the sensations we link to an experience in our nervous system. In order to follow through on a decision to break a pattern or set of patterns, you must link more pain to *not* changing than you do to making the change. You must then link pleasure to the new set of patterns.

Mind This!

Our society is obsessed with disengaging pain and responsibility from the consequences of action. The Menendez brothers kill their parents in cold blood. That's OK, the parents were mean to them years ago. Poor boys! But decisions lead to actions, actions have consequences, and you are responsible for those consequences. If those consequences are painful, so be it. Without pain, there is no change and without change there is no growth.

And you need to rehearse the new empowering alternative again and again. This can be done with mental imagery as effectively as with physical rewards because the brain cannot tell the difference between vivid imagination and external sensory input.

The next step is to set up a schedule to reinforce your new behavior. How can you effectively reward yourself for succeeding?

At Sea World, if a dolphin is rewarded with a fish each time it performs a successful jump, it may become habituated and may lose its drive to perform. The reward becomes expected, so it stops being effective as a reward. Trainers know this. If they're trying to teach the dolphin to perform five jumps, they start out by rewarding it after each jump. But to avoid habituating the dolphin, they soon change the pattern of reward: the fish is sometimes given after the first jump, sometimes after the fourth, and so on. The dolphin is never sure which jump will be rewarded. Any jump could be the one that earns it the treat, so the dolphin jumps with a will.

These insights from the worlds of snails and dolphins are directly applicable to you as you try to change your behavior. To sum them up for you to use:

➤ Be clear about what you want and why you want it. This allows you to develop effective rewards for reinforcement. For example, you want to quit smoking because you want better health.

➤ Get leverage on yourself: Associate more pain with not changing than with the change. This can be as simple as keeping your cigarette pack in an extremely inconvenient place so that getting a smoke is a lot like work.

➤ Practice the new behaviors that you want to adopt. Remember, using visualizing techniques counts just as much as physical practice. Perhaps you've decided to replace the cigarettes with the money you would pay for them in a big glass jar. For a two-pack-a-day smoker, that's about five cents every 20 minutes. Imagine the coins mounting up.

➤ Find a new empowering alternative that replaces the pain of changing with the pleasure of the change. In our quitting-smoking example, you could use the accumulated change to treat yourself to a brunch at that great, non-smoking restaurant you always wanted to try out.

➤ Vary your schedule of rewards, to make sure that your new empowering pattern lasts.

Mind This!

Having trouble gaining leverage to break a particularly strong association? The greatest leverage you can create for yourself is the pain that comes from inside, not outside. To get true leverage, ask yourself pain-inducing questions. "What will this cost me if I don't change?" Imagine what life would be like in 5, 10, or 15 years if you do not change. What will you lose? The second step is to use pleasure-associating questions. What will I get if I do change? What will life be like then? What will I gain?

If we try many times to make a change and fail to do so, this simply means the level of pain for failing to change is not high enough.

Faulty Connections

How do faulty or ineffective stimulus-response mechanisms get established in the first place? Blame it on your brain. Each time you experience a significant amount of pain or pleasure, your brain will search for the cause and record it in your nervous system to enable you to make better decisions about what to do in the future. These cause-and-effect associations provide the bases for your responses to events, circumstances, or problems.

To find the cause of a pleasurable or painful experience, your brain looks for certain things:

➤ It looks for something that appears to be unique to the experience.

➤ It looks for something that seems to be happening simultaneously with the experience.

➤ Your brain looks for consistency of association *with* that experience.

If all these criteria are met by something that occurs simultaneously with the pleasurable or painful experience, the brain assumes that it is the *cause* of that experience.

But causality is a difficult thing to nail down, and the brain can make mistakes. For example, let's say a baby is crawling on a tabletop and falls on a blue carpet, hurting itself. Now the baby is sprawled on the carpet and the baby's brain looks for the cause of the pain. The blue carpet is unique and immediate to the experience. But this only happened once, so causality isn't immediately assumed. But if, the next day, the baby again climbs on the table and falls on the blue carpet, that blue carpet may be assumed to be the cause.

This example may sound silly, but in fact, many of our stimulus-response associations are based on just such faulty reasoning. They form the core of the common phobias that so many of us live with. And because most of us never review and reconstruct our conditioned responses, we simply accept them as our masters. We may not be happy with the results, but we are stuck in a script that may in fact have been written long, long ago. But you can change this: Re-evaluate the pain or pleasure you have linked to various behaviors, and replace those that interfere with your development of a more effective intelligence.

The Least You Need To Know

➤ Take control of the decision-making process.

➤ Decisions have consequences: You are responsible.

➤ The triad of effective intelligence begins with decisions, so– practice making decisions.

➤ Decisions lead to change, and change is necessary for growth.

➤ Change must be reinforced with conditioning.

Part 2
The World Talks to Us

The raw material of your effective intelligence is the data you receive from your senses. Part 2 takes you on a guided tour of your individual senses and explains just exactly how your brain processes the information they feed it. From your visual world to your sense of touch, you are constantly receiving important data, from which you construct your vision of the world.

But you're not a passive recipient of all this information—not if you don't want to be. You can actively take charge of your senses, teaching yourself to observe more, feel more, comprehend more—if you only take the time to learn the processes by which your brain works. In this part of the book, you'll learn all about those processes, and you'll learn simple exercises that you can use to maximize your sensory awareness, thus enriching the field of data you can use to make decisions and pursue your goals.

In addition to learning how to increase your ability to gather sensory data, you'll also learn how to take charge of your brain's processing powers. You'll learn to work with your brain's natural tendency to organize the data it receives, and you'll discover the secrets of maximizing your effective brain power.

What You See Isn't Always What You Get

What is light? In 1910, half of the scientific community was insisting that it was a wave of energy, the other half was just as convinced that it was a particle. Einstein, then a lowly junior-level professor, came along and said that maybe it was both—that maybe light was composed of particles that moved as waves. He came up with that insight by thinking outside any of the normal compartments of knowledge and relating information in a new way. In 1919, an international team of scientists working together proved that Einstein was right.

Why all the fuss? Well, two reasons. First, Einstein's insight provides an example of the effective use of intelligence to solve a problem. Second, his insight was about one of our important sources of information—information we use daily to do our own problem-solving.

We are a very visual species. Although our ancestors seemed to rely more on the sense of smell, today we are primarily moved by light and sight. We want to see things *with our own two eyes*! We say "Seeing is believing." We've even got a whole state (Missouri) that takes it as its motto "Show Me!" But how does the human brain process visual information?

The Eye as a Camera: Just Point and Shoot

A video camera takes 30 pictures a second; each frame having between 400 and 800 individual dots or pixels. The meshing of those frames provides a moving picture of the world around us that feels three-dimensional. Impressive, but our eyes are many times more detailed and much faster than any video camera on the market. Let's look at how they work.

Figure 8.1: Cross-section of the human eye.

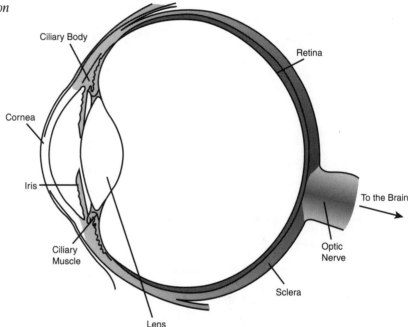

As you can see in Figure 8.1, the human eye is a series of barriers through which light has to pass. In the front of the eye is the cornea. This is a resilient structure that protects the eye from injury and (usually) lets light come through without resistance. Light then passes through the lens, where it converges onto the retina, the neural sensing organ of the eye. The job of the lens is to make sure that the rays of light converge exactly where they are supposed to—on the plane, or flattened portion, of the retina.

What you're looking at, however, is never a single item. Your eye has to manage to provide information about a variety of objects at varying distances from it. That means that in a single viewing, your eye has to shift rapidly, changing its focus so that it can perceive not only close-up elements of your visual field, but also figures that are located further away. It does this by changing the shape of the lens.

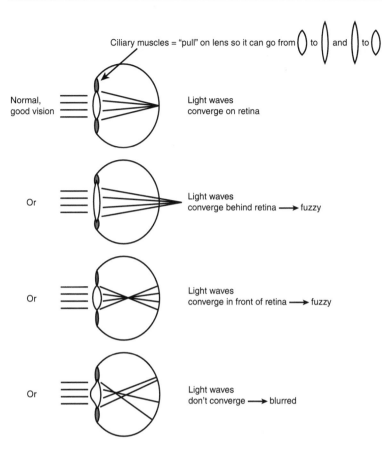

Ciliary muscles = "pull" on lens so it can go from ( ) to ( ) and ( ) to ( )

Normal, good vision — Light waves converge on retina

Or — Light waves converge behind retina ⟶ fuzzy

Or — Light waves converge in front of retina ⟶ fuzzy

Or — Light waves don't converge ⟶ blurred

And lens shape is a dynamic process. If you want to rapidly shift focus between an object that is far away and one that is close up, you must rapidly change the shape of the lens. This process is very fast, with many oscillating adjustments possible in a single second.

Skill at shifting focus is very important for your eyes to elicit a full and fully useful image of your environment. What does this mean for increasing your effective intelligence? The skill is one that you can enhance, if you take the time and make the effort.

Brain Food

You see this shifting focus every time you watch a movie, TV show, or commercial. The actor in the foreground talks, and the camera focuses on his face. His co-star in the scene speaks from the background and the camera shifts to her, bringing her image into clearer, sharper focus. The camera shifts back and forth between the two characters in the scene, featuring first one, then the other, as is called for by the script.

Complete the following exercise:

Focus your eye on the tip of a pencil, preferably one with a picture attached to it—the picture will help you maintain your focus. Move the pencil tip away from you as far as your outstretched arm can go, then back to within six inches of your eyes. Repeat this motion at least ten times. Keep your focus on the pencil tip, or the picture. Do this at least five times a day. If your eyes start to hurt—good. It means that the muscles that change the lens shape are being tested and conditioned.

Let's now move beyond the lens and look at what happens to the light when it hits the back of the eye. It bounces off the sclera—sort of a reflective backboard, then gets dumped into the biological basket—the retina.

The Brain Starts Here

Light entering the eye is reflected by the sclera, hits the photoreceptor cells in the retina, and the processing of light information begins. These photoreceptor cells come in two flavors: rods and cones. Rods, like *film noir* aficionados and retro-TV watchers, deal with black-and-white vision only. Individual rods register different shades of gray. Cones, which work with color, are of three types: those that respond to red, those that respond to blue, and those that respond to green.

So rods and cones act like the pixels on a TV screen, breaking up and reintegrating the images received by the eye from the environment. But a TV picture is actually made up of about 400 pixels or dots, while the rods and cones in the retina handle thousands. There is a problem, however. Because the image comes from a signal that is bounced off the sclera, it is inverted and flipped upside down when it lands on the retina. It still has to be transformed, within milliseconds, into a right-side-up, uninverted, faithful reproduction of the original visual image.

Figure 8.3: Cross-section of the retina.

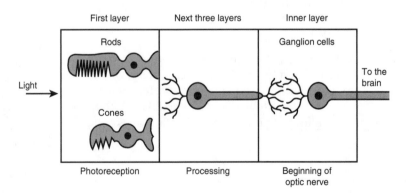

Figure 8.3. shows that the retina is organized into five layers. The photoreceptor cells make up the front layer, the retinal cells that process visual information are in the middle, and ganglion cells bring up the rear. These cells are nerve cells, and their axons make up the optic nerve, which is the nerve that sends visual information to the brain.

Mind This!

"Eat your carrots, they're good for the eyes," mothers tell their children. Well, Mom was right. Carrots contain a great deal of vitamin A, an integral player in the process by which we see—it's what the photopigment rhodopsin is made of. When light hits rhodopsin, the light breaks it apart. When this reaction occurs within a particular rod, the breakup of the rhodopsin is registered as white.

What form does this information take? Visual information is transmitted to the brain via the ganglion cells, each of which has a receptive field that represents a specific portion of the surface of the retina.

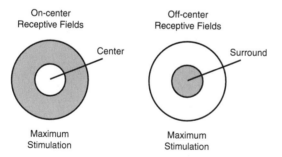

Figure 8.4: Two receptive fields.

Receptive fields in a ganglion tend to be round, and come in two types: on-center and off-center. Figure 8.4 shows an on-center ganglion cell responding to light in the center of its receptive field by firing at an increased rate. Light striking the area around the center makes the firing drop back to a more normal, at-rest rate. An off-center ganglion cell works in the exact opposite way: it increases its firing rate when light hits the outer portion, and slows up that rate when light hits the center.

These cells thus measure light according to the degree of *contrast*; they do not measure the absolute degree of illumination in your room or visual field. In fact, an increase in general diffuse light causes a very weak response in these ganglion cells because, as diffuse light increases, it increases equally in both the center and the surround and therefore the contrasts in an image are reduced. The practical effect of a system that measures contrast this way can be seen in Figure 8.5.

Figure 8.5: Effect of contrast on perception.

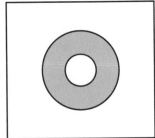

Notice in Figure 8.5 that the gray looks darker when surrounded by black, and it looks lighter when surrounded by gray. This is an effect of greater or lesser contrast (gray on black provides a greater contrast than gray on gray does).

But we do need to know more than just the contrasts. For one thing, we need to measure the absolute degree of illumination so that our pupils can dilate or constrict to sharpen our focus on a visual image. For this purpose there is a whole other set of ganglion cells, specifically devoted to gathering this necessary information.

The middle layers of the retina have to do a great deal of information-processing to go from the pixels seen in the photoreceptor cells to get them into shape for use by the ganglion cells. Where there is processing, there is always the opportunity for distortion. From the ganglion cell layer, information flows up the optic nerve and diverges into two complementary pathways.

The Low Road and the High Road Between the Brain and the Eye

Visual information that takes the *low road* is information that you need to perform the physical tasks of seeing: pupil constriction and dilation, and lens expansion or contraction. Your eye sends this information to the brainstem, where motor nuclei are stimulated, touching off the physical responses that help you see.

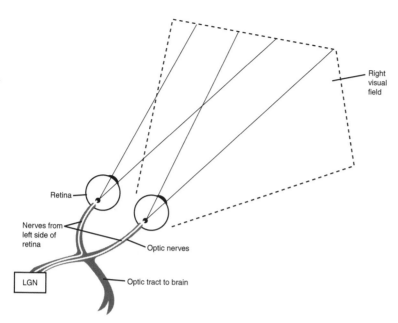

Figure 8.6: The high road of visual information transmission.

Visual information taking the high road is information about the actual image you're looking at. It gets to the brain through the optic nerve, and then on through two optic tracts. Information from parts of both the right and left eye are combined into two sets of signals that are sorted out into two separate *visual fields*, right and left. The information encoded in the right visual field is then shipped off to the left side of the brain; information encoded in the left visual field gets sent off to the right side. In the process, the upside-down and inverted image that originally gets dumped on your retina gets flipped back to right-side-up.

Each visual field is serviced by both eyes. In this way, information from the two eyes is mixed. However, there are also pieces of information, sent to the brain, which represent input from each *eye*, not each visual field. This is important for depth perception.

Depth perception is divided into near-field (less than 100 feet away) and far-field (greater than 100 feet). Near-field depth perception requires two eyes. The eyes are approximately 2.5 inches apart, and therefore have slightly different views of an object. You can prove this to yourself: pick an object to view that is less than 100 feet away from you. Close one eye and focus on the image, and then open the closed eye and close the open one. Shift back and forth between eyes rapidly, and you'll note that the image seems to jump slightly sideways. This happens because each of your eyes is oriented to the image from a slightly different position at the near distance.

Complete the following exercise:

Put an eye patch over one eye, and wear it for an hour or so. Notice how you see less depth than you would with two eyes. Notice also that over the course of the hour, your single eye gets better at recognizing two-dimensional detail.

Far-field depth perception does *not* require two eyes. When objects are greater than 100 feet away, both eyes are essentially looking straight ahead, and the distance to the object mitigates any minor differences in orientation from one eye to the other. In this case, the brain relies on *monocular depth cues* (such as a previous familiarity with the size of an object, distribution of shadows, or illumination) to make judgments about the depth and contour of the image.

So, there's distortion at the point where an image is received in our retinas (the image is inverted and upside down), and there's potential for distortion while the image is being processed on its way to the brain.

Brain Food

In the movies, people see stars when conked in the noggin. This actually occurs: it results from the stimulation of the occipital cortex as it bounces against the skull. Nerve cells in various cortical columns are stimulated to randomly fire, which creates false and incomplete images that take the form of light flashes, or stars.

Still more distortions can happen during the process of reorganizing the visual image in your primary visual cortex. The visual information moves on through several other synaptic stations for further processing. Along the way, the final picture of the world is systematically assembled. Finally, we arrive at the association cortex, where all these reassembled *video* signals are mixed with the sound track that's been arriving from the ears, the vibrational info from the skin, and so on. In the end, you get a kind of director's cut of the movie in the mind.

But, you'll note that at every step of the way, there are opportunities for distortions in the signal. There are at least eight different synaptic stations that the visual data has to cross, not to mention all sorts of substations, where transmission failure and distortion can occur.

Visual perception is often compared to a camera, but that implies a strictly faithful reproduction of the original image once it's been handed on to the brain for processing. That just isn't so. The brain doesn't just passively take the image it is given—it customizes it. To understand what this means, think of a movie scene when the hero approaches the foreground from the background. The hero's image gets larger as he gets closer to the camera lens, but your brain doesn't interpret it in quite those literal terms. You don't perceive the approaching hero as actually getting bigger—you take your cues from the visual image, combine it with your experience and expectations, and come up with the judgment that he's staying the same size, but simply getting closer. The approach only gives the *illusion* that his image is increasing in size.

By examining illusions, we can get an idea of some of the principles that the brain uses to customize our visual world.

Figure 8.7: Optical illusion: a vase or faces?

Take a look at Figure 8.7. Do you see a vase, or two faces gazing at each other? Maybe you can alternate between the two, but you *can't* see both visual possibilities at the same time. The brain has to impose order on its visual input, and one way to do that is to organize an image into object and ground. As soon as you choose one possible figure as the object, the remaining figure immediately disappears into the background, or *ground*. (More about the processing of visual information in Part 3.) But you can train yourself to be able to recognize either possibility, and to switch back and forth between them at will.

Beauty Is in the Eyes of the Beholder

More specifically, beauty is in the *brain* of the beholder.

Complete the following exercise:

Try to enhance your color appreciation. Look at any object, person, or animal for five seconds, turn around, and write down all the colors you saw. Now, look again more closely. You'll see more colors, guaranteed. In your first quick glance, you selectively registered the dominant contrasts and colors. By taking a longer and closer look, you find much more variety.

Your appreciation of beauty is affected by many factors. In the movie world, the "golden hour" is an hour just before sunset. Colors are enhanced and look richer at this time. The sky is bluer, grass is greener, and sagebrush acquires a deep yet intimate shade of brown. Sunlight really *does* have different qualities as the big yellow ball moves from the eastern horizon to its setting place in the west. And there is a specific time of day when our perceptions of its quality change.

Complete the following exercise:

In the mid-afternoon (around 2 p.m.) of a day when the sky is clear and you have a good view of the western horizon, take a companion and spend a few hours together, just observing the scene. Each of you should make a record of the time of day when the colors of the familiar objects change and take careful note of *how* they change. See how closely your observations of color and time match those of your companion.

The point is that we perceive objects very differently, even if they are not physically changing. This depends on many outside variables such as sunlight and perspective. Similarly, these qualities may affect your brain differently, having an effect on your mood, your judgment, or even many of the decisions you make. The more you can consciously affect reception, the more you can take control of the power of effective intelligence.

The Least You Need to Know

➤ The eye is a very sophisticated camera.

➤ Visual information is initially picked up as pixels and then transmitted to the brain as doughnuts.

➤ We see mainly the contrast between different light intensities, not absolute intensity.

➤ Visual information meshes with other modalities in the association cortex to make a "movie" in your mind.

➤ You can train your visual system to gather relevant information that helps to enhance your effective intelligence.

Hearing the Silence, and a Lot More

See no evil, hear no evil, and you might as well add experience no reality. Our ears enable us to connect with our fellow Earthlings, whether they be human, animal, or vegetable. Most people would say that their sight would be the most devastating sense to lose, but losing your hearing will definitely make life most lonely. Sounds are everywhere, all the time—all we need to do is tune in. Stop boasting to your fellow campers and turn down the radio on your next wilderness outing at twilight. The symphony of the woods will be sung to you by coyotes, crickets, frogs, mosquitoes, birds, gophers, and your own inner voice.

As Beethoven's slide into deafness progressed, he left the streets of Vienna and composed out of a cabin in what was then the Austrian wilderness. His Pastoral symphony evokes sounds of nature and the experiences of the people who live close to it. Images of babbling brooks, singing birds, rolling hills, thunderclouds, rainbows, and earth-connected country dancers have never been more clearly painted with musical notes.

Of Megaphones and Microphones

We all know that our brains hear from the headphones that we call ears. But we have internal "ears," too. In our quest for greater effective intelligence, we can train both our external and our internal ears to provide us with a higher caliber of sound information.

The ear is a funny-looking appendage, hanging there on the side of the head. But the externally visible part of the organ is only part of the story. Most of the action that we call "hearing" is accomplished in the much more discrete parts of the organ, cozily tucked away inside our heads.

The ear is divided into three parts, conveniently named the outer ear, the middle ear, and the inner ear. The outer ear is a 19th century megaphone connected to a 21st century microphone, the eardrum. Sound funnels in from the outer ear and hits the eardrum as waves. Each wave of sound has a specific frequency (pitch) and amplitude (volume). Just as the eye turns the wave-particle phenomenon called light into electrical signals between neurons, the middle ear translates sound (a wave traveling through the air) into pulsations of fluids that fill the inner ear. This is illustrated in Figure 9.1.

Figure 9.1: Cross-section of the ear.

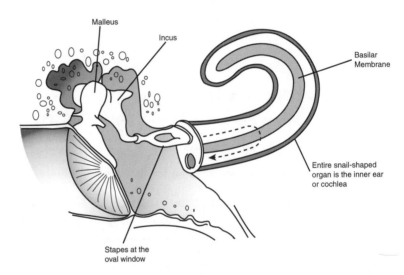

Sound is gathered by the outer ear and produces vibrations in the tympanic membrane, or *eardrum*. These vibrations then travel through three little bones, which are called the hammer, anvil, and stirrup because that's what the bones are shaped like. Once the vibrations reach the stirrup, the little bone responds by passing them along to the inner ear through a membrane called the *oval window*.

When the oval window vibrates, it transmits these vibrations to the fluid that is contained on its inner side, cupped in a structure called the cochlea (*the snail*). This vibrating fluid sets up the signals that are ready to be picked up, coded, and transmitted by the nervous system.

The cochlea is curled up like a snail's tail; its general anatomy is seen in Figure 9.2. Its inner surface is lined with several types of cells, the most important of which are the outer hair cells. These cells have hairs on top of them that move when fluid moves past them. Cells are not specific for certain frequencies, but patterns of cell firings are. How does this occur? The answer is complicated, but we'll go over a few simple concepts.

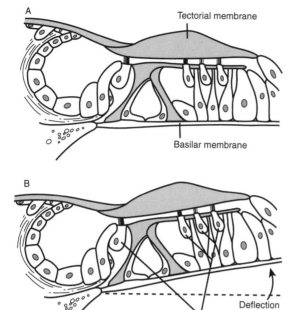

Figure 9.2: Cross-section of an inner ear cell.

The simplified diagram in Figure 9.2 shows a cross-section of the basilar membrane, the hair cell, and the tectorial membrane, a stationary membrane overlying and attached to the hair cell. The basic mechanism of sound transduction involves the displacement of the basilar membrane by a sound wave conducted through the cochlear fluid. When this happens, the hair cell moves too, but the tectorial membrane does not. This results in a bending of the hair, which stimulates a release of neurotransmitter to the auditory nerve.

But how does the ear distinguish sounds of differing frequencies? When a sound of a certain frequency hits the oval window, a wave of displacement travels along the basement membrane. This is similar to the way a wave travels down a rope or a whip when it is *snapped* from one end. The location of the peak of the wave is different for each frequency, giving a characteristic *signature* and enabling the brain to tell the difference between different frequencies. Loudness is determined by the amplitude of the wave.

This response can be influenced, however. Hair cells have differing lengths of *hairs* that can influence the way sound is recorded. It also appears that hair cells can change their shape as well as the length of the hair. Finally, internal electrical properties of each cell can change to make it more or less likely that a message will be sent to the auditory nerve. The point is, once again, that even at the level of the receptor, the acquisition of

Brain Food

The whole process of hearing can work in reverse. The ear can actually produce sounds that can be recorded from the outer ear. Hair cells may move, causing a fluid wave in the opposite direction, vibrating the oval window and ultimately working its way back to the eardrum. The subsequent vibration of the eardrum produces a sound. This may be a cause of some cases of tinnitus, or ringing in the ears.

sound information from the environment can be modified. This is built into the system! All of this helps the brain customize its view of the world.

Signals from the basilar membrane go up the auditory nerve, synapse at a few places in the brain stem, cross over to the other side (about half of them do this), say hello to other sense modalities in the thalamus, and then move on up to the temporal lobe of the cerebral cortex (next door to the hippocampus). High-frequency and low-frequency sounds separate out at this point because each has a separate primary reception center.

Sometimes sound at a certain frequency feels "bad," and this is an individualized response. Pretty much every-body will cringe when fingernails meet blackboard, but other reactions to sounds are by no means as universal. Some people voluntarily listen to singing chipmunks; others can't bear anything but cool jazz. In some brains, seizures can be set off by just the right frequency of sound.

How to Hear What Is Being Screamed into Your Ears

Our basilar membranes and brains are conditioned to being able to hear sounds with frequencies from about 20 to 20,000 cycles per second (Hz). Can we train ourselves to hear higher and lower pitched sounds? Can we train ourselves to hear subtle differences between frequencies? Can we train ourselves to listen to more than one musical, voice, or nature track at the same time? Yes, yes, and yes.

Where do the ears learn? The structures in the eye that regulate its behavior or changes (like lens-widening or, pupil-dilating) are a lot easier to spot. And, knowing where they are, you can take a page from Andy's training manual and set up exercises that will eventually result in restructuring your optical architecture and improve the quantity and quality of the visual information you receive. That's not so straightforward when it comes to your hearing. Still, we know that a well-trained auditory system likely involves increasing the number and complexity of neural connections in the cerebral cortex—after all, that worked for Andy, back in Chapter 4.

Healthy use of the auditory system makes it a more sensitive and useful microphone to the world. Musical ability and appreciation runs in families, partly because of genetics, but mostly through exposure. People who grow up in talkative families learn the musicality of speech and develop the skills that can help them become great actors, playwrights, and directors. Kids who hang around mechanic shops learn more than just what gizmo is connected to which widget—they learn to *hear* when an engine isn't sounding right.

The other side of the coin—abuse it, lose it. When lazy cover-band musicians try to compensate for their inability by playing louder on stage, the crowd pays the price. Ever wonder why forty-year olds who went to too many pick-up bars and rock concerts in their twenties and thirties utter, "What did you say?" as often as your grandfather did on his 75th birthday? Loud industrial noises, on and off the job, do nothing to help make an urban welder, machinist, or stockbroker into a musical Einstein, either.

Natural stress is the best environment for any sense-modality workout for whatever sense you're working on improving. Although the sounds generated in a natural environment are ever-present, generally speaking, they are non-intrusive. If this is true for the other senses, it seems only logical to assume that it's true for working on your hearing skills.

What Does It All Mean?

Natural stress is a veterinary term. For example, horses have to eat and drink. One could keep these animals in their stalls and bring them food and water. But an environment that promotes natural stress—one in which they would have to walk to the barn to eat and down to the river to drink, stimulates their senses all along the way.

Complete the following exercise:

Go to a crowded restaurant where there is lots of talking. Eavesdrop on as many conversations as you can. Once you get good at it, try to listen to two conversations at the same time. Close your eyes, and see if this makes a difference in how well you can track multiple conversational threads.

Training the Ears Inside Your Brain to Sing by Themselves

Have you ever found yourself listening to a song inside your head, and it gets *louder*? Relax, you're not auditioning for a three-year run as star patient in a psych ward. You are *visualizing* sound—a rather misleading term for the spontaneous actualization of your natural aural skills.

This is what the stone-deaf Beethoven did, in what the musicologists called his *third* period, and look at the results. Three major symphonies, each more intense and more intricate than the one that preceded it. Add a whole bunch of sonatas, string quartets, oratorios, and a concerto or two. We listeners who do have ears always notice that Beethoven's third-period music is far better than what he turned out in the first two periods of his life, when his hearing was intact.

Complete the following exercise:

With eyes closed, put a multi-track orchestral piece on the CD player. Listen to the whole piece from start to finish. Now, listen again, focusing on just one instrument. Continue until you've given your ears and mental attention to every instrument you can find to focus on. Now, listen to the entire piece again, for the big picture. During this final hearing, do you hear *flaws* in it that you would correct that weren't apparent on the first hearing? How would *you* conduct, rescore, or play this piece? Can you hear and feel the ringing *silence* between and behind the notes?

Writers of dialogue for screen and stage do auditory visualization constantly. You have to hear the lines spoken in the head before you can justify putting them onto paper. And a real writer's brain is never on vacation—it's always pulling information in from the environment. The girlfriend of one of the staff writers for *Star Trek* playfully moans that her boyfriend is always in analytical mode when the TV is on. The same writer hung out in pizza joints in NYC when he was writing for *Fame,* trying to get a feel for how kids talk.

But you can condition your ear, even when you are *not* consciously analyzing what is being said around you. Many great drama writers keep the TV going in the background when they are cleaning the sink, filling out their tax forms, or even calling their girlfriends.

Hearing with the Brain and Hearing with the Heart

Einstein says, "Without science, spirituality is blind. Without spirituality, science is lame." All creativity involves cooperation between the spiritual and scientific parts of the brain. And that should give you a clue about how we learn and how best to teach. How many of us learned to hate reading because, long before we had a chance to get caught up in a well-told story, we learned to hate the *mechanics* of the process that took up the whole first few years of reading lessons. The emotional engagement was sacrificed for the scientific understanding.

Sid Fields, guru of every screenplay writer on a steady paycheck east of Jersey and west of the Sierra Nevadas, reminds his readers that "Screenplay is structure." Even the most unstructured art form has structural rules to it, determined by how we have been trained to hear them. Jokes are always most effective if delivered according to the rule of threes (two set-ups, one punch line); stories that move us always have a defined beginning, middle, and end; as do each of the two-minute scenes in a 120-minute movie. Great scriptwriters feel and transmit human emotion, but they do so with the application of their mastery of the craft. So do musicians. Primal screams just aren't good enough (as the sales figures on early Yoko Ono records make clear).

Complete the following exercise:

This is one you'll want to repeat over several evenings. Listen to the symphony of the woods. Sunset is the best time to do this because it is a time when creatures get dead quiet, then begin to *talk* to each other. (Yes, our furry friends have happy hour after a hard day's work, too.) When you first arrive, breathe deeply, and (if possible) spend time doing meditative exercises. On your first evening out, identify as many sounds as you can. Notice how the quality and quantity of sounds change over the course of your visit. After several such field trips, notice how you seem to be able to hear with *bigger* ears, and that the number of sounds you come to recognize as familiar (even if you can't name just what *made* them) has increased.

The Harmonics of Sound—Not Just for Musicians

Ever wonder why some people can only sing lead, but not harmony? Yes, a lot of it has to do with ego. But even if you want to be head of the rock and roll band, you have to be able to write for or direct the background singers, and to do that you have to be able to be a background, harmony, or second-fiddle player yourself.

In the western world, sound is divided like the keyboard. Eight white keys in an octave, five black ones. The notes define the melody. The chords around the notes provide tone for the melody, a chord being one note higher than the melody note and a second note below that of the melody. Major chords sound simple; minor chords more *exotic*.

Every note has a chord around it. Musical Einsteins hear chords, not notes. Catch the subtle movements of the hand of a musical Einstein as he/she hears a new melody. The fingers will play the chord around the note on the invisible keyboard on the knee. The same major chord progressions (C to E, C to F, C to G, G to F, and then C to F) are behind 90 percent of the many rock, country, and blues songs that made it out of the garage and onto the stage, tape deck, or CD player.

Complete the following exercise:

Watch a movie, one that is audio-busy. Robert Altman's classic flick *M.A.S.H.* is a good example, or you could pick a more contemporary, high-paced, action thriller. Try to identify as many background sounds as you can—a train chugging along, water rippling, footsteps, and so on. Now rent an action feature from the boring, low-budget section. Notice how many of those incidental sounds are missing? How does this affect the feel of the film?

Complete the following exercises:

1. Listen to a one-note melody. Try to sing, hum, or play harmony to it; first going high, then low. Now, do it with major and minor chords.

2. Clank objects around the house. What notes to they correspond to on your piano or guitar? Experiment with ways you can make sounds from nonmusical objects. Go up or down a note or two on the very grand scale.

Hearing the Silence

There is a silent sound of human creativity that cannot be measured or recorded, but can be felt by everybody.

Remember the last time you were out in the woods and connected with the wilderness experience; or listened to some music that you felt in the center of your soul; or experienced intense, intimate love with someone you will always remember (and perhaps are still with)?

It is "The Sound of Silence"—a loud sort of hush or a ringing in the ears that you can always hook up to. It's as much a part of your auditory surround as all the noisier inputs of our busy world. But it's one of the hardest ones to hear. Its subtlety keeps it hidden from most of us, but for if you want to increase your effective intelligence, learning to hear it is probably one of the most important skills you can develop.

How to hear the silence? Close your eyes, concentrating your visual attention on the point above the bridge of your nose (the *third eye*). Breathe deeply from the diaphragm, slowly, focusing your physical energy on the chi point just below the belly button (umbilicus, for you science guys). Make the world around you stop and listen to it. Oh and, yes, if you've managed it this once, you can open your eyes and still hear it.

The Least You Need to Know

➤ The human ear detects sound by changing sound waves into mechanical displacement and then into the chemical and electrical signals that are the language of the brain.

➤ Your perception of sound can be customized, even at the level of the ear.

➤ You can condition your ears to hear more than you normally do through exercising your auditory abilities.

➤ Overstimulating sound can make you deaf in the ears, and in the head.

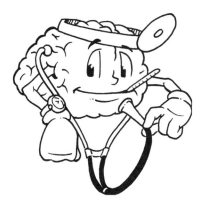

Chapter 10

See Me, Feel Me, Heal Yourself

In This Chapter

➤ Receptors for vibration, temperature, touch, and electricity

➤ Using those receptors to increase sensitivity to the world

➤ How the body customizes sensory information

Good vibrations, positive energy, connecting with others and yourself. These are not just New Age Party election promises; they are based in biological reality, and they are inseparable from the development of a more effective intelligence. Touching may be the swiftest form of communication. A simple touch can be interpreted in so many different ways. The gentleness or roughness of a person's touch is often taken as being indicative of personal interactions to come. The firmness and length of a handshake can set the tone for the entire meeting or maybe the entire relationship. Cold hands…warm heart?

And the right to touch someone is carefully guarded. Different types of touch are clearly recognized—divided not only by the location of the touch, but also by its quality. There are still many mysteries surrounding the sense of touch, but its place in our psychological and emotional lives is clear.

Good Vibrations: The Pacinian Corpuscle

No one really knows *exactly* how we detect things like pressure, vibration, and electrical fields. But there's one kind of specialized nerve ending that displays special properties designed for multiple tactile-sensory purposes.

Figure 10.1: The Pacinian corpuscle.

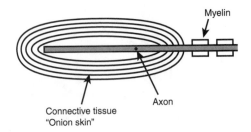

The Pacinian corpuscle is an onion-like cellular capsule around a naked nerve ending in the skin. It enables the nerve ending to pick up vibrations around the skin, pressure on the skin, and (possibly) electrical charges close to it. Pacinian corpuscles are found in several places; nature has carefully placed them where they are needed most. They are highly concentrated on the tips of our fingers, which are the main sensors we use to feel the world.

Use Your Head

Lots of us treat our fingertips as expendable. Calloused hands are a badge of honor in a working-man's bar, but they limit the range of work you can do because the sensitivity is gone. Take the veterinarian who boasts about how he did five C-sections on cows in minus-30-degree weather without gloves. Then ask him to perform veterinary acupuncture. Acupuncture point detection requires fingers that can listen to the electricity (lowered skin resistance to current) in the specific points that have to be needled.

Another place having large densities of Pacinian corpuscles is the sole of the foot. This may seem a little odd, but remember that the shoe-wearing, asphalt-walking modern version of humankind is a fairly recent development. It makes sense to have vibration sensors on the bottom of your feet if those feet are one of the first points of direct contact you have with your environment—tromping down a path, wading through a stream, or tip-toeing across a rocky beach.

"Feeling the vibes" is another one of those sayings that are based in biological fact. In fact, Pacinian corpuscles are highly concentrated in the belly skin. These come in handy as vibration receptors when you're a lion on the Serengeti plains, lying on the ground, listening to the ground for rumbling of zebra herds that will provide you with your next meal. As for us, consider the last time you went to a live music performance and felt the music in your gut. Sound is vibration, and the gut is the largest and most exposed vibe detector we've got.

Running Hot or Running Cold?

Ever been sweltering in a supposedly air-conditioned room, while your fellow inhabitants smile in comfort? Or, in reverse, been perfectly happy with the temperature of the room, while everyone else is desperately gulping tall cold ones and searching frantically for a fan? Well, blame it on your (or their) receptors for hot and cold. These receptors are located in one-millimeter patches throughout the skin. Thermal stimulation of these areas will elicit feelings of hot or cold, depending on the specific receptor.

Two interesting points can be made here. First, your perception of how hot or cold something is depends on what part of the body touches it. Different parts of the body have different numbers of receptors and thus different sensitivity levels. Second, each receptor is hard-wired. In other words, regardless of what the actual stimulus is, if a cold receptor fires off, the sensation will be interpreted as cold. This is just another example of how the body projects an imperfect view of the outside world, even at the level of the receptor. Imperfect, but *effective*.

Warmth is mediated by warm receptors in the range of 32-45 degrees C. Over 45 degrees, the sensors do not fire very much. Instead, sensors that mediate pain, called nociceptors, take over.

Touch Me in the Morning

Another receptor involved in picking up *miscellaneous vibes* from the outside world is the hair follicle receptor. This simple structure is responsible for that indescribably delicious feeling you get when a warm breeze blows across your body on a lazy summer day. These receptors cover most of our bodies (a little less on Sinead O'Connor or Telly Savalas look-alikes).

But let's not discriminate. Hairless skin, like that found on our fingertips, contains several sensitive receptors for touch. These receptors, also called *mechanoreceptors,* come in two varieties: *rapidly adapting receptors* (there are two of these— Meissner's corpuscle and Pacinian corpuscle) and *slowly adapting receptors* (another pair—Merkel's receptor and Ruffini's corpuscle). Rapidly adapting receptors resemble the starting gun and the checkered flag, responding at the onset and often at the termination of a stimulus, but having nothing to do while the stimulus is in progress. Slowly adapting receptors respond continuously to a persistent stimulus.

Brain Food

Cold receptors are normally activated from approximately 1 to 20 degrees C below normal skin temperature (which is about 34 degrees C). Higher temperatures do not activate cold receptors, with one exception. If a temperatue of 45 degrees (hot) is applied selectively to a cold receptor, the sensation is registered as cold. OOPS! The system is hard-wired and mistakes can be made.

What Does It All Mean?

Pacinian corpuscles mediate the sensation of vibration. *Meissners corpuscles* mediate low-frequency vibrations, felt as a gentle fluttering in the skin (sometimes called fluttersense). The precise role of the other mechanoreceptors still baffles scientists.

Figure 10.2: Five receptor areas for the sense of touch.

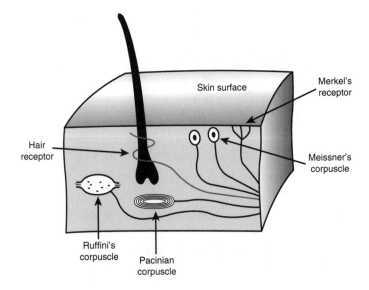

As you see, these receptors differ from one another in the timing of their response to stimuli. They also differ in the size of their receptive fields. The receptive fields of Meissner's and Merkels receptors are small, on the order of 2-4mm, unlike Pacinian corpuscles and Ruffini's corpuscles, which sometimes cover as much as one third of the surface area of the hand.

Why does this matter? Receptors with large receptive fields will have poor two-point discrimination. In other words, they will be less useful in determining the shape of an object by touch or figuring out whether you are holding two jellybeans or one, purely by feel. This is illustrated in Figure 10.3.

The point here is that by varying the size of the receptive fields or the number of receptors per square inch, your perceptions of the shape or number of objects can be changed arbitrarily. This, in turn, will change your internal representation of the world.

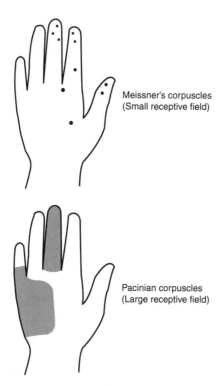

Figure 10.3: Receptors in the human hand.

Meissner's corpuscles
(Small receptive field)

Pacinian corpuscles
(Large receptive field)

Territoriality Among Neurons

Tigers will urinate on the boundaries of their territory to warn others to stay away. Luckily, neurons are more civilized and less messy. Over the years, each spinal segment has assumed responsibility for sensation from its own region of the skin, called its *dermatome*. A map is provided in Figure 10.4.

Sensory information from each dermatome flows up sensory nerves to the *dorsal root ganglion*. This ganglion is a collection of the cell bodies of these nerves, located very close to the spinal cord. This information is then relayed north to the thalamus and beyond. Pathways to the brain first go up the ascending spinal cord tracts, most of them crossing over to the other side of the body. Temperature, pressure, and vibration-detection pathways are relatively distinct, but there is alot of mixing within the spinal cord and within the tracts themselves.

Next stop—the thalamus. Each tactile sense modality ends up in a separate nucleus, and then they mix up again as they are prepared for relay to the primary sensory cortex and a chat with the homunculus.

Figure 10.4: Map of dermatomes.

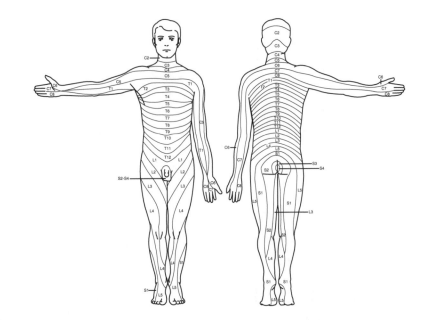

The Man in Your Head

When sensory information reaches the primary sensory cortex, it is neatly divided among the cortical cells. But there is no equality here. The nervous system begins to make some judgment calls and to customize information yet again. Certain parts of the anatomy are deemed to be more important than others; they therefore get the lion's share of the available space and cells.

Feeling the Electricity with Your Fingers

Can we sense other phenomena through our somatic sensory organs? The Chinese claim they have been doing this for centuries. It is a biological fact that our bodies generate electric fields. The entire discipline of acupuncture is based on the fact that there are *channels* (called *meridians*) that carry electric current (called chi) along the skin. There are about a thousand acupuncture points on the skin, which have skin resistance that is about three times lower than the skin around it. Those points are called acupuncture points, and they represent *stations* along the meridians where energy from one meridian system can cross over into another.

There are thought to be fourteen meridian systems, twelve of which dive deep into the body's internal organs, along very specific routes that carry electric fields to organize the activity of the tissue around them.

Great acupuncturists feel this electricity in their fingers instinctively; others have to develop this ability through years of practice. In addition, the acupuncturist feels small, subtle changes in skin temperature, skin texture, and skin pliability.

Mind This!

The most sensitive parts of your hand are the tips of the fingers, most specifically, digits 2, 3, and (to a lesser extent) 4. Thumbs are best used for holding needles, not detecting points. Thumbs are far less sensitive.

Try This at Home

Try the following exercises:

1. An acupuncture point is a small electric *pulse* (usually 1mm. in diameter) in the middle of a gully-like, soft depression in the skin (usually 1cm. in diameter). Run the tip of your index finger up the arms, legs, and back of someone you know and try to identify as many acupuncture points as you can. Connect the dots into what seems to be a meridian system. Check out your findings with an atlas of acupuncture points or one of those acupuncture dolls.

2. Move your fingers slowly toward someone else's body until you feel a heat/electric *aura* on their exposed skin. Do this with several people. Now, close your eyes and do it again. You will be surprised—you CAN see their body profiles with your fingers.

3. Find a nature area that is enriched with water, preferably with underground streams. Walk through it with leather-soled shoes, and then barefoot. Can you feel anything different with your feet? Can you feel where the water is and walk to it, even with your eyes closed? The answer will probably be "yes."

4. Crank the stereo up (from speakers in the room, not phones on your ears) and try to hear the music with your whole body. To make things more interesting, put earplugs in your ears. Have someone else turn the bass levels up and down, and see if you can tell when they are doing it.

The Least You Need to Know

➤ You have receptors in your skin that detect vibration, pressure, temperature, and electrical changes in the outside world.

➤ These receptors are found in high concentrations in your hands, feet, and belly (gut).

➤ The number, quality and distribution of receptors greatly affects your ultimate experience of the world

➤ The body is divided into dermatomes—the brain then creates a disproportionate map of the body, according to the importance of each part to maximal NE.

➤ You can train yourself to feel the vibrations and touch the electricity.

Chapter 11

The Nose Knows: Taste, Smell, and Effective Intelligence

In This Chapter

➤ The nose and tongue as sensing organs

➤ How we learn with those senses

➤ How Einsteins of many kinds use taste and smell as standard gear on their journey to Stellar Intelligentsia

We've seen it before, and it is imprinted into our brains. Throughout the ages, large noses have been associated with intelligence and wisdom. Likenesses of Socrates, Sherlock Holmes, Ben Franklin, and George Washington have triple-A olfactory detectors between their all-knowing eyes. And Einstein's oversized honker was nothing to sneeze at.

Does this mean we should pick people for admission to medical school or positions of public responsibility by checking the size of their noses? Of course not. But the senses of smell and taste are not to be underestimated. They contribute greatly to our vision of the world.

The Nose—Sensors and Pathways

The Martian description of the human nose would be a two-holed appendage to the skull that leads to the throat, which leads to the windpipe (trachea) that goes to the lungs. Lining the nose is a layer of nerve cells that *transduce* chemical information (from odiferous substances) into the electrical language of the brain.

Brain Food

The ability of humans to distinguish between different odors is extraordinary. We can detect thousands of different chemicals in concentrations as low as a few parts per trillion.

What makes an odor activate the nose to tell the brain that the air has definitely changed? We don't know. Though billions of dollars are spent every year on making deodorizers, room fresheners, perfumes, and colognes, no neurochemist can really tell you why a rose usually smells sweet and why the garbage dump behind the florist shop smells rotten. Suffice it to say that, to some extent, fragrant versus sickening is in the nose of the beholder. Or perhaps it in the brain of the beholder.

What is known is that odorants (chemicals that cause odors) first become trapped in the mucus that overlies the olfactory receptor cells in the nose. These cells are nerve cells, but differ from most other neurons because they are regenerated approximately every 60 days.

Figure 11.1: Olfactory receptor.

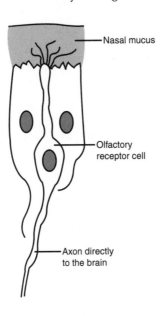

Nasal mucus

Olfactory receptor cell

Axon directly to the brain

Through some as yet unidentified mechanism, these odorants then cause an increase in the frequency of action potentials, which are sent through the axons of these cells to the brain.

But how does the nose identify the thousands of different odors in the world? It appears that there is a whole family of olfactory receptor cells, and that each cell is responsive to one or several different odorants. Information from these cells then enters the brain directly and makes synapses on the cells of the olfactory bulb.

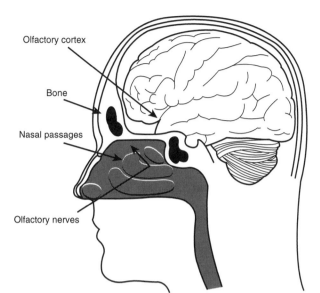

Olfactory cortex

Bone

Nasal passages

Olfactory nerves

Figure 11.2: Processing olfactory information.

Notice that when it comes to the processing of odor information, we skip a normal stop on the sensory express superhighway—the thalamus. Olfactory information is the only sensation that bypasses the neurological customs officer at the "gateway to the cortex" and makes a back-door entrance into the cranium.

The olfactory bulb has a complex organization. Suffice it to say that different populations of brain cells respond to different odors. When the odor becomes stronger, more cells in the olfactory bulb fire, thus providing a measure of the strength of the stimulus. Extensive processing and customization of olfactory information takes place within the olfactory bulb before it is ready to share this information with the rest of the brain.

Why do odors carry such an emotional punch? When someone smells a rose, that information is transmitted directly to the olfactory lobe, processed, and customized. The package is then express-mailed directly to the limbic system, the most ancient portion of your brain system that controls emotion. This produces a raw emotional response.

A duplicate package is sent to our old friend, the thalamus, to be relayed to the thinking part of the brain, the cerebral cortex. This is a good thing because the cortex has a chance to analyze the smell and impose a more reasonable response than your limbic system is likely to come up with.

Use Your Head

The axons of the olfactory receptor cells in your nose are very fragile, and project through a series of tiny holes in your skull (the cribiform plate) to the olfactory bulb. These connections are commonly destroyed in car accidents. When you hit your head at high speed, the brain continues to move and bounces around inside your skull. Meanwhile, your skull has stopped and the axons are pulled apart. Once your sense of smell is lost in this fashion, it does not return. So buckle up!

The Nose as a Tool for Effective Intelligence

Like all other senses, a varied, challenging environment helps us learn. Not only can dedicated gardeners tell the difference between the fragrances of tulips, roses, and dandelions; but they can differentiate how mature the plant is. Veterinarians working around low-budget human shelters learn how to "smell" parvo and numerous other diseases in the excrement of the unwanted furry creatures that cross their path. Pathologists can often smell a dead body, and tell you the time and cause of death without putting a single tissue sample under a microscope.

There are many other uses for the nose in smelling for the source of human troubles, and with time and practice the sense of smell can be made more acute and therefore more useful as a diagnostic tool. Brilliant criminal investigators smell what the camera can't see at crime sites. Doctors, whether they are trained in Eastern or Western medicine, can smell acetone on the breath of patients with diabetes and the characteristic "uremic mouth" that accompanies advancing kidney disease.

But you can still be fooled. First of all, sensitivity to smell may vary as much as a thousandfold between individuals. Some people have specific deficits in the ability to distinguish odors, lacking only the ability to smell specific odors. Small seizures can cause olfactory hallucinations, usually involving undesirable odors. And the ability to recognize odors is extremely susceptible to habituation: we all know smokers who can't sense the scent of tobacco in their clothes (although it's obvious to every non-smoker in the room).

Pheromones, Conditioning, and Smelling the Roses

"Pigs can't smell. Men are pigs. Therefore, men can't smell." It is a biological fact that porcine creatures that are male can't smell. In the mating ritual that precedes breeding, the gilt (female pig) does all the smelling.

Sense-of-smell sensitivity *does* seem to vary according to gender, even among humans—or, at least, the different sexes seem to apply the odor information provided by their noses in different ways. There is good evidence, for example, that women use their sense of smell to communicate in rather mysterious ways.

A case in point—pheromones, which are odiferous substances that are released by one person and affect the behavior of another. In animals, pheromones are often used to attract a mate. It is not certain whether this is true in humans as well, but examples of the human pheromone effect are well-known.

If women are housed in a single dormitory facility for several months, something can happen to their menstrual cycle. They begin to synchronize by ovulating and menstruating at the same time of the month. The "alpha" woman—the woman whose cycle all the others begin to follow—signals something to the others to make their 30-day cycle shorten or lengthen.

The reason for this is not known. We know it is not because the "alpha" woman has a louder CD player and a bigger collection of Michael Bolton albums. It probably has to do with pheromones—smells. What that smell is, however, is not known.

Mind This!

Pheromones can mean big money. Think of the riches that would accrue to the inventor of a perfume made from the human sexual pheromone.

There is another aspect to smell that is very primal, and stays with us for a lifetime. When we first smell something, the experience is almost immediately tossed into a mental box marked pleasant or one marked unpleasant (stronger words have been known to be used). Do you know why? The short answer is *conditioning*, just like Pavlov's salivating Russian dogs.

Yes, Pavlov knew. We are conditioned to associate smells with emotional responses, usually at a young age. The smell becomes the *anchor*, immediately conjuring up experiences from the past. Some of these can lead to odd associations. If the agonies of a dysfunctional family plagued you when you were a kid, and your parents were florists, the smell of flowers may conjure up associations with tension. And if you have hay fever, the smell of green grass makes you want to clam up, not open your nostrils to the fresh spring air (not just because of your allergic reaction—you'll associate the very smell with physical discomfort). If you had a great childhood growing up in the Bronx , the smell of bus fumes in the Iowa town you are stuck in now is the odor of the gods. And don't forget the smells from the kitchen—the ravioli, calzones, and lasagna that you associate with the comforts of your childhood home remain richly evocative throughout your adult life.

Complete these exercises:

1. Close off the other senses and focus on the one you want to develop. When you are blindfolded, comfortable, and in a quiet place, have someone present as many different objects as they can to you with distinctly different odors. Try this with twenty objects, some that you know (e.g., onions, garlic, rose petals), and some you don't know (the newest lotion or perfume from the New Age drug store, for example).

2. The next time you walk into a new place, take a whiff of it before checking it out. Take notes on what you smell.

3. Go to that patch of woods you went to for the "hear the silence" exercise in Chapter 9. Now, smell the air. Make notes about its nature, strength, quality, and character. Is it fragrant? Unpleasant? While you're at it, take note of the environmental conditions. Is it rainy, foggy, clear, windy, smoggy? What time of year is it, and what are the plants and animals doing? Go back there at different times of the day and during different seasons. See if you notice a difference.

The Tongue—A Tool for Listening and Talking

Normally, we don't sample our environments with our tongues. Besides being very messy and painful, it would be hygienically dangerous. But the tongue is used for more than just talking.

The tongue and its taste buds are the brain's microphones for "listening" to the symphony of tastes in the world around us. Without it, eating would be like taking a pill when you are ill, something necessary, but certainly not something to center entire romances around. The old adage is correct:"The way to a man's (and woman's) heart is through the stomach." And humans aren't alone. The easiest way to catch horses is with halter in hidden left hand and food in outstretched right. Even when they know what's coming, they still think that a few bites of granola or a chomp on a carrot is worth being under the control of a human for an hour or two.

Taste buds are strange creatures. They live barely two weeks, and then die, only to be regenerated. As sensory receptors, taste buds are also involved in transduction (the transformation of chemical substances to electrical signals), in much the same way as are the olfactory receptor cells. This transformation occurs in the *afferent* nerve.

What Does It All Mean?

An *afferent nerve* is any nerve that carries information away from sense organs toward the brain. An *efferent nerve* does the reverse, carrying information away from the brain—to a muscle, for example.

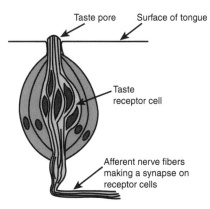

Taste pore   Surface of tongue

Taste
receptor cell

Afferent nerve fibers
making a synapse on
receptor cells

Figure 11.3: Taste bud cross-section.

Taste buds are embedded in the tongue and communicate with the surface via the taste pore. Unlike the olfactory receptor, the receptor cell does not send processes to the brain, but has synapses that connect it with the afferent nerve. From here, taste information finds its way to the thalamus, and then is relayed to a special area at the bottom curve of the parietal lobe—just under the strip where touch, vibration, position, sense, and pain are felt.

Something to keep in mind here—taste and smell are often linked in the brain, but they are different sensations before the brain mixes them up. If you don't believe that modalities mix in the brain, imagine smelling freshly baked cookies and not eating them. Think about the last time you had a favorite dessert on your palate when your nose was plugged up with a common cold.

Brain Food

According to Taoist traditional medicine, there are five basic tastes: salty, sweet, sour, pungent, and bitter. In the west, only four are typically recognized—salty, sweet, sour, and bitter.

Complete this exercise:

Have someone peel an onion, a potato, and an apple. Place them on your tongue. Do this blindfolded, with your nose closed up. Notice how they all taste "neutral."

103

The Least You Need to Know

➤ Smell is a complex sense that goes directly from nose to cerebral cortex, and then to centers that control the emotions.

➤ Odors are often anchors that conjure up complex emotions because of conditioning earlier in your life.

➤ You can use smell as a tool in your job, recreation, and life mission.

➤ We need more pheromones.

➤ Taste and smell are different senses that use different brain pathways, but they are often closely linked.

Pain and Pleasure: Two Sides of the Same Coin

"No pain, no gain!" Just an NFL Today ad campaign? Well, athletes and coaches know that the sensation we call "pain" can be your best friend. It is an indicator that the system has reached its present limitation. When muscles don't get enough blood to meet the increased demands on them, the body begins to produce lactic acid. Lactic acid activates "pain" receptors in the muscle, and makes us feel like our legs or arms are on fire. The sensible thing to do is to stop when it hurts, right?

Not necessarily. While it is true that pain often serves as the body's early warning system that something is wrong, it signals other things as well. Muscles get larger and more effective with increased use, particularly when you push yourself beyond the "pain barrier." Ask any endurance swimmer or runner what happens when you grunt out and "hit the wall," but push on through to the other side. You wind up in the "zone" where the pain disappears and you find an extra surge of energy you never knew you had. And if you keep on working at that level, you also end up with a highly conditioned body you never dreamed you could have.

What Is Pain, Anyway?

Good question, with a very complicated answer, but you really only have to get a grasp of the basics. First, the sensation of pain is a result of *nociception*: the process by which the brain receives signals that indicate tissue damage. These signals are generated by special nerve receptors, called *nociceptors*, which specialize in specific tactile sensations (they came up briefly in Chapter 10).

Pain receptors ring the alarm bells, blink the lights, and wave the red flags when they register that something is wrong. Whether or not you actually *feel* pain is a different matter, however. We already know that signals from all the other sensory systems are routinely distorted and customized, and pain is no different. Witness the football player who plays with a broken hand or the wounded solider who drags his buddy to safety. Once again, we see that the brain does not run a democracy. Events are weighted. Decisions are made. How about a closer look?

Lets start with the pain receptors. These are free nerve endings located within the skin, joints, or (most often) muscles that are activated by changing temperature, or physical or chemical damage. How does this activation happen? When tissue damage occurs, there is "panic in the streets." The damaged tissue sends chemical messengers running in all directions. These inflammatory chemicals bind to nerve endings, causing them to become sensitized and start firing. Even the nerve endings themselves join in. They release a peptide called substance P, which in turn sensitizes other neighboring nerve endings. The result? A tidal wave of signals comes roaring up the nerves toward the spinal cord. Figure 12.1 shows how this works.

Figure 12.1: The sensory mechanism of pain.

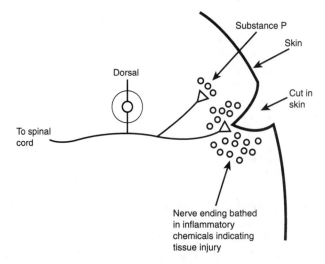

In the spinal cord, pathways cross over to the other side and eventually find their way to the thalamus. The red flag has been raised, but you do not feel "pain" yet. First, the impulse must reach the cerebral cortex, the thinking brain, and enter your consciousness. Once there, it is translated into a recognizable sensation: "Ouch!"

Or at least that's how it happens in theory. Reality is quite a bit messier. First, the presence of nociceptors is not necessary for you to feel pain. People who have had an arm or a leg amputated will often swear that they still have pain in that hand or foot. The limbs are gone, but this *phantom pain* is very real. No pain receptors here, just the remains of severed nerves feeding the spinal cord and brain false information.

Second, even with a full set of nociceptors firing madly away (frantically signaling "Damage here! Damage here!"), your brain may not be paying the slightest bit of attention. This is what's going on when that football player keeps charging down the field, playing through a serious injury. But if the pain receptors are doing their job, how is it that your brain can sometimes ignore it?

Well, the brain has a snooze button. Maybe, for whatever reason, it doesn't want to hear that right now. When that's the case, your brain can activate *descending inhibitory pathways*. These pathways originate in the midbrain and go down to the spinal cord. When they are activated, they effectively close the door on all the noise that the sensory receptors—including pain receptors—are making, letting the brain get some shut eye. In other words, not only can the brain customize any information it receives in any way it pleases, it can also tightly control the messages that make it in the first place.

In addition to all these internal maneuvers, the brain can direct you to take action to modify a pain response, changing the nature or intensity of the sensation. Let's consider what happens when you press down on a hand or foot that has been recently slashed, burned, or bruised. Oddly enough, pressing on an injury makes it hurt less—a biological fact. One of the reasons—the nerves that carry information about pressure are large-diameter, myelinated, rapidly-conducting cables. These nerves, when stimulated, activate an inhibitory interneuron in the ganglion just outside the spinal cord. This inhibits further transmission of the pain impulses to the brain, effectively "cutting it off at the pass."

And the brain can manipulate pain in the opposite way as well. It can generate the sensation of pain without any external "pain-causing" stimulus at all. In 1906, Drs. Dejerine and Roussy described several cases of severe pain resulting from strokes occurring in the thalamus. The patients had aching shooting pain in the limbs, and reported feeling numbness, burning, and other painful sensations; but the injury was in the brain, not in the location on the body where the pain was being felt.

There Are Some Pains with Which the Brain Cannot Be Trusted

Playing around with the sensation of pain is all well and good, but there can be no room for fooling around when your foot is on fire. For situations of real physical damage and danger, the body has developed a system of defense that usually bypasses cerebral control.

Let's say you accidentally place your finger in boiling oil in a frying pan. This is no time for shenanigans; you've got to get your finger out of there. The body adapts a "shoot first, ask questions later" attitude. First, the message comes up from pain receptors and thermal receptors, and gets relayed directly into the spinal cord *motor neurons*. These neurons are responsible for contracting the biceps and moving your whole arm back. At the same time, you want to relax your *triceps muscle*. This muscle has the opposite effect on the elbow, and if it contracted, the elbow joint wouldn't move because the biceps and triceps would cancel each other out.

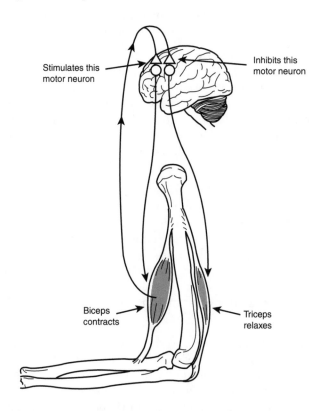

Figure 12.2: Neural connections of arm muscle to the brain.

Stimulates this motor neuron

Inhibits this motor neuron

Biceps contracts

Triceps relaxes

The incoming axon carrying the information about the frying pan also sends a branch to an inhibitory *interneuron*, which in turn makes a synapse on the motor neuron for the triceps, telling it not to contract or to relax. Your arm is pulled away from the point of danger without any decision having been made by your brain—it hasn't even been informed yet about the problem.

Yes, reflexes mostly happen below the neck. The spinal cord and brain stem do the work, by-passing your brain entirely. But even your reflex responses can be changed, if you take the time and make the effort. Learning how to fall, a skill that most martial-arts students are taught early in their training, is an example of how you can train new reflex responses.

Normally, if your body senses that it's falling, your reflex is to throw an arm out in the direction of the fall to cushion the impact. But that can result in a broken arm. Far better to take the brunt of the crash on your shoulder and roll with the impact, but that's not what your reflexes want to do if you leave the decision up to them. Through practice, however, you can retrain those reflexes (as martial-arts students do), in effect reprogramming your reflex response to one that is more to your liking.

Brain Food

Have you ever noticed that when you touch something hot, your arm pulls away a moment before you are aware of any pain. This illustrates the point. The brain is informed as an afterthought, by receptors that sense the movement of your arm and by the sensation of pain that eventually works its way up to the boss.

The Opium Den in Your Skull, or Sometimes the Brain Is a Smoky Room

Dulling pain and/or giving pleasure has been heavily linked to the release of endogenous (that is to say, normally-occurring) opium-like substances called *opioids*. Synthetic opioids include drugs like morphine, codeine, and heroin, and they all have pain-killing properties. The endogenous opioids made in your body come in three classes and activate at least three kinds of receptors, each of which specializes in blocking different types of pain.

Mind This!

"I saw the lion just in the act of springing upon me... He caught my shoulder as he sprang and we both came to the ground below together. Growling horribly close to my ear, he shook me as a terrier does a rat. The shock produced a stupor... It caused a sort of dreaminess in which there was no source of pain nor feeling of terror, though I was quite conscious of all that was happening... This peculiar state is probably produced by all animals killed by the carnivora; and if so, is a merciful provision by our benevolent creator for lessening the pain of death."(David Livingston, Scottish traveler and explorer.)

Use Your Head

All scientific advances can be abused. In South Africa, ketamine (a pain blocker) was given to wounded soldiers so they could go back into battle and not feel the pain. Most of them got shot again and didn't come back for another injection.

There are times when being preoccupied with pain would be so distracting to the organism that the perception of pain simply *must* be temporarily suspended. That's when the body produces its opioids. Stressful situations, like "fight or flight" reactions stimulated by the release of adrenaline during a life-threatening emergency, can cause the body to put aside the reaction to pain until the immediate danger is removed.

And the brain can avoid registering pain—even though the pain is biologically present—by disassociating itself from the body. Certain drugs do this, such as ketamine. It prevents pain information and many other kinds of impulses from getting to the cerebral cortex through the thalamus. If the message can't get through, the brain doesn't have to acknowledge that it's there.

Complete this exercise:

The endorphin "high" can be used to rocket to more effective intelligence. The next time you feel this rush, go immediately to performing a task or practicing a skill that you want to develop. Take note of how much better and faster you work when you have just had the endorphin rush.

A Kick in the Butt

The brain can play with psychological pain as well. "Sticks and stones may break my bones, *but words will never harm me.*" Maybe, maybe not. Psychic pain can be just as crippling as any physical pain, but just *what* causes psychic pain is highly variable from one individual to the next. That's because your individual brain decides what will cause you psychic pain, based on experiences and associations you've built up over your lifetime. Changing your susceptibility to psychic pain requires changing your frames of reference—the filters through which you interpret the things that happen to you.

The Brighter Side of Pain

Everyone knows that pain can be bad—that is, unpleasant and undesirable. But pain can serve a more positive purpose: It can be a tremendous motivator.

All According to a Plan

Collectively, the sensory systems described in the previous chapters constitute our window to the world. Because effective intelligence is based on accumulating information and increasing your ability to apply that information to achieving your goals, it's obvious that the first problem you need to solve is how to increase the quantity and quality of the information at your disposal—information that you receive through your senses. Although the solutions are all different, the problem remains the same. How do you construct a series of detectors that can give you a useful picture of the world?

Notice that we said useful, not accurate—this is an important point. The world that the brain constructs inside your head is a completely utilitarian one. It is there so that you can make decisions and take actions that will allow you to survive. But intelligent beings want more than mere survival: they want to flourish. Goals are much more complex; hence, more and higher quality information is necessary; processing must be more flexible and abstract; output must be faster and more dexterous. We must learn from our mistakes and use this information to make better and better decisions in a never-ending cycle of improvement.

But it all starts with sensation. Which natural phenomena, and what properties of those phenomena, should our senses be measuring? How often should they be measured? How sensitive should our detectors be?

Windows to the World

Even though all sensory systems are different, they have many things in common. They are all open to the world, and respond to a physical stimulus that originates outside of the brain and spinal cord. Once this stimulus is received, it must be *transduced* into the electrical and chemical language of the brain. This information is subsequently logged and hopefully utilized. Much of it will not enter consciousness, but those bits and pieces that *do* must be mixed and matched, and formulated into a perception of the world.

Brain Food

We also receive information from within the body; from blood vessels, internal organs, etc. This information is used to regulate blood pressure, heart rate and the like. Most of this does not reach consciousness. However, biofeedback studies have shown that if we allow blood pressure information to reach consciousness with the aid of a continuous digital display, we can influence it consciously. Give the brain an inch and it will take a yard.

What Does It All Mean?

Submodalities describe various qualities of modalities, For example, visual submodalities include motion detection, color perception, depth of field, and definition of shape.

Meaningful Modalities

To provide the raw material for the brain to form a world view, receptors have been designed to measure certain qualities of a stimulus. Principal among these is *modality*, and each receptor is relatively *modality-specific*. For example, sensory receptors don't "see" light. They detect electromagnetic waves, react to certain properties of these waves, and begin to convey this information to the brain. When a sound wave hits the ear, the hair cells detect changes in the fluid dynamics of the inner ear. If you place a hair cell in the eye, it will not be able to pick up information about light and similarly, a photoreceptor cell from the retina is as useless in the ear as using a sun reflector in the dead of night.

The five modalities of vision, hearing, touch, taste, and smell are well known to us. Each modality has many *submodalities*, and these are responsible for the richness of our sensory experience.

Intensity Issues

Receptors also respond to the *intensity* of a stimulus. An important concept here is the *sensory threshold*, the weakest stimulus that can evoke a response. And that's where you can step in, in your quest to increase your effective intelligence: This threshold is variable, and can be changed with practice. In other words, through using the exercises in this book and other exercises like them, and by presenting yourself with a busy and challenging environment, you can improve your ability to detect even slight changes in the external world.

How Long Has This Been Going On?

Receptors also measure the duration of a stimulus. If a stimulus persists, the sensation usually fades. Witness the disappearance of an odor after one spends some time in a room. Similarly, if you keep your finger in a tub of warm water, the sense of warmth will fade. However, the sense of warmth will not fade at the interface between the cooler air and the water. As we also saw in the visual system, sensory receptors are very sensitive to *contrast*.

Location, Location, Location

Finally, sensory stimuli can be localized to certain parts of the body. Each somatosensory receptor (thermal receptors, pressure receptors, etc.) has a particular *receptive field* from which it receives information. So when a rogue neurologist pricks you with a pin, the particular receptive field that the message came from can determine the location of the stimulus. This is not this simple in some sensory systems. Localization of sound or visual objects is a little more complicated and occurs mostly at higher cerebral levels.

Brain Food

Consider a runner at the starting line, ready to leap ahead at the sound of the starter pistol. Suddenly a kid in the stadium blows a bubble and the snap of the bursting bubble causes the entire line to push forward. The runner has made a mountain out of a sensory molehill by lowering the stimulus threshold for that sound. But this is not an effect on the *absolute detectability* of the ear; it is a change of the *criteria* that the brain uses to determine the significance of a stimulus. Under other conditions, the relatively insignificant noise would have been ignored, even though it may have been picked up by the ear.

Sensational Stimulation

The important thing to remember is that all our sensory systems can improve and perform better with practice. In fact, we need sensory stimulation to fully develop our sensory apparatus. What happens when an infant is brought up in a sensory-deprived environment? Basically, neuronal connections don't form. Dendritic trees stay simple, dendritic spines are undeveloped, axons don't sprout out where they should, and synaptic disuse kills a whole lot of connections made in the womb. Places in the brain that develop after birth, such as the hippocampus, have a circuitry system that looks more like the telephone system in 1930 Kansas City than 1998 Manhattan.

The Case for Challenge

"Long periods of boredom, punctuated by brief moments of terror." Sound like an optimal environment for development of effective intelligence? Of course it isn't. No one learns in such an environment. In case you're wondering, this quote is found, one way or another, in every diary in any war. But there is good news. Most of us live in the DMZ of sensory experience.

What lies between boredom and terror? A magical area called challenge. Challenge meets us when we commit to leaving the comfort zone, with eyes open and game plan intact. We are well equipped for sensory challenge and have lots of built-in safety nets when we soar out of "same as always" land up into the unknown.

You've already seen that sensory systems adapt. Even our snail buddy, Andy Ayplasia, has a sensory nervous system that won't let him get into too much trouble. Every sensory nerve ending, in Andy and in you, has the capability to accommodate changes in the environment. If sensory input becomes too intense too fast, the frequency of action potentials firing off to the spinal cord slows down. If things get too quiet and you need to hear the difference between a hush and a whisper, your sensory endings turn up the gain on their sensitivity dial.

Your brain does not like rapid change, however, so it tries to keep things from getting too out of hand—it interprets and represents your sensory input in terms that you're likely to be comfortable with, so you generally get a world view that meets your basic expectation.

So, your brain and sensory neurons do their best to save you from boredom and terror. Sometimes they turn down the volume, sometimes they fill in the gaps when things get slow, and sometimes they give you a road map with landmarks to guide you through unfamiliar territory.

Living the Good Life

Your biology is designed to keep you from boredom and terror. But between these extremes lie unlimited possibilities. It is up to you to create and manage a challenging life—and that means a life in which you continually refine and develop your sensory systems. After all, sensation is not only a window to the world, but also a doorway to the brain. Improving the quality of the input that passes through that doorway allows you to make better decisions and vastly improves your effective intelligence.

Creating a more challenging environment most often starts with taking action. A soldier in the movie *The Magnificent Seven* said that in order to win, "you have to fight, fight some more, then keep fighting 'til you forget what you are fighting for." The point is that thought alone does not equal action, and without action, there can be no effective intelligence.

Environmental Awareness

Challenging environments, rich in sensory information, enable you to develop your effective intelligence because at least two things happen. First, you increase your ability to handle multiple inputs—you develop the capacity to handle more and more varied stimuli. This improves your *cognitive flexibility*—the ability to quickly and effortlessly move from one input to another. This is one of the most useful skills you can have in this fast-changing world.

Second, you become aware of more of your surroundings. The greater your awareness of your environment, the greater your ability to respond quickly and appropriately to changes in it. And that's not just changes in your physical environment—your increased awareness includes changes in your technological, emotional, and intellectual environment as well. The faster we can react *effectively*, the better we will be able to "apprehend facts in such a way as to guide action towards a desired goal."

Mind This!

As you begin to take more action and increase the complexity of your environment, you run the risk of becoming more impatient or easily discouraged. To avoid this, always keep a number of projects going at once. Make sure that every long-term, difficult project is balanced by a short-term, easier project. When one project becomes overwhelming or discouraging, you can let it rest and lift your spirits by concentrating on another that is working.

But, you may ask, to become a super-sensing machine, don't you have to be in a quiet, peaceful place? That's hard to come by in this hectic modern world.

Complete this exercise:

Pick an outdoor cafe on a street that is not too busy at noon, but "bumper-to-bumper" with rush hour pedestrian and motor traffic after 5 PM. On two separate visits—once at lunchtime, once at the end of the workday—take a seat in the restaurant, order a large cappuccino, and put on those Italian secret agent sun glasses. Pay attention to what's going on at the tables around you. Take note of what you pick up about the customers in the restaurant during rush hour versus the "quiet" time.

Well, if you are trying to hone the *sensitivity* of your senses, retreating to a cabin in the woods might a good way to go. But if you're working on cognitive flexibility, you really need a busy environment—one that gives you the creative "buzz." But you need to pick the *right* environment for you—one that's rich in sensory inputs but not *so* busy that you feel threatened.

Complete this exercise:

Find yourself a book of readings like they use in first-year English classes—the kind with essays and stories, each with a series of questions at the end. Take it with you on a day trip to a more-or-less rural, quiet setting, and read one chapter while you're communing with nature. Answer the questions at the end of the chapter and see how well you do. Now, take the same book to a bustling cafe in town and read another of the essays while you're surrounded by the hustling crowd. Again, take the test. Note whether or not your performance in answering the questions was better, and if so, which environment allowed you to do your best.

Ever wonder why kids insist on studying with the TV or radio on, or why you see people reading complicated texts in a crowded subway? For some people, the increased volume of sensory stimuli in a busy environment will also heighten their ability to *take in* information. For others, the increased volume of input leads to their developing greater efficiency at cutting out distraction. They develop a greater ability to concentrate on the task at hand. In quiet environments, sometimes the tiniest sounds can turn into major distractions. Your reactions are, to a large extent, based on your familiarity with your environment. A country mouse in the city will probably be very distracted by all the noise—sirens, traffic sounds, street noise of all kinds. But a city mouse in the country will be just as distractable when the frogs in the pond start singing and the crickets are chirping all night.

Complete this exercise:

Make a few observations "on the run." Take note of changes in your awareness of things around you in the following situations:

➤ A sporting event in which you are *playing* (effective intelligence is an ACTIVE process). Does your level of awareness differ when you are ten points ahead, ten points behind, and tied with your opponent with two minutes left?

➤ Work, during the middle of the day versus the end of the day. What factors affect your level of alertness?

➤ A nature experience, maybe river rafting, when you are "row, rowing your boat gently down the stream" versus battling the white water in what seems like a sequel to *Deliverance*.

➤ Times when your friends or family are all healthy versus times of illness.

Depending on your circumstances, your brain will use different criteria when deciding what is and what is not important to notice. The criteria it uses has a definite impact on the quantity and quality of information you have at your disposal—which is important for developing more effective intelligence.

Lace It Up Tight, Doc

"Lace it up tight, Doc. I got a war to fight," said John Wayne to the doctor on the beach at Normandy in the movie *The Longest Day*. During periods of stress and urgency, when it is life or death, we turn up the gain on all our skills. Urgent situations seem to kick our effective intelligence into higher gear, sparking levels of performance we'd normally never even try to attain. But how do you go about inspiring that kind of peak performance without waiting for the next major catastrophe to strike (and who really wants a catastrophe, anyway)? Believe it or not, you can learn to do this for yourself.

Complete this exercise:

Set up a "things to do today" list for tomorrow. Now, increase the number of things to do by 50%. Now, decrease the time frame to do them by 50%. Now, the easy part—DO THEM. At the end of the day, check off every item on your list that you actually got around to doing. Keep doing this daily, increasing what you expect to do beyond initial goals till you get a sense of your "I shouldn't" brain limitations and your "I can" brain expectations. Keep copies of the original lists, checking off what got done and what didn't. After a few days, compare your first list (both for length and for number of tasks accomplished) to your later ones. You'll see a steady increase in your ability to get things done.

The Least You Need to Know

➤ Sensory systems have different solutions, but the problem is the same; providing effective input for your use in achieving your goals.

➤ You can increase the effectiveness of your sensory systems with practice.

➤ A challenging environment will allow for constant refinement and development of sensory systems.

➤ Increased urgency in your life turns up the gain on your effective intelligence, inspiring you to greater accomplishment than you'd normally think possible.

Chapter 14

Now Hear This: You Get to Paint Your Vision of the World

In This Chapter

➤ Heightening your level of attention

➤ Choosing what to pay attention to

➤ The importance of cognitive flexibility

➤ Using control of your focus to become more intelligent

Attention!

Now, stand up straight, shoulders back, head forward, eyes straight ahead. Focus intensely on these next few words. *Take command of the sensory information that reaches your consciousness.*

How are you going to manage that? Learn to manipulate your attention and your focus.

Attention is your primary tool for keeping a steady stream of information coming in, and for effectively using that information as you try to achieve your goals. But if not properly managed, it can also work against you by elevating the most mundane stimuli to superstar status until you're too distracted to get anything done. Fortunately, life doesn't have to be like the old *Outer Limits* TV show: in real life, you *do* control the horizontal, you *do* control the vertical... In this chapter, you'll see how.

Just Because You're Paranoid, It Doesn't Mean They're Not Out to Get You

Let's examine attention more closely. When a soldier comes to attention, he shuts out all extraneous stimuli. All that exists for him (or her, for that matter) is self-confidence and a constant vigilance for target stimuli (like the commander's voice). The singular purpose of mind seen in the Queen's Coldstream Guards in London or the Marines guarding the Tomb of the Unknown Soldier are extreme examples of tight voluntary control of sensory input. These men pride themselves on their ability to ignore all distractions.

The essence of this vigilance is a kind of controlled paranoia—always being prepared for the worst by seeking to sensitize yourself to the slightest change in the environment that could herald that disaster. But this attentiveness has a selective aspect as well—note must be taken of the slightest details, but only true threats can be allowed to inspire a response.

For the Coldstream Guards, the primary task is to protect the Queen of England. The only environmental information important to them is information that relates to this duty. If it doesn't relate, it is not let in. On the other hand, the tourist standing beside one of these Guards and posing for a souvenir photo has an entirely different focus on the world. Both are receiving nearly the same environmental stimuli—they're standing right next to each other, after all—but their experience of the world around them couldn't be farther apart.

The fact is that we are constantly bombarded with more sensory input than we can possibly handle. We all have internal censors that distort reality to suit our needs and expectations by manipulating our focus and attention. Much of the stimuli in our environment never reaches our consciousness—we'd all be overwhelmed with such a vast quantity of raw data—but that which *does* get through has a particularly profound impact on our behavior. And as you'll soon see, all sensory input competes fiercely to be chosen as the thinking brain's pet.

Brain Food

Militaries over the ages have known that the way you carry yourself has a tremendous effect on your state of mind and consequently on which things in your environment you choose to focus. Try it now. Stand up straight with your shoulders back, take a deep breath and let it out slowly. Keep your head forward, and your back straight, firm as the Rock of Gibraltar. This simple exercise in posture will result in a state of heightened awareness and freedom from distraction.

Guardians at the Gate

There are two ways of controlling information that becomes conscious. You know by now that all sensory input originates in the sense receptors, gets onto local roads pointing toward the brain, and eventually ends up on parallel super highways speeding toward the thalamus. After converging in the thalamus and mixing slightly, this information is sent to the respective areas of the cortex for more processing, and then mixes again in the association area to form the "movie in the mind."

So where is the decision made about which information wins the race for that moment in the bright warm light of consciousness? One school of thought casts the thalamus as judge and jury, taking advantage of the sensory bottleneck that happens there to decide what information gets passed on to the boss, the cortex. It's a lot like a bureaucracy: The cortex may be the president of the brain, but the bureaucrats like the thalamus really run the show.

But maybe there's a way to make the bureaucrats work for *you*. Maybe you can establish voluntary control over what information the thalamus collects and collates, so that you get to make the final conscious decision about what is and is not important.

Mind This!

How important is it to make the right decisions about the relative importance of sensory information? Well, let's say you're crossing a street in a quiet little town. Out of the corner of your eye, you see a leaf falling off a tree and a tractor-trailer approaching you at the same time. You choose to avoid the leaf. Suddenly you get flattened by the Mack truck rumbling down the road.

Even when your thalamus is busily playing censor over the information it passes on to your brain, even unattended information is often sent along for processing to a high level in the cortex. You can prove this to yourself. Tune your radio to an all-talk station, sit nearby, and try to read a book. Even though you are trying very hard to attend to the words on the page, you'll probably find yourself reading the same paragraph over and over. The unattended stimulus, the radio, must be reaching a cortical level because it is entering your consciousness and distracting you. If the thalamus were cutting it out, you'd never have known the radio was on.

There are limits to how much you can attend to at any one time. And it is more difficult to attend to sources of information when both are presented to the same modality than when they are presented to separate modalities. So, trying to focus equal attention on a painting *and* on the details of the room it's in simultaneously is very difficult. And even when the modalities are different, if the competing information has to be processed using similar codes or shares similar semantic content (like trying to read while listening to talk radio), your brain will still find it hard to attend to both at the same time.

Use Your Head

Your brain really doesn't like to try to process competing inputs—and if it tries to do so, it gets stressed out. Try to avoid such situations: Turn off the TV when you are having a conversation. When you need to be creative, steal away to a quiet room and try to find some uninterrupted time.

In addition to systems for general levels of alertness, there are separate networks of systems within the brain that mediate selective attention. These systems seem to have three major purposes:

Maintaining the alert state.

Orienting to sensory stimuli.

Detecting "target events," whether in real time or from memory.

For example, if you're looking straight ahead but want to focus on your kid brother, who is standing off to your right, you'll shift your eyes so that your brother's image lands smack dab on the fovea, the central and most sensitive part of your retina. This is where direct straight-ahead vision lands and is the place on the retina where the object of our attention is usually processed.

But suppose you're in a lecture hall and you're paying attention to the professor. The professor moves over to the right by fifteen feet; you move your eyes to the right, so that the image of the professor still lands on your fovea. In shifting your gaze, however, you now notice a conversation going on between two students who are off to the edge of your new line of sight. Even though the professor occupies the central point of your focus, it *is* possible to attend to those students instead, even *without* moving your eyes. Although the object of your attention is *usually* processed in the fovea (currently occupied by the professor), you can in fact attend to almost any object in your visual field without moving your eyes simply by making that *choice,* cortically.

Mind This!

There seems to be a limited number of channels available for processing each type of information, and your brain would prefer that we keep a sign-up sheet.

Keeping the Mental Camera on Close-Up and Wide Angle at the Same Time

You're at the office on a normal, hectic day. Your coworker down the hall yells out to you "Hey! I have Jones on the phone, he wants to know why the goods haven't arrived yet!" Meanwhile, you've got a client on your own phone and he's asking if you can ship his widgets in blue instead of red and still make delivery on Friday. While you're answering, you're entering the order on the computer and figuring out what you're going to say to Jones.

Just another day at the office? Maybe, but it's also a demonstration of *cognitive flexibility*.

Throughout human history, this flexibility has *always* been an important survival skill. If you're only focusing on the bear's right paw, and he's getting ready to swipe you in the head with the left one, you're not likely to survive the experience. You need a broader field of focus—you need to be able to attend to multiple sensory inputs.

We almost never have the luxury of facing only one problem at a time. That's why cognitive flexibility is so important. But juggling multiple sensory inputs—and making simultaneous (or nearly simultaneous) decisions about them all doesn't leave room for much more than simple *reaction*. At the end of a hectic day, how often have you felt like you've just been spinning your wheels, taking care of business, perhaps, but getting nothing creative done? That's because you've been so busy dealing with the sensory inputs that you just don't have time to come up with new ideas.

What Does It All Mean?

Cognitive flexibility refers to the ability to rapidly switch your attention back and forth between multiple sensory inputs.

Studies show that it is difficult to be in a complicated, overly- challenging environment and think creatively. The reverse is also true: the generation of ideas from long-term memory and the development of complex new ways of looking at things are tasks that interfere with the detection of new signals. Most of us need some quiet contemplative time to generate new ideas.

But how much is enough? As Einstein would say, it's all relative. We're back to our snail pal, Andy, here: If you've become habituated to a busy environment, you may need only a little time away—say a weekend at the beach. If, on the other hand, you're an introvert who's used to a much slower pace, you might need two weeks in the country to recover from a high-intensity period of challenge.

Managing Modernity

Modern work and home environments are complex and challenging, requiring constant shifts in attention. Take a simple social event: You're looking at someone at a cocktail party, and then you suddenly shift your attention because you've just noticed that a friend you haven't seen for awhile has just entered the room. How does that shift in attention play out in your brain? Even before you move your eyes to focus on the newcomer, your parietal lobe (in the cerebral cortex) first has disengaged attention from your present focus. Your midbrain then redirects your attention to the new area, and another part of your brain restricts the input you receive to this new focal point. Only then do the parts of your brain that deal with moving your eyes get into the act.

All this takes time, but not much. In the time it takes to sip a drink, you can assess the external aspects and potential internal attributes of a human being who could change your life, without even being aware of the processes by which you do so.

The big point here is that many of the things we do that we take for granted, that seem to occur so seamlessly and easily, actually occur as a discrete series of steps within your brain. Like microprocessors in computers, your brain handles these steps rapidly—though the actual speed varies from person to person. The good news is that we aren't stuck with the speed we have right now—if we understand *how* the brain accomplishes the steps, we can improve our performance. *That* is effective intelligence.

Even a Great Movie Is Built One "Frame" at a Time

Although we can become fairly adept at handling multiple inputs in rapid succession, the brain is not built to handle two inputs coming in simultaneously. This seems to produce a great deal of interference in the brain. This is true, whether the information is from the same sensory modality or not. It even happens when one or both inputs arrive purely from memory.

Successful screenplays are written so that only one main thing happens on center stage at any time. The same thing is true about a symphony, a novel, or even conversations. There are lots of things going on in our brains and our lives, but they don't all occupy our center of attention at any one time—something is always predominant.

Mind This!

Challenging, complex new environments can, and often *do* produce novel ideas. The trick is how you manage both your internal and external environments. Use the new environment as an opportunity to test new associations among things that you already know, and you can end up generating new ideas. There's truth in the old adage: A change is as good as a rest.

Now That You Have the Power, What Are You Going to Do with It?

So how do we choose what we want to attend to? Normally, the focus of attention is determined by two things: the events around you, and your current goals or concerns. Of course, both your environment and your internal goals and concerns constantly change, and constantly compete for attention.

Remember, attention is gold. It is a very limited resource. The skill you need to develop is to be able to micromanage your day-to-day input and macromanage the overall course toward achieving your goal. In other words, you must be able to see both the forest *and* the trees. The skills that let you do this appear to be mediated by the frontal lobes.

Although much of what you choose to attend to is under your voluntary control, there are some instances where attention is *not* voluntary. For example, we can pay a great deal of attention to what is going on in our dreams, but we seem to have very little control over them.

Not until we wake up. At that point, if we remember our dreams, we can start to consciously customize their meaning. Even in cases where we have no voluntary control over focus or attention, as when we're dreaming, we *do* have control over how we want to place this in our memory and how much subsequent focus we want to place on that memory.

Vigilance

Chance favors the prepared mind. Life often seems to involve a large element of chance. In reality, however, intelligent people—people who are adept at guiding action towards a desired goal—are constantly on the lookout for opportunities to move things along to their own advantage. They know where they want to go and have an idea of the sorts of circumstances or environments—in other words, sensory inputs—that will get them there. So they are vigilant in their search for these inputs.

The military has spent a lot of time studying the particulars of vigilance. It makes sense: the people who are assigned the task of protecting, defending, and dying for us *must* be interested in finding out how to keep alert enough to spot potential threats, even when nothing much is going on. Military studies (among others) indicate that vigilance seems to involve active participation by one part of your brain; while another part—the part that is usually involved in handling multiple simultaneous stimuli—is, effectively, turned off.

What this indicates is that when your primary task is to wait for infrequently occurring signals, you increase your effectiveness (your vigilance) if you empty your head of any ideas that might interfere with detection. Alertness comes with a price tag: you are more likely to respond to a stimulus, but you are also more likely to make a mistake.

Brain Food

"You can't see the forest for the trees," is an adage that we have certainly heard time and again. Actually, it turns out that different parts of the brain are used to see the forest and to see the trees. Try it yourself: On your computer (or typewriter), make the figure of a large "A" out of a lot of little letter As. If you look at it, attending to the little As, you won't really see the big one, and vice versa. It appears that the left temporoparietal junction of your brain processes local information (the small As), whereas the right cortex processes global information (the large A). Get in the habit of using *both* sides of your brain!

Selective Attention

The brain treats internally generated images the same way as those originating from the outside world. Patients who have strokes on the right side of their brain, particularly in the parietal lobe, often neglect the left side of their body. They can still move everything, but they will only eat food on one side of their plate, and shave or apply makeup to one-half of their face. In the external world, all things are as they have always been. What has changed is the internal perception of things. Recognition of things on the left side of the body and the left side of the visual field simply no longer reach consciousness.

Interestingly enough, this neglect syndrome not only causes a failure to attend to the left side of the external world, but also causes a failure to attend to the left side of internally generated visual images. If one of these patients is asked to imagine him- or herself in a well-known public place and told to describe the scene, people with neglect syndromes will only describe the right half of the scene.

So the same mechanisms that control selective attention when you are looking at the world also control selective attention of the "mind's eye." The brain does not distinguish between the two. This is a very important property of the brain, allowing us a great deal of flexibility in our pursuit of intelligence. It allows us to gain "experience" by using only our imagination. And it lets us call upon our memories, edit them to our liking, and then reincorporate these new edited versions into memory as the "real thing."

What You Focus on Becomes Reality

Whatever we focus on becomes our reality. Focus on something horrible in your past, and you will feel horrible. Focus on something good, and you will feel good.

Complete this exercise:

Close your eyes, sit up straight, shoulders back, big smile on your face. Now in your mind's eye, go back to a when you were happy, really happy. See what you would see when you were happy. Hear what you would hear. Vividly re-create the time in your mind. Add color, tone, and richness to the sounds. Now, note your feelings. Have you re-created, at least in part, the happiness of the original time?

Reality can also be altered by a change in perspective. Say you were to walk into a room with a video camera during a party and focus on a couple in the corner who are arguing. When you played the videotape later, what would be a viewer's impression of the party? If, instead, you focused your camera on that couple in the center of the room who were dancing and laughing, your videotape viewer's perception would be much more positive. Same party; different focus—different perceptions. Remember, what we are actually doing when we focus our attention on something is allowing it, instead of some other alternative view, to reach consciousness.

And it's not just the subject of our attention that determines our perception: it's also the amount of context we allow into the picture. Two-bit dictators and national news media use this technique frequently to manipulate meaning. Let's say there are 20 roadrunners demonstrating loudly against ACME Corporation for selling destructive devices to Wiley E. Coyote. A narrow view might make it look like the city is awash with angry menacing birds. A wide view may show relative calm with the exception of a small ring of avian troublemakers.

So what's the point? Quite simple: You can't always control what happens to you, but you *can* control the meaning you ascribe to the events because meaning is often a matter of focus. Suppose a woman is waiting for her husband, Fred, to come home at night. He said he had to work late that night and would be home at 8:00, but it's now 9:00, and she hasn't heard from him all evening. Before she begins to fret in earnest, she has to make a choice about her perspective—her focus. She can focus on any one (or all) of the following "facts:"

a) Her husband is a womanizer.

b) Her husband has been working long hours lately to make extra money for their son's college tuition.

c) He has had three accidents in the last three years, all of them at night.

d) The car is 10 years old and not very reliable

e) Tomorrow is their 25th anniversary, and he may not have a gift yet.

The relative weight she gives to each of these five bits of information will have an effect on her state of mind: she could be jealous, worried, proud, or happily anticipating an anniversary gift.

Complete this exercise:

Go into a room full of people who are talking amongst themselves, and eavesdrop on a conversation—just one. Look around the room as you listen. Take note of how what you hear affects what you see. If you are hearing a conversation about fashion, do you take sharper notice of what people are wearing? If it's money talk that hits your ears, do you suddenly find yourself noticing who's paying for the drinks? If it's a medical conversation, are you suddenly more aware of your own aches and pains?

All this is to say that what you focus on will affect the reality you create for yourself. Ask yourself what thought, idea, or perception is central to your view of the world, and how does it affect the rest of your perceptions and your actions?

See how far off-stream you get when you have no focus, no "center stage." Relate a story about your last vacation to people who have never heard about it. Switch topics continuously, purposely getting off-track after every sentence. Notice the effect that your disjointed narrative has on your listeners during the course of your tale. Does their interest begin to fade? Do you notice that they start to tune you out?

Next, try relating the story of that vacation, this time focusing on a single, interesting, but minor point. The unpleasant customs agent, perhaps, or the less-than-perfect weather. Explicitly relate every element of your tale to this point—let no other event take over the "center stage" of your tale. Again, note how your audience reacts. Do they begin to seem impatient? Probably not. Can you maintain their interest? Probably.

Finally, begin a new narrative of your vacation story. This time, before telling the tale, think about the main theme or lesson learned during your trip. When telling the story, relate all the events of your vacation in light of this main theme, *but never explicitly state that theme.* You should discover that, even though it's left unstated, the theme serves to organize your tale, making it more coherent and therefore more interesting to your listeners. This is what focus is all about: It permits a mass of otherwise unrelated information to be fitted together into an organized framework that makes sense.

The Least You Need to Know

➤ You control access to your conscious mind.

➤ The ability to rapidly change our focus is called cognitive flexibility and is a valuable skill. However, most creative thought requires contemplation.

➤ You can only attend to one thing at a time.

➤ Different parts of the brain look at the forest and the trees.

➤ Focus often controls the meaning you give to events.

➤ What you focus on becomes your idea of reality.

Part 3
The Huddle Before the Next Play: Processing

Now that you have a good idea of how your senses gather information from the world around you, it's time to focus more closely on just what your brain does with all that data. Part 3 is all about taking what you learn and maximizing your understanding of it. You'll learn all about your brain's "central processing unit" to find how to pump its effectiveness up not just one, but several notches. From sight to sound, from memory to muscles, you'll learn everything you need to know to vastly improve your effective intelligence.

And you'll add a whole new dimension to your understanding of intelligence—an awareness of how you can go beyond the simple world of sensory input to enrich your brain power by calling on your brain's capacity for fantasy. Imagination—the creative use of fantasy—is perhaps the most powerful tool you can develop in your quest to increase your effective intelligence. Here's where you'll learn how to harness that power.

Chapter 15

The Movie Inside Your Mind: Far More than the Ocular Camera Sees

In This Chapter

➤ How color charts become so complicated

➤ How the brain uses color

➤ How the "movie in your mind" is created and why it is in Technicolor

➤ What we can do to improve our visual sense

There is an old saying, "The map is not the territory." What we see, hear, feel, smell, and taste are representations of the real world, but they're not necessarily *accurate* representations. Every visual image you have is like an interactive moving picture, in which you're the writer, director, and actor. You've already seen how much customization of information occurs *before* the information of your senses reaches your cortex, but that's only part of the story.

The Brain as Set Designer

Set designers talk about colors in ways most of us (except interior decorators) would never think to do. Can *you* see the difference between sunset yellow and canary yellow? Probably not—but people in design-related fields can. Is this because they've got better eyes? Not really—you can blame this one on the brain.

Color has a number of properties. Certainly we have all heard of the three primary colors, red, green, and blue. All other colors are combinations of red, green, and blue, or so goes the conventional wisdom. But is this an objective, physical fact? No. It's all a trick of the brain.

What Does It All Mean?

All *waves* have several primary characteristics, including *wavelength* (which determines the frequency) and *amplitude*. The frequency is the number of wave cycles per second. The amplitude is the height or strength of the wave, and the wavelength is the length of one whole wave.

Early nineteenth-century scientist, Thomas Young, suggested that the eye was composed of cells that responded to each of the primary colors, red, blue, and green. A century and a half later, in 1964, the research team of McNichol, Wald, and Brown found that some human photoreceptor cells, called cones, do indeed have specific photopigments that preferentially absorb red, blue, or green light. (*Rods* have another pigment that responds to the presence or absence of light, irrespective of color, giving us information about form and movement, mostly in glorious gray. You learned about rods and cones in Chapter 8.)

The gift that the world presents to these cells is an electromagnetic *wave* called light, offered in a variety of frequencies. It is our brain that turns that wave into what we know as *color*.

Figure 15.1: Lightwave cycles and frequency

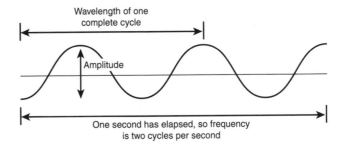

Primary colors are "primary" because they are the wavelengths to which our eye is maximally sensitized. As we discussed in Chapter 8, color vision begins when the electromagnetic information contained in light is converted into the electrical language of the brain. Cones, the cells in the retina that are responsible for detecting color, respond to all wavelengths that fall into a certain range (from 400 to 700 nanometers), but respond most strongly to one of three specific wavelengths. Your brain translates these three wavelengths into blue, green, and red.

As Figure 15.2 shows, the sensitivity of each color-specialized cone overlaps with the others. This means that light of every wavelength between 400 and 700 nanometers will stimulate a different combination of three cones. Each combination is like a key that unlocks the perception of a different color (or hue) in your mind.

Your brain is able to distinguish approximately 200 hues, but hue is only part of the color-perception story. In fact, color has at least two other qualities. One is *saturation*, or the richness of hue. This will change, depending on the background against which the color image is viewed. Certain backgrounds will make a color jump off the page—in this case, the color is highly saturated. Against other backgrounds, the same color will appear less striking—the color is desaturated. All 200 colors can have approximately 20 distinguishable steps of saturation.

136

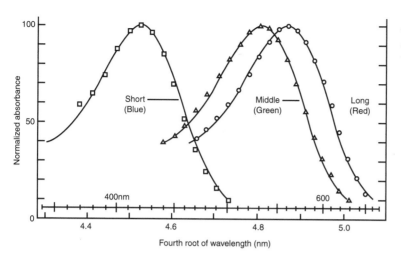

Figure 15.2: Cones specialize in different color wavelengths.

Finally, your brain can measure a color's *brightness*. Brightness is the total light energy that hits the eye. We all have at least an intuitive knowledge of the concept of brightness and how it affects the appearance of colored images. For example, you've probably noticed that an orange image begins to look brown if you see it when the lights are turned down. There are approximately 500 distinguishable steps of brightness.

> **Complete this exercise:**
>
> Have an objective demonstrator put a sheet of one color in front of you, shining minimal light on it. Name the color. Now, try this with different colors, altering the intensity of the standard room light you flash on it. Are the colors different, depending on how well they are lit?

So now you know why a set designer can create an incomprehensible language of color that isolates and identifies variations that the rest of us don't register. There are approximately 2,000,000 different color gradations, based on variations in hue, saturation, and brightness. People in the design industry just recognize more of those variations than the rest of us. They have to—it's their job.

Color Me Effective

Although you may think color is there just to make things look good, it has a more practical use—it helps make us more effective. Color provides the natural world with extra contrast, so that it is easier for our brains to distinguish one object from another. Your eyes *could* differentiate between objects solely by other means, but then the possibility of error increases.

For example, your eyes can perceive, and your brain can judge, differences in brightness. But sometimes those differences are very small. For example, if a rose is lying on a wooden floor, chances are that the brightness of the light hitting the rose is similar to that hitting the floor. Trying to measure the minute differences in the brightness of light emanating from these two objects would not be very reliable—you might not see that there were two objects.

So, in addition to contrast in brightness, the brain uses differences in color. Using color gives the brain about 2,000,000 different combinations to choose from. This gives the brain a much more effective way of distinguishing one object from another.

So how does your brain build a Monet from the raw material fed to it from the retina?

First of all, colors compete with each other for space in your mental image of the world. For color vision, cells in a part of your brain called the lateral geniculate nucleus (LGN), known as *concentric single-opponent receptor cells,* represent the world as doughnut-shaped receptive fields. These receptive fields will either have a green- or red-sensitive "on" center, with a red- or green-sensitive "off" surround. Alternatively, they can have a green- or red-sensitive "off" center, with a red- or green-sensitive "on" surround. The color sensitivity and on/off status of the center are always accompanied by their alternative status in the surround. For example, a cell with a red-sensitive on center will always have a green-sensitive off center.

By the time this information reaches the cortex, the brain has taken the processing to the next level. Here, we see cells called *double-opponent cells.* These cells represent the world as doughnut-shaped receptor fields that are simultaneously stimulated by red and inhibited by green in its center, with the reverse being true in its surround.

These cells will respond the same way to either a green light in its center or a red light in its surround. To see how this works, place a gray stone on a piece of green paper. The stone will appear to take on a red tinge. The green in your visual field (the paper) dominates the surround, making the cell fire. This makes the center of the cell register red. (When green is "on" in the cell's surround, red is "on" in the cell's center.) When this message reaches your brain, it fills in the red while processing the image.

In the first example, the stone is gray, not red. The brain just *created* an image of red that had nothing to do with the wavelength of light emanating from the scene, but has everything to do with the brain's construction techniques. Filling in the red made reality conform to its rules, not the other way around. By now, you should expect this sort of behavior from your brain.

Brain Food

The experiments on double opponent cells were done by inserting a very small electrode into the brain until it impaled a cell in the cortex. These are extremely small. The test subject (human or animal) was then given objects of different colors to look at until the implanted electrode measured an electrical reaction in the cell. The particular color that kicked off the electrical reaction provided clues about the type of receptor that was pierced by the electrode.

There are three additional classes of double-opponent receptor cells that use various combinations of red, blue, yellow, and green. Although this is very complicated, its purpose is to show you that the visual image is broken down into component parts and then built up again. Try to follow this, but don't worry if the specifics escape you.

Remember, what we're doing here is taking an inverted map of the world that is projected on the retina, turning that map into information resembling doughnuts, sending that back to the brain, and asking the brain to reconstruct that image within itself. Because we are first breaking the image up into its component parts and then putting it back together again, we have an opportunity to add things, remove things, or otherwise move reality around.

All the King's Horses and All the King's Men

The whole process is similar in concept to an exercise that is very popular in directing workshops. The exercise involves taking one script and having each director make the story happen in different ways. Oh, such a difference an individualist view can make!!! The same scene might turn out as high Greek tragedy, drama, comedy, satire, and farce. And each interpretation can work, even though not a word of the script is changed.

At one such workshop, the script used was a scene between da Vinci and the model he used for the Mona Lisa. Three different directors shot the scene, each using an identical script. One saw Leonardo and the model as being involved in a torrid affair. Another went the conspiracy-theory route, using the dialogue to show the couple plotting to kill Leonardo's patron (his model's husband), the Duke. A third portrayed the model as distraught at the absence of her beloved Duke, feared dead in a war. In this treatment, the dialogue was interpreted to show the model seeking, and the artist providing, emotional comfort.

Deconstruction always carries a risk. Have you ever taken something apart—a watch, a radio, your car's engine—only to realize that you're not really sure how to put it back together again? The possibility that reconstruction won't give you a 100-percent accurate version of the original is always there. When your brain is doing the reconstruction, that same possibility of error exists. And strokes, tumors, and other diseases can increase the chance of error, resulting in bizarre interpretations of the world.

The Wiring: Old Ideas Verified by New Technology

If you recall, visual information is relayed from the retina to cells of the LGN. When excited, these cells generate a signal and send it along to the primary visual cortex, where a big change occurs.

Things begin to change when visual information reaches the cortex. First, the primary visual cortex transforms the concentric receptive fields into linear rectangular fields that have definite boundaries. Each field is directed by a single new type of cell. This

Brain Food

Only 20% of the neuronal information that reaches the lateral geniculate nucleus actually comes from the
retina. The other 80% comes from
different parts of the brain, many
from feedback connections. This 80%
has the capacity to greatly modify the
20% of input from the retina.

new type of cell in the primary visual cortex is sensitive
to lines and boundaries, and it is also sensitive to the
alignment—the axis of orientation—of those lines. As
was true about colors, different cells are specifically
sensitive to particular alignments. So now, the visual
landscape being processed by your brain is represented
as a series of short-line segments of various spatial
orientations, rather than just as a series of dots of
contrasting shades. This is just another step in the
reconstruction of the visual image.

Groups of these cells are organized into more complex
cells as the brain continues to build our version of the
world.

Understand that the information processed in your
visual cortex is built up, step-by-step, through increasingly complex neural structures. First come the groups
of ganglion cells in the retina. Next, the information goes to the more complex cells in
the lateral geniculate nucleus. The information passes from there to simple cells in the
cortex, and then on to more complex cortical cells.

In addition to color information, information on motion and spatial relationships, and
detection of form is also needed to re-create a version of your visual landscape. These
three different types of information arrive in your brain along three separate and
distinct pathways. Let's look at each of these types of information in turn:

System 1: Detection of motion and spatial relationship

➤ It contributes to binocular vision or depth perception.

➤ Because this system is important in motion, its neurons respond rapidly but only
transiently.

➤ It is insensitive to color and therefore responds only poorly to contours or
borders that are discernible only on the basis of color contrast.

➤ Lesions in this pathway result in a selective deficit in motor perception and eye
movements directed towards moving targets.

System 2: Detection of color

➤ Neurons form varying degrees of doughnut-shaped visual fields that react to the
three primary colors.

System 3: Detection of form (and, to some degree, color)

➤ Neurons in this system are sensitive to the orientation of edges.

➤ Because a great deal of information about shape is derived from borders, this
system is important for the perception of shape.

Once the cortex receives information from all three systems, it can take the complicated process of reconstruction to new levels. All of this is very open to customization during the process of constructing a visual image. (Some of these tricks can be mimicked by a camera.)

Complete this exercise:

To turn yourself into a homegrown Cecil B. De Mille, all you need is a video camera, a few lights, and, if you have them, some colored cels (cellophane or glass that is tinted with a distinctive hue). Fool around with shadows, colors, and distributions of light. See how you can be made to look like everything from a monster, to a man with a mission, to a mobster with a mad obsession, to an angel who got cast in a gangster flick by mistake—it's all in the lighting. Once you understand how the brain puts your world together, you can begin to manipulate it.

And When the Connections Aren't There...

In biology, as in every other part of life, for everything that goes right something can, and usually does, go wrong. All sorts of problems can emerge.

Take *agnosias*, which is an inability to do something, even when you've got all the skills required to get it done. Agnosias can occur in any of the three major systems.

System 1: Motion and spatial relationships. Stereoscopic vision problems—the inability to see where objects are in space relative to each other—can be caused by cortical lesions on the right side of the brain. These and other lesions can impair your ability to gauge motion and spatial relationships between objects. These kinds of problems don't require a brain tumor or a hit on the head to materialize. We ALL are somewhat brain-damaged because the brain's connections are always breaking down and brain cells are *always* dying. But all of them involve skills that we can improve with effort.

Complete this exercise:

Work on your ability to judge distances. You will need a length of string, some sticks of various lengths, a long measuring cord, and a referee you can trust. Head out to a flat field with no obvious landmarks to provide frames of reference. Place the sticks, one behind the next, into an even field at various distances from where you intend to stand for the test. The sticks should stand at randomly varying heights (that is, not tall-to-short, or short-to-tall). Guess the distance of one of the sticks from where you're standing. Your referee can tell you the proper answer. Now, make guesses about the distances of all the other sticks, as well.

The skill of judging motion and spatial relationships includes the ability to judge distances. This includes judging distances of stationary objects as well as objects in motion. The inability to follow an object in motion can result from a lack of communication between the occipital cortex, where the visual information comes in, and the temporal cortex, where it gets assembled into the movie in the mind. And speaking of movies...

Complete this exercise:

Train yourself to follow the action. Get a video camera; find a soccer, basketball, or hockey game; and then shoot away. Follow the ball/puck and the action around it, keeping in mind that the object being thrown, kicked, or hit across the frame has to stay in the center 1/3 of the frame. Sound impossible? Once you get your camera eye, you can do it. You do it with your ocular camera—your eye—already

---

What Does It All Mean?

Agnosia refers to the inability to perform a familiar task, even though all the skills necessary to perform the task are intact. For example, the inability to recognize faces, even though your eyes are working well, is an agnosia.

System 2: Detection of color. Color blindness comes in many forms. There's the familiar red-green color blindness, in which these two colors are confused. Color agnosia is the inability to associate color with the object in question—as in associating red with an apple, for example. If the problem also involves the speech area, the sufferer may recognize the color but be unable to come up with its name.

System 3: Detection of form. Agnosias for form and pattern recognition include a subcategory specifically concerned with facial recognition. People with this type of inability can *describe* someone in the greatest detail, but will still fail to recognize that person when they see him or her on the street.

Complete this exercise:

Try this. Take a picture of someone you know very well and put it on a 40×40 line grid. Now, cover up all but 5 percent of the grids, spacing them evenly. Recognize the mystery guest? Reveal another 5 percent of the squares and have another go at it. Keep at it until about 80% of the squares are gone. You would be amazed at how many people still don't recognize the photo, even if it is of themselves.

The Least You Need to Know

➤ There are over 2,000,000 possible colors.

➤ Your brain recognizes color as a way to more clearly distinguish objects from one another.

➤ The visual world is deconstructed and then reconstructed in your brain.

➤ There is a great deal of room for customization of your visual image during the process of reconstruction.

➤ Visual skills can improve with practice.

Chapter 16

Listening: An Active Process

In This Chapter

➤ How the brain deconstructs sound

➤ How the brain localizes the source of sound

➤ Hearing the silence

➤ Effective listening skills

When asked what sense is valued most, most people say sight. But it's lack of hearing that makes us feel most alone, most out of contact with the world outside our heads, the world we must be in contact with to make the movie in our mind have meaning.

Technical aspects of sound are also taken for granted. But anyone who's attended a film festival or a showing of student films at the University of Anywhere can tell you that the thing that most sets aside a B movie is a bad soundtrack.

In Part 2, you saw that the ear is something far more than a megaphone in reverse. It's more like a mini-sound studio. And, just as you've seen with the other senses, it is fully capable of being made a more efficient and effective tool to increase your effective intelligence. It's time to take a closer look.

More Than Just a Game of Cerebral Telephone Tag

You now know that your inner ear picks up sound vibrations from the outside environment and detects them through a row of sensory "hair cells." Sounds of certain frequencies activate receptor cells close to the eardrum, while others seem to stimulate cells located further away from the middle and outer ear.

Brain Food

From a technical perspective, your ears and brain are better than anything made by Sony, Fuji, or even the reincarnation of Alexander Graham Bell. You are capable of hearing sounds with frequencies between 20 and 20,000Hz (cycles per second), and you can localize sound to an accuracy of 1 degree. Your ability to detect differences in sound intensity (loudness or amplitude) is also astronomical—your brain has literally a million settings on the loudness detection band.

The next signal relay station on the way to the brain is the cochlear nucleus.

This nucleus consists of two separate types of cells, named for their shape. The first type, "bushy" cells, react to an incoming sound signal by immediately firing off a response. The second type, "stellate" cells, seem to take their time responding to an incoming message, but when they do get around to it, they can respond by firing off multiple response signals.

The "why" of this process is complicated. Current thinking is that the bushy cell tells us when the sound is starting. The tiny time difference between when a sound is heard in one ear and when it's heard in the other helps us localize the sound. But the frequency of sound, ultimately felt as a tone, is most likely transmitted by the stellate cells.

Sorting Out Audio on the Cerebral Sound Board

From the cochlear nucleus, information about sound finds its way to the brain through lots of relay stations. Along the way, some fibers want to take a synaptic rest stop; others send their axons straight on through. Also, signals often cross over from one side of the brain to the other.

But it's even more complicated than that. You're not just registering and distinguishing individual sounds. You're also reconstructing the whole sound experience, and figuring out where it's coming from.

Mind This!

All musical information is processed by the same pathways from the ear to the cortex, but from there on, different components of music are actually handled by different parts of the brain. Experiments show that tone, harmony, and rhythm are processed separately and then recombined into a cerebral symphony.

Sound Perspective: Eyes on the Sides of Our Head

"Keeping things in perspective" is more than just good day-to-day emotional advice. It's also an important skill of your auditory system—one that allows you to tell where sounds are coming from.

Locating a sound source is something we appreciate in movies. When the scene includes someone speaking from a position down the hall from the central character, the world we are watching makes more sense if the voice has less volume. Wise editors know this, and will vary the volume of noises and voices so that they make sense, given the relative on-screen location of their sources. They mimic our perceptions in real life, in which we must know if sounds are coming from behind our eyes, below our heads, or above our cranial vaults.

Take the example of the owl. How does the owl hear where its prey, the mouse, is? It needs to be accurate in three dimensions and within less than one degree, or it will never manage to capture its lunch. It locates the sound of its prey on the right by comparing it to sounds arising on the left. The sound generated to the right of the owl will hit the right ear first.

We do the same, relying heavily on specialized ear structures to help us tell the difference between sound coming in from one ear or the other.

Complete this exercise:

Amaze yourself. Have someone you trust blindfold you. Once you can no longer see your helper, have him or her make sounds at an equal distance from your body in an arc all around you. (It's best to use a sound maker that consistently produces the same tone, volume, and quality of sound, like a clicker.) See how well you can locate the sound. You'll be quite surprised at how accurate you can be. But now repeat the exercise after having inserted an earplug into one ear. You'll still be able to hear, but your ability to locate the sound will be dramatically reduced.

The Intelligent Ear and the Doppler Effect

Ever notice that the pitch of a sound gets higher when it approaches you, and gets more "bassy" when it moves on? Think about a car with horn on full blast, whizzing by you. The differences in the sound as it approaches, as it passes you, and then leaves you behind is called the *doppler effect*.

But the doppler effect is about more than motors, whistles, and sound sensations. It is very physiologically and physically real. Basically, what happens is this: As an object crosses your path from far to near, the frequency of the sound waves from it increases. The pitch seems to go higher. Then, as the object leaves, the frequency of sound decreases, making it sound more like a bass.

Complete this exercise:

Find a friend who can hold a note steady and have him or her stand about 50 feet away from you. Put on a blindfold and have your friend sound and hold a note while steadily approaching your position, then passing behind you and continuing on. Notice that the pitch of the note changes? Repeat the exercise with variations in the rate of speed with which the singer approaches you and note the differences in sound quality.

Use Your Head

This isn't smoke and radio DJ mirrors here. When we attune our ears to it, and adjust our brains to trying to predict how fast the object is moving, and to/from what location in space, we use the Doppler Effect to "hear" where a person is coming from and how fast. We combine visual and auditory information for this.

Brain Food

"A play consists of silence broken up by periods of dialogue." So says Henry Woolf, master drama teacher at the University of Saskatoon and former actor, whose credits include *Gorky Park, A Lion in Winter,* and *Rocky Horror Picture Show.*

Hearing the Silence—Prelude to Hearing the Sound

Most studies reveal that we actually register only one-third of everything we hear. There's nothing wrong with our ears—it's just that hearing is not quite the same thing as listening. And effective listening is a skill that can be improved.

If you learn to focus on the silence around you before attending to the noise, you can increase your sound sensitivity. When you actively experience silence, the nerve endings responsible for picking up sounds become sensitized—the better to hear the sounds that *do* intrude on the scene.

Conversely, a lack of silence between listening periods lowers our ability to discriminate between sounds, comprehend words, and retain concepts. Top 40 radio DJs in the United States and Canada are ordered to "keep the hits happenin'" by playing them back-to-back, without even a second of quiet between them. The result is an "arousal" level in the listener described as "upbeat." But with this kind of "upbeat" comes a price. The audience hears all the hits, but can't listen to them as effectively as if there were those golden two seconds between songs.

Complete this exercise:

Have a friend pick the opening (vocal) chorus from three songs with a similar tempo and tone, but different words. Play them back-to-back, without silence in between them. Recite the words. Now, try the same thing with three different songs, but this time insert four seconds of silence between cuts. Take note of how much more you can hear, lyrically and musically.

The Most Effective Earplug—Your Mouth

"Just shut up and listen!!!" It may be rude, but it's good advice.

Dolphins are probably the underwater counterpart to humans. They are mammals, breathe air through two pairs of lungs, are very easily trainable, can learn the language of another species (ours), and have an advanced language of their own, which they use to speak to each other.

But in one sense, dolphins have an edge over humans: they can talk and listen at the same time. Most of us can't. Try listening to what is going on in a room while your mouth is actively in gear, formulating sentences, extending requests, relating facts, and issuing commands. Yes, overlapping conversations are part-and-parcel of every Woody Allen film, hot political debate, and emotionally-expressive family Thanksgiving dinner. And, yes, lots of things get settled, lots of new things get found out, and lots of skeletons bash their way out of the cranial closet. So, you say, we always listen when we talk? Not hardly.

Listen to a well-crafted film with overlapping dialogue. Woody and his mother, lover, and therapist are always talking over each other, but each character makes his or her important point or hits the word of emphasis when the other character is between sentences, words, or syllables. This syncopated rhythm does not have to be scripted or timed by a metronome. It happens, naturally, in everyday human conversations.

But when this give-and-take is not present, you get something more like the talking-head news shows, where everyone is shouting everyone else down: No one is listening, and nothing gets resolved. Obviously, the communication style that is most effective is the one that gets something done—the style that allows the give-and-take of information and impressions. And this is a skill that can be developed or improved.

Complete this exercise:

Recruit two friends. Ask Person A to hum a series of ten ten-second songs—the hum should be in a medium-volume monotone. Meanwhile, you and Person B read a script, alternating turns of speech at roughly 10-second intervals, at medium to high volume and using full vocal expressivity. After two minutes of dialogue with B, try to name the tunes that A was humming. Most people hear less volume and make out less detail about the sound when they are talking. By repeating this exercise, however, you can increase your ability to attend to the humming, so that you can pick out the tunes.

With training, you can learn to improve your abilities of listening, even while you are talking. But in fact, what you are doing is developing the skill of hearing *between* your words and retaining what you hear.

How Much Do You Listen?

There are two kinds of people in the world: talkers and listeners. Most of us, unfortunately, are better talkers than listeners, and we pay a real price for this—in lost information and lost opportunities.

The oldest, and still most effective, trick in any reporter's handbook is to listen. The skilled journalist knows that people love to talk about themselves. Want someone to spill the beans, reveal the hidden agenda, give you the "only for privileged ears" goods? Get them talking about themselves while you just listen. The interviewee's ego opens the floodgates of information, often leading him or her to reveal things that would never otherwise be said.

Complete this exercise:

Carry a tape recorder around in your pocket for an entire day and record the conversations you have with others. At the end of the day, measure how much time is spent in each of the following categories for each conversation:

➤ Listening to the other person (L)

➤ Talking to the other person (T)

➤ Listening-to-talking ratio (L/T)

➤ Overlapping conversations

When does the L/T ratio change? Does it increase or decrease? Does this happen at the beginning or end of the conversation? How does this relate to the other person and what was being talked about? After doing this once, do it again with a stopwatch in each pocket, one for talking, one for listening.

An interesting hierarchy is reflected in a person's listening-to-talking ratio and when it changes in a group conversation. The most junior member often talks first, or close to first. Intermediate members dominate the middle of the conversation, often representing two opposing views. The elder or dominant member usually speaks last, with a few well-chosen words.

ACTIVE Listening: A Lot More than Being Polite and Quiet

"If I'm not talking loud enough, listen harder." These were the words of Dr. John Opdyke, a slow-talkin', deep-thinkin' Texas-bred cardiovascular physiologist at New Jersey Medical School to a smart-aleck New York medical student in the back row. Is the command "listen harder" something that can be obeyed? Yes, and with good biological reasons.

If you remember, sound is transmitted through the middle ear by the vibrations of three small bones, including the malleus. The capability of the malleus to vibrate is controlled by two muscles, the tensor tympani and the stapedius. If they both tense up, less sound gets through to the inner ear, where the neural sensors are located.

The stapedius and tensor tympani muscles both reflexively contract when we get blasted with loud sound. When we "listen harder," we probably force the muscles in the middle ear to relax so that they respond better to vibrations in the outer ear and transmit more of this information to the brain.

"Prick up your ears," the saying goes. Actually, what it means is to practice active listening. You do this naturally. Think about the last time you had a conversation with someone you deeply respect. When they talk, you *really* listen, although you may not be consciously trying to do so. This close attention is something that you can learn to extend to everything you hear.

The Least You Need to Know

➤ Sound information is deconstructed and reconstructed.

➤ Two ears are necessary to localize sound.

➤ Listening is an active process: We can train ourselves to become better listeners.

➤ Active listening is enhanced by also hearing the silence.

➤ Talking is far more effective when listening skills are developed.

Memory and Magic

Remember "cramming" for a test in high school? The word is pretty accurate: When we memorize, we "cram" things into our heads in specific sequences and contextual slots, and we recall those things according to sequential and contextual cues. For example, when a veterinarian hears the words "calf diarrhea," his or her automatic response will be to think: "E. coli., rotavirus, coronavirus, BVD." These are some of the most common microbes that afflict calves, and so this automatic response will usually allow the vet to make a correct assessment of the problem. Specific drugs and vaccines are available to treat and prevent each of these conditions, and the vet can make a reasonable choice among them. But the association of illness with a likely microbe tells the vet nothing about where the microbe came from, or how it does its work on the calf's system.

Why would this matter? Well, take that same vet—trained and experienced in livestock diseases common to, say, western Canada, and drop him or her into the Thai jungle during an outbreak of gastrointestinal disease in the local buffalo herds. The standard "E. coli., rotavirus, coronavirus, BVD" response to the reality of a bison calf dying from diarrhea-induced dehydration won't go very far. The microbes that commonly afflict the livestock population of western Canada are very different from those indigenous to the Thai jungle environment. The vet who will excel in this new environment will be one who has an understanding of how the intestinal tract works; how microbes, toxins, and diet changes affect it; and who can see beyond the textbook answers to real-world problems.

Use It or Lose It

"An unused fact is a lost fact," so says chairman Peter Flood of the Western College of Veterinary Medicine when he addresses a class of anatomy students. And it's true. Think back to your own experiences in school. When you studied by rote memorization, you might have gotten high scores on your tests, but how many of those memorized facts were still with you a week after the final? And have you ever noticed that when you took the time to think through the things you were trying to learn, your test score might have been a little lower, but you still knew the information weeks, months, and years after the class was over.

Time spent memorizing something you can look up is highly ineffective, and discouraged by the wisest teachers. True, you don't want anyone doing brain surgery on you if he has to look at a textbook in the operating room to remind him of the structure of the brain. But the best neurosurgeons around still consult anatomy atlases before going into the operating room to refresh their memories about minute details and to affirm cutting strategies. And wise physicians *do* occasionally look at the dose recommendations on the drug bottles instead of relying on their memory for the medications that go into your body.

Complete this exercise:

Pick up one of those double-language dictionaries used by language classes (English and French, English and Spanish). Pick out ten words or phrases to learn. For five of them, try simple memorization: say them to yourself, drill yourself on them, but do *not* speak them aloud to another human being for 48 hours. At the same time, take the other five words and carefully read them (and their English definitions) three times only. But use them in conversation with other people whenever and wherever you can, during the next couple of days. At the end of the two days, get a friend to test you on your recall of the whole set of 10 phrases. Which five do you find it easiest to recall?

Short-Term Memory and Intelligence: A Mismatch Made in the Land of Ignoramus

Memory is *not* intelligence. There is only a slight relationship between the ability to memorize and the ability to perform. Take two actors: Marlon Brando and George C. Scott. Both are "brilliant," right? They both give life to the words of a script and bring meaning into our humdrum lives through their performances. You might think that they have great memories—after all, they have to learn all those scripts, right? But you'd only be half right.

Mr. Scott is a Shakespearean actor with a quick mind that can memorize anything. But Mr. Brando's memory is not quite up to that speed. When Brando and Scott were cast against each other, Scott had to carry cue cards around for his co-star because Brando kept forgetting his lines. The movie worked, both men turned in stellar performances, and the producer made money—but oh, the difference in how each actor approached his role.

And how about Wilfred Brimley, the brilliant character actor who costarred in "Cocoon?" He was recently featured in Disney's *Summer of the Monkeys*. But though he infused life and definition into every line, he never delivered a line the same way twice.

Mind This!

Great actors don't go "off script" at every whim. Instead, they combine spark, spontaneity, and consistency. Henry Fonda was famous for working out a scene at rehearsal, then delivering the same thing, line for line, gesture for gesture, take after take, and scene after scene.

For learning to be available long-term, thinking *must* occur before memorizing. This enables us to internalize what we learn and communicate it later to others. Rote memorization alone is ineffective.

Complete this exercise:

See what happens when you try to memorize something you don't care about. Get an audition piece from a play or film, or passionate political speech—something with some emotional teeth in it. Before you memorize the lines, try to figure out and feel the emotions behind the words. Call this "Piece A." Pick another piece (call it "Piece B"), but this time make *no* effort to find the emotional meaning behind the words. See how long it takes to memorize the words to piece A versus B.

"She's a walking encyclopedia," is said as a compliment for someone who can spout out a factoid to every "hard" question. We give such people straight As in school, kudos at cocktail parties, and promotions at work. But an encyclopedic knowledge of facts is not the true measure of intelligence—it's what we do with the facts we know that makes all the difference.

Brain Food

You lose something important when you put memory in front of thinking—you lose the miracle of *wonderment.* Einstein spent a large portion of his book, *The World as I See It,* criticizing people, programs, and institutions that force rote memory on school children. But even Einstein had to memorize sometimes—without having memorized his times tables he could never have redefined the universe in the mathematical language of genius.

So, while memorization is a sometimes-necessary tool, how can we make more effective use of our memories?

Memory Processing

How does the brain take short-term experience and put it into long-term memory? No one knows for sure, but there are some general observations we can make about how the process works.

Repetition of stimulus: We learn best when we have regular lessons, optimally every day, and at the same time every day. Rodents will learn to find the location of submerged platforms in a water tank if they are tossed into the water for three successive days. They do far better than animals that get five such exercises spread over ten days. Any horseman will tell you that the equine beast learns best if its lessons are given four days in a row. Miss a day and you often have to start all over again—the horse will forget everything it has already been taught.

Incubation time. You can think of the hippocampus as the library of your mind, but it takes time for it to put new information onto the bookshelves. For each new "lesson" to be maximally incorporated, the hippocampus needs twenty minutes of "off-time" from the stress of new stuff. This may explain why ten to fifteen minute breaks between one-hour lectures have evolved as the rule of thumb in most educational institutions.

New information must be incorporated with the old. You can't memorize what you can't understand. Your brain likes order and relatability—and that's true even for the most eccentric and artistic of geniuses. If new information relates to what you know or can be *made* to relate to what you know, it will more quickly find a home in your mental library.

A receptive mental state. For both memory and learning, your brain requires that certain conditions be met.

For example, extreme terror at exam time is not a productive emotional environment for incorporating information into long-term memory. The librarian at the hippocampal library can only file new "books" at a certain rate, and she doesn't like to be rushed. A panicked cortex, throwing information all over the place, will only confuse the filing process.

Information that doesn't move us emotionally, or for which we have negative associations, is not going to be remembered as well as stuff we really like. Sometimes, you can trick the brain into liking information that it will otherwise resist acquiring. For example, try munching on your favorite snack food while studying for exams in courses you hate. It works.

Complete this exercise:

Mark off ten stories to read in the newspaper. Nibble on a food you like while reading the first story and headline. When you move on to the next one, don't touch that snack. Alternate back and forth like this as you read the remainder of the stories you've marked. Now, have someone ask you what each headline was about, and quiz you about the articles you just read. See how well you recall the articles you associate with snacking, in comparison with your memory of the "snack-free" readings.

Now, try the same experiment, but this time eat something you *don't* like while reading.

One thing to keep in mind: Memory is a process that is different for everyone. Here are some hints you can use to strengthen your ability to memorize.

Compartmentalizing the Chaos

When you are trying to learn new information, make an effort to understand what is presented. Ask yourself some directed questions: What does it mean? What are you expected to retain and what is extraneous detail? What would be useful to keep and apply to your everyday life? If you're trying to learn a large amount of factual detail, say, from a passage in a medical textbook, breaking each paragraph down into a list helps.

Help your hippocampal librarian out. Make the categories into which you divide new information as simple as possible. A wise medical lecturer knows that even doctors will retain no more than four points after a twenty-minute lecture. That's why people slap up summary slides with things to remember in four bulleted "points." The eye is spared unnecessary verbiage and gets just the facts.

Any actor worth his SAG card breaks down every line into two or more emotional "beats" (changes in emotion or motivation). Each beat lasts about five seconds. Key emphasis words in each sentence are identified. Each beat carries with it a specific motion or gesture, sometimes as little as a shifting of an eye or the lifting of an eyebrow. In rehearsal, they say *and feel* the lines. The immediate result is an intellectual, emotional, and structural under-standing of what the scene is about. The ultimate result is a strong, nuanced performance.

Use Your Head

Learn in context—it's always more effective. Actors can usually only memorize their lines if they know what the lines mean. They seek "motivation": How do these words relate to the plot line of the play or the emotional makeup of the character? Rote memorization *is* possible, but it takes a lot more work and makes for a far worse performance for the actor, director, and audience.

Identify the Information with More than One Sense

Those of us with "photographic" memories retain what we see. Auditory memorizers can hear a 30-minute sitcom and recite it back, bad joke to worse joke, to a happy conclusion. Really good massage therapists and chiropractors remember a patient by the tightness of their muscles more easily than the name on the bill. Jazz musicians hear a melody once, and then improvise countless variations.

Each of us tends to rely on one of our senses more than the others when we try to memorize something—and the particular sense used varies from one person to the next. But what happens when we try to combine the senses, enlisting more than one in the memorization process?

Use Your Head

Whenever you've got something difficult to learn and need to retain it, reinforce your retention by involving more than one sense in the learning process. While you read, take notes, repeat aloud what you're reading, and try to write the material in your own words. You'll keep the information longer this way.

Take a medical student—let's call her Jenny. Between Jenny and a lucrative practice that heals thousands of people a year lies Harold, a skeleton with more than 200 bones that need to be memorized by name, shape, and function. The exam will be a written affair, but she wants to retain the information long past the exam date, for use in real life when she takes up her future practice as an orthopedic surgeon.

Jenny could sit herself down in a study room with an unabridged copy of *Gray's Anatomy* and memorize every word of the 220 pages dealing with the skeletal system. That might get her past the exam, but it will do little for her long-term retention of the material.

Let's say that her immediate task is to learn about the humerus, the bone that connects to the shoulder socket. She reads about it in the book, then touches it, feeling every bump and notch, naming each of them by speak-

ing the word. She sketches the bone, coloring the humerus green, drawing insertions of where extensor muscles go with dark red, flexors with light red, and the pathway for nerves with yellow. She moves the bone, taking note of where and how it connects to the scapula at the shoulder and the radius and ulna at the elbow. She sees how much pressure she has to exert with her hands to break it, imagines what the broken bone would look like, and how she would fix it. She glides her fingers along the surface to feel the different textures of the bone's shaft and the specialized areas on either side that connect it to tendons, muscles, and other bones. She knocks on it to hear how hollow it is. Her nose detects a faint odor of blood coming from the small amount of red marrow inside it.

Having done all this, Jenny's ready for her cortex to kick in. It quickly gets to work, sorting through all the sensory data that Jenny's been providing to it, and integrating all that with the passage in the medical textbook. All this related material gets dumped into the hippocampus, where Jenny's cortical librarian files and cross-references "humerus" under the sensory categories of sight, sound, touch, tensile strength, and smell.

Incubation Time and Recall

When you're trying to memorize something, it's a good idea to take breaks—but only if they are the right kind of breaks, taken in the right sequence. According to psychological testing, the following sequence, followed without interruption, is most effective when trying to incorporate new information into long-term memory.

1. Examine the information. Use as many senses as you can. Read it, say it, feel it, color it, smell it, move it around, visualize it, and appreciate its connections to other information. This session should be no more than one hour, with the idea of incorporating one block of information at a time (don't try to memorize an entire book in one reading).

2. Brain rest. Immediately after each examination session, clear your mind completely. There are many ways to do this, but one of the best is to close your eyes in a quiet room and concentrate on a single sound or image. The essential point is that you do not allow any new information to come into the brain for 10 minutes (20 is better, but 30 may be too long). An alternative way to clear your conscious mind is to go to sleep immediately after your examination session, without doing or looking at anything else.

3. Mindless activity. On ending your trance or sleep session, busy yourself with something mindless for a few minutes—something as simple as a household chore like doing the dishes works well for this stage. Don't do anything stressful, and certainly avoid anything that requires you to actively learn or memorize anything.

4. Recall. Try to recall the information you examined in step one. No cheating. See what you know, and identify what you don't know. Engage as many senses as possible in this effort at recall. For example, if you're learning a portion of a script, don't just say it or write it, *perform* it.

5. Confirmation and assessment. Go back to the original information source. Re-examine it, again using all possible senses. Mark out what you missed in your attempt at recollection—focusing on key words, concepts, or images.

6. Start the whole process over again. Three successive repetitions are best—you'll find that by the third time, you will have memorized far more than you think you were ever able to. When you can recall it letter-perfectly, move on to the next learning task you've set for yourself.

Overlearning: The Only Way to Keep Your Memory

Sometimes we get cocky. We think: "I know this stuff; I'll ace this exam; I don't have to study." So you sit back and relax, then submit yourself to the trial by fire and get burned. You really didn't know it after all.

Mind This!

To reinforce the memory, it is vital to go back to the memory grindstone two to three times after you have successfully recalled it. You may feel you've already got the material down cold, but you want to make sure to move it from short-term to long-term memory. Repetition is the only way.

Your memory can play tricks. What you know today, you may not still know tomorrow. To make your new knowledge stick with you, you often have to go over it again and again. This grind is called overlearning, but if you do it—and then do it again—soon after the first perfect recall, it stays with you for life.

The Least You Need to Know

➤ Memorizing is not the same as learning.

➤ A certain amount of memorizing is required to develop effective intelligence.

➤ The brain is better at learning than memorizing.

➤ You can memorize and learn at the same time.

➤ Memory retention can be retained for life if you do it right.

Chapter 18

Converting Brain to Brawn: A Class Act

In This Chapter

➤ Planning for action

➤ Visualizing action before it happens

➤ Right side versus left side of our brain

➤ How the cortex sits in judgment of our actions

You know the old Zen riddle: "If a tree falls in a forest and no one hears it, does it make a noise?" Maybe yes, maybe no. But you live in a world full of people. If you go about it in the right way, you can certainly make yourself heard—and felt. In fact, you have to because that's what effective intelligence is all about: initiating your plans and visions in the real world. Remember: Intelligence isn't just about thinking great thoughts or plans. It's most of all about *doing* something with them. Even the best and most noble plan without action is daydreaming, and effective intelligence is about making your visions happen in the world, not just in your head.

So, no matter how cerebral you are, every plan you make requires that you take an action to be effective. But what of the plan? Action without careful planning is chaos. Where does this planning take place?

Association Cortex: What's Up with So Many Circuits?

Big plans involve many small actions. Consider how many small motions of the hand are needed to play Beethoven's Emperor Concerto or be the fiddler at a Celtic music festival. No time to think about where your fingers are between the lightning movement of notes lasting 1/16th of a second. No time to think consciously, but a great deal of planning goes into the process, nonetheless.

To begin to understand how this works, let's take another look at the roadmap of the brain. Your primary *sensory* cortex collects information from the various senses, giving you the raw material from which you construct your plan of action. Your primary *motor* cortex sends signals that make the plan happen by making muscles move and priming reflexes associated with those movements. It *looks* as if the motor cortex is doing all the work, but it's really only the delivery boy. The actual packages of information are processed elsewhere in the brain—in the *association* cortex.

The association cortex is biologically defined as an area of cerebral cortex that receives information from one modality and mixes it with information from another modality. This part of the cortex is located in several areas of the brain. It takes the processed video picture from your eyes and mixes it with sound from your ears, taste from your mouth and tongue, touch from your skin, and smell from your nose to create the multimodal movie in the mind.

Figure 18.1: The association cortices of your brain.

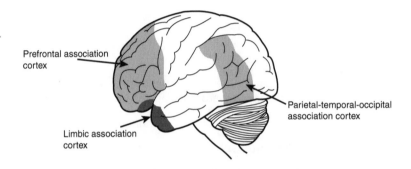

Prefrontal association cortex

Parietal-temporal-occipital association cortex

Limbic association cortex

Brain Food

Andy Aplysia is an impressive creature in his own right, particularly to his girlfriend Andrea. But he can only react to the world around him; he can't think too much. There is no association cortex in his nervous system. Move on up the evolutionary trail to Ricky Rat: about 10 percent of his cerebral cortex is association. The cat that eats the rat has about four times more association cortex. In humans, over 90 percent of the cerebral cortex is association.

Specialized areas of the association cortex, called *premotor areas*, are located in front of the primary motor areas. These specialized spots make things happen more effectively by coordinating movement and fine-tuning the reflexive actions that increase the smoothness and effectiveness of any particular action.

Ever notice how one couple on the dance floor seems to have only a *technical* mastery of the steps to, say, a waltz; while another just seems to be a natural, executing the steps as if the music was right *inside* them. The difference between the two couples is a difference in smoothness of motion. This smoothness comes from the dancers' conscious sense of rhythm, their timing, and their ability to fit their movements with the ones made by their partner. All of this is coordinated by the association cortex. And it can be improved upon by rehearsal. In fact, any smooth performance of *any* movement, on the stage of Lincoln Center or on the stage of real life, involves the rehearsal of action.

Mind This!

When you're moving your finger, activity in both your primary and premotor cortex is enhanced. But if you first take the time to anticipate and *visualize* finger movement, only the premotor cortex is pumping with circulatory juice. The planning is done in the premotor cortex and actual movement is the province of the motor cortex.

So, what does rehearsal entail? Constant feedback and adjustment is the game here. It is the association cortex that directs the action, collects information from all of your senses, and decides what to do next. But it doesn't stop at using only immediately-received sense information. It also adds memories of past performances, experiences, and emotional information from the limbic system to the mix.

To illustrate this, let's return to hammering that nail into the board. As you lift the tool in preparation for the swing, your eyes stay fixed on the nail. Your premotor cortex has already predicted the trajectory before you've even started swinging. You begin to swing the hammer as the muscles in your hand and arm keep a constant flow of messages going to your brain, informing it about how much they are being stretched. And your brain is constantly monitoring the situation, judging where you are in the swing—at the bottom, where you're still gauging the point of impact; or at the top, where you're ready to let the hammer rip forward at full speed.

Use Your Head

Premotor problems don't prevent people from doing actions, but they do make doing those actions far more difficult. In the case of the guy with the hammer, he might not only miss the nail, but possibly the wood as well.

Motor Cortex: Just Where Are the Engines Under the Cerebral Hood?

The stimulation of specific nerve cells in your head make your limbs, digits, and other parts of your anatomy move in very specific ways. And, just like Dr. Frankenstein's experiments, this stimulation is accomplished by electrical charges. But unlike his "monster," *you* don't have to get hit by lightning to be energized into action. The area of the brain that is most directly involved in making your body move is called the motor "strip." Each subarea of this strip is assigned to a specific body part and regulates the action *of* that body part.

All this information funneling into one place makes the association cortex an ideal place for the seat of thinking, judgment and other higher functions, which are all necessary for making intelligent plans.

Judge but Not Jury

In science, people feel very strongly about ideas. But for an idea to graduate to the status of accepted truth, there have to be a number of tests. The original spark for the idea can come from anywhere—and usually does. But although that original insight may be generated without the benefit of a closely reasoned chain of logic, its acceptance by the wider world requires that rigorous proof be provided.

What does all this have to do with effective intelligence? Well, we are all capable of both the insightful spark *and* the logical proof. But these two aspects of intelligence are very different and depend on very different skills. In fact, they're even accomplished by very different parts of the brain—if you're right-handed, the intuitive leap is the province of the right half of your brain and the closely reasoned logic is the fruit of the left half.

The importance of logical reasoning is easy to see. It may be a slow process, but that's to be expected because it bears the intrinsic burden of discovering proof, constant questioning, and an ongoing reassessment of a given idea or concept. The end result of the process is the drawing of conclusions that enable us to better predict and maybe manipulate the natural world. Within the brain, the scientific process is carried out through a process of trial-and-error as associations are made, acted upon, or discarded if the fit isn't right. Effective intelligence, too, demands that we plan actions, execute them, and assess their results in light of our desired goal. But we all know that there's more to what we call thinking than cool logic.

And that brings us to the contradiction between logic and emotion, mental siblings that are generally considered to be opposites. But although reason and passion are different, they are not necessarily opposed. They serve different roles: one as the director who has to be in control of everything, the other as the actor who can give vitality and expression to the script.

Different cultures place varying values on how much passion should drive reason and how tightly reason should ride herd over the more emotional animal inside us. Some cultures are far more comfortable with recognizing the mix of passion and reason than our own Western one is. In our culture, too much intensity is often seen as objectionable. This is the phenomenon that comedy workshop leader Judy Carter refers to when she tells students that you should put the "f" word (with all its emotional intensity) into your act when getting it ready, but take it out when you get on stage. Her advice is about something more than just avoiding offending the sensibilities of people who prefer not to hear "bad" words— what she's talking about is a way to *control* the expression of intensity: You keep the fire in your routine by getting it ready in all its raw emotional expressiveness, but once you get on stage, you channel it so that it ignites the room instead of hitting a wall of resistance that bounces it back into your face.

Use Your Head

Don't mistake strong language for strong communication skills. You can get your points across effectively with the mildest of words—delivery, focus, and a well-chosen vocabulary are far more effective than vehemence or vulgarity.

The great comics might use words considered vulgar on stage, but most do this sparingly, if at all. And if your goal is to be known by as many people as possible, there is a limit to how many "bleeps" you can get away with. Even Howard Stern generally finds a way to say the "bad" words without actually saying them. The point is to use passion internally in any way that feels right for you, but always seek to control and channel its energy when you let it out of its cage. You must be the master at all times.

Logic may set out a reasonable course, but it's only one part of the human experience. Although passion will give you the energy to get through adversity, see your goals to fruition, and lead others along the way; if it's uncontrolled, it will only trip you up. You need to have both functions available for your use. And that means working with both sides of your brain.

Right versus Left: Always an Unbalanced Political and Cerebral Debate

Throughout this book, we have been talking about the brain as if it is a single entity, but when you look at things from the central sulcus, the grove between the hemispheres, you notice that you have not one, but *two* brains. One on the right side, the other on the left. They look alike, act alike, and feel alike—or do they? There is alot of talk in the popular press about the necessity to use both sides of the brain. What's that all about?

The next time you get a new hat that you want to fit just right, take note of the size on the right and left side. One side of your brain is larger. Measurements of brain sizes show that in all of us, one cerebral hemisphere is larger than the other.

Brain Food

Have you ever felt that you were "of two minds" on a subject? The phrase may be more accurate than you think. When the connections between the hemispheres are knocked out, the two sides of the brain cannot communicate. One boy, who had the connection between the two sides of his brain severed to prevent epilepsy, was asked the following question: What do you want to be when you grow up? The left side of his brain answered, "a draftsman." The right side said, "a race car driver!" The two sides of his brain often disagreed, and his mood improved when they felt the same about an issue.

What Does It All Mean?

The *corpus collosum* is a structure in the brain that acts as a bridge between the left and right sides of the brain.

But there is an even bigger functional difference that goes well beyond a simple difference in size. As we noted earlier, in right-handed people, the left side of the brain is the part that is generally more concerned with speech, and linear and logical thinking. The right side takes a more emotional approach, being more concerned with musicality, spatial reasoning, and other non-verbal artistic abilities.

Yet, our two brains do have more similarities than differences. Sensory information from both sides of the body reach both sides of the cerebral cortex. And there is a neuronal bridge between the left and right side, the *corpus collosum*—a one-inch wide, six-inch long bundle in the middle of the brain that has one job—to keep left and right talking to each other.

Keep Your Perspective

Your brain must categorize input in order to make sense of the world. It loves labels. But labels are dangerous when they become fixed—once we assign a permanent interpretation or label to a concept, person, or thing, we lose the ability to change our perspective about it. Until we become supersensing machines, we will never have all the raw facts. Even then, there are still things about "knowing" that we will never know, so locking ourselves into a single perspective or interpretation of the facts may feel comfortably safe, but it stops us from growing and learning.

There's only so much data we can collect and process before we run out of time and exhaust the capabilities of our senses, so when we're trying to make sense of the world around us we have to make the best guess with the tools we have. Hippocrates had a papyrus sheet, the touch of his hand, some knowledge about what ingesting plants does to people, and not much else. But from these few tools, he fashioned the precursor of Western medicine. Cajal, grandfather of modern neuroscience, had an old microscope that wouldn't be worthy of being a six-year-old's biology toy today. And it wasn't as if Einstein could check in with the guys at the nuclear accelerator lab in 1905 when he was envisioning his Theory of Relativity. Still, he managed to come up with insights that still withstand the challenges of scientists that came after him.

What we need to do to effectively process all the information, sensory data, and experience we pick up in our lifetimes is to develop a healthy grasp of the "big picture." (This is a concept that actor Peter O'Toole tried to pass on to his graduate student in the humanistic comedy about scientists, *Creator*.) A universal perspective is often the most useful. The question is this: how do you go about developing such a perspective? You try to walk in the other guy's shoes. You look at a problem from as many sides as possible. Your association cortex takes it from there, and when action is the appropriate response to the information you've been gathering with your senses, it gives you the proverbial green light and monitors what you do to make sure everything occurs according to plan.

The legs are moved by neurons at the top of the strip, the arms are moved by areas in the middle, and the facial muscles and tongue are manipulated by nerve circuits originating at the bottom. The size of the body part matters little in relation to the number of command neurons in the motor strip. Instead, it's all about how important the body part is and how intricate its actions are. The tongue and fingers have more representation in the cortex (and have more neurons driving their muscular engines) than the legs do, which don't require as much cerebral fine-tuning. (A more complete accounting of the way the body executes cerebral commands will be given in Chapter 20.)

The Least You Need to Know

➤ The association cortex is where action is planned.

➤ Voluntary action is initiated by the same part of the brain that constructs our view of the world.

➤ There are clear differences between the two sides of the brain, and they may have different opinions about a subject.

➤ Judgment, reasoning, and other "higher" functions are mediated by the association cortex.

➤ Ideas are tested and refined by trial-and-error in the real world.

Chapter 19

Visualize a Compelling Future

In This Chapter

➤ How the brain can create its own world view

➤ Using your brain's power of visualization to set your goals

➤ Manipulating your visualizations for fun and profit

Even though you've got a sensory system so potentially accurate that it makes anything made by NASA look like a tinker toy, you possess a brain that can get very creative when creating its vision of reality. Truth is, it doesn't even need to rely on information from the outside world. Your brain can entertain itself quite well all by itself, thank you very much. When you were young, you did it with your imagination. As you got older, you developed a new skill, called visualization. In either case, it's a wonderful and useful trick.

The *real* news here is that you can make visualizations work for you. They allow you to dream the dreams that inspire you to move forward. Your dreams help give your life meaning, both in the "Kansas" of your mundane world and in your personal dream version of the land of Oz. To see how this works, let's look at one type of creative reality produced by your brain, the hallucination.

The Hallucination as Proposed Reality

Hallucinations make us *see* the music that comes into our ears and *feel* the texture of a Michelangelo statue with our eyes. Our sensory modalities can be mixed and matched to our liking. How do we do this? Well, here's where all that information about how your brain works will come in handy. Take a minute to remember all the areas in the central nervous system where your sensory modalities intermingle—where they, in effect, "talk" to each other: the spinal cord, thalamus, and cerebral cortex.

Brain Food

Society's treatment of visualization is highly context-sensitive. Take people who see visions. If their hallucinations are of saints, we call the seer holy. If they are of white puffy rabbits wailing out blues riffs, we call the seers weird. If they are of fireballs in the air and mass destruction, we call the seer dangerous.

How does your brain create hallucinatory worlds? The answer is simple: It appears to borrow the very same image-generating apparatus that it uses to create ordinary, representational images from sensory information. True, the images you create in your head are fuzzier and more difficult to hold onto than those derived directly from sensory input. But, those creatively produced images nonetheless follow similar rules.

For one, they employ the principle of perspective—of relative distance. For example, in a wholly visualized (as opposed to directly observed) view of a known scene—let's say a farmhouse with a barn and stable—the relative distances between objects in your imagined view of those structures will stay the same as it is in real life! Let's say that in the real world, the stable is twice as far away from the house as the barn. If you visualize the scene and then visualize yourself walking to both the barn and the stable, it will take you twice as long to get to the stable. In other words, there seems to be a scale map of the world in your head that corresponds to the scale of objects and distances found in the real world!

Second, your sensory abilities and disabilities in the real world are replicated in the world of your imagination. A study of brain-damaged patients disclosed that those who tested out as color-blind would report a color-blind view of the world, even when reporting the color of objects from memory.

What Does It All Mean?

Color blindness is the partial or total inability to distinguish one or more of the chromatic colors—that is, the primary colors. It's a condition that affects more men than women. Red/green color blindness is very common.

Other perception problems of interpreting real-world sensory data are also replicated in visualized or imagined scenarios. For example, some brain-damaged patients have a disconnection between visual and verbal color assessment. They can perform purely visual tasks (such as matching color samples) and purely verbal color-identification tasks (such as answering questions like, "What color is associated with envy?"), but could *not* perform tasks that combined the two skills. So, if asked to look at a particular color sample and provide its name, they just couldn't *do* it. And they couldn't do it for an *imagined* color sample, either.

The point is that the image you make in your head is treated the same way and is subject to the same rules as the images generated from outside stimuli. If you have flaws in the way you process sensory material from outside, you'll reproduce those flaws when generating your imagined worlds, too. This is why, many times, your brain apparently cannot tell the difference between imagination and "reality." Your imagination can produce images or sensory experiences that are just as arousing, enraging, or bliss-inducing, as anything that can be experienced in the "real" world.

Manipulating Your Own Magic Carpet

In his 1960 book, *Psychocybernetics*, Dr. Maxwell Maltz discusses the goal-seeking qualities of the brain. He suggests that visualization is the most potent way to activate the brain's potential and that it is the most potent way to activate the brain's natural tendency toward effective intelligence. For instance, when you want to pick up a pen, you don't think about the sequence of events necessary for doing this (which muscles you should use, the sequence of flexing and extending those muscles, and so on). You simply give your brain the order ("Pick up the pen!"), and your brain finds a way to achieve that goal.

However, picking up a pen is a simple task. For longer-term or more abstract goals, you can substitute an actual visual image (the pen) with mental imagery. So, for example, if you are aiming for that career in stand-up comedy, your brain might generate an image of you standing onstage before a wildly applauding crowd of laughing fans.

Maltz postulates that the brain treats these visualized images exactly as if they are from the outside world. The brain provides itself with a clearly defined goal, expressed in a multimodal visualization. The more vivid the imagined representation of your goal, the more clearly that goal is defined. There are some obvious practical applications that follow from this. By repeatedly visualizing your goals, you can enlist your brain's natural tendency to automatically plan for the accomplishment of a set task or goal—give it an order ("pick up pen" or "get that stand-up career off the ground"), and it'll find a way to fulfill it.

> **Complete this exercise:**
>
> Throw a real rock at a real tree a few times and make a note of how often you hit your mark. Visualize doing it perfectly over and over again. Then try throwing a few more real rocks at real trees. You'll see that your accuracy will improve as if you had *actually* practiced hundreds of times.

Fine-Tuning the Third Eye

What kind of world do you imagine when you let your imagination have free rein? Is it in color? Is there a soundtrack, and is there sensaround sound? How about smell—is the world of your imagination rich in aromas, both good and bad? Can you feel the ground beneath your feet, the sun on your skin, and the wind in your hair?

171

Mind This!

The more detailed your visualizations, the more likely they are to be logged as experience or to clearly define your goals. The more senses you can call into play, the more "real," and thus the more effective, your visions will be.

Complete this exercise:

Close your eyes and go back to a time when you were feeling wonderfully happy. Imagine yourself there, in the scene. Do the same for a time when you were very sad. Compare the differences between the two imagined scenarios—particularly the differences in your sense-impressions. Is the happy scene more brightly lit? With pleasant sounds and comforting smells? Is the sad one darker? Accompanied by loud sounds or ominous silence? Now try applying some of the positive sense-impressions to the negative scene. Manipulate the light and "soundtrack." By doing this, you can begin to get a handle on your internal representation and begin to change your feelings.

For example, you can make a sad scene less sad by adding color, brightening things up, or bringing the image into closer focus. You can train yourself to do this deliberately, eventually becoming able to manipulate the internal representations that you associate with various feelings and behaviors in your life.

Working with manipulating your visualizations is a direct route to improving your brain's effective intelligence. It helps to begin by concentrating on one aspect of your powers of visualization at a time, at least to start. For example, you can practice manipulating pictures in your mind. Imagine a scene, and then ask yourself the following questions, concentrating *only* on the visual aspect of the experience:

Is the imagined scene moving or static?

Is it in color or in black-and-white?

Is the image above you, directly ahead of you, or beneath you?

Is the image bright, dim, or dark?

How close is the image to you?

If the image is moving, do you perceive that motion as fast, slow, or somewhere in between?

Is your focus consistently drawn to any particular element of the image?

Is the image central to the scene, or is it off to the right or left?

Is the image life-size, bigger, or smaller?

Are *you* in the scene, or are you watching from a distance?

If the visualized scene is in color, is there any one color that has a strong impact on you?

Is it a three-dimensional or two-dimensional image?

Now, keeping the same visualized scene in mind, explore its sound component:

If you are in the scene, are you speaking? Listening to others?

What specifically do you say or hear?

Are certain words or sounds emphasized?

Where are the sounds coming from?

How loud are they?

What is the tonal quality of the sounds?

Are the sounds harmonious? Cacophonous?

Are the sounds regular or irregular?

Are voices inflected or flat?

Are there any unique qualities to the sounds?

Now, move on to consider the more physical and tactile sensations in your visualized scene:

During the visualization process, do you feel an increase in tension or relaxation?

Is there movement? If so, in what direction? How fast?

Do you sense textures?

Is there a vibration?

Do you sense an increase or decrease in physical pressure?

How about temperature? In the scene, do you register heat? Cold?

Are your physical sensations steady or intermittent?

If your visualization features a specific object, does that object change size or shape? Is it heavy or light?

Powerful associations can be established between events and your internal representations, and these associations can have a major impact on your behavior. For example, if you notice that you respond negatively to certain people, foods, places, or situations, chances are, these people, things, or events are linked to negative internal representations. But, as

173

you saw in Chapter 7, you can learn to understand and manipulate these representations in order to alter your responses. Improving your skills at doing this gives you greater control over your responses to the world.

What Gives Us Such Flexibility?

Use Your Head

Be careful of the images you place in your mind. Today's media expose us all to vivid depictions of all sorts of negative images: death, starvation, autopsies, murders, war, and countless other evils. Your brain has a huge appetite for imagery—it will internalize what you feed it. Be choosy!

Visualized images are most likely created by the cerebral cortex, the Grand Magician of the brain. As you already know, both your cortex and your sensory system use the same processing equipment—but your cortex is a master of illusion. The difference between the flexibility of sensory-generated images and internally generated images is like the difference between me and Mickey Mantle at the plate. We may both be holding the same baseball bat, but there's a world of difference in how we each are able to use it.

Most scientists believe that the brain has an image generator somewhere, but no one's been able to give it an exact cranial address. Studies on brain-damaged patients suggest that image generation is probably most strongly associated with left-brain activity, but that association is not 100 percent.

Our skills in generating mental imagery were probably initially evolved to enhance our powers of perception, and they were only later pressed into the service of our imaginations. You know from your own day-to-day experience that your sensory system tends to fill in gaps in the real world: Have you ever proofread a letter and failed to notice missing words because your brain just filled them in for you? Or how about this: You think you're about to taste a spoonful of whipped cream, but discover the spoon holds yogurt instead. Even if you *like* yogurt, your first reaction is likely to be an unpleasant one. That's because your brain seems to form a set of expectations before an experience, and will tend to add its own two cents to your perception of it.

The Least You Need to Know

➤ Your brain uses the same apparatus to create visualizations as it does to interpret data from your senses, and it can't tell the two of them apart.

➤ You can use vivid visualization techniques to help achieve your abstract or long-term goals.

➤ Effective intelligence is selective about the images reaching the brain and the editing that happens in the cerebral editing room.

Part 4
We Talk Back

Learning how to increase your ability to gather information from the world around you is only half the story of effective intelligence. True, you live in a world that's always talking to you, but equally important is the fact that you are always talking back. Verbally, physically, emotionally—you are always engaged in a two-way communication with your environment. For most people, much of that communication is done unthinkingly. For the truly effectively intelligent, it's important to take charge of the process.

In Part 4, you'll learn what you're really saying to the world, by word and by deed. Once you develop a full understanding of how you communicate, you can then work on improving your message so that it better reflects what you truly want and mean to say. You'll learn how to bring your spoken word into sync with your body language, and you'll discover how to direct the conscious and subconscious messages you're sending to others, so that you can most clearly and effectively express yourself.

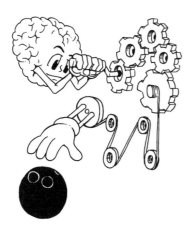

Chapter 20

The Intelligence of Brawn: How Brain Moves Muscle

In This Chapter

➤ The mechanics of using a hammer

➤ Antagonism in the motor system

➤ Communicating by the way you walk

➤ Writing a motor program

"A journey of a thousand miles begins with the first step," the Chinese proverb goes. Ancient proverbs such as this retain their vitality because they are useful and because their application produces desirable results. We in the West have adopted this adage as a motivational tool—we use it to keep ourselves from getting overwhelmed by the size of a task we face by focusing on the first few elements rather than the larger whole. But it works equally well as a metaphor for the mechanics involved in increasing your effective intelligence.

How does this work? Let's take a simple example: the mechanics of physical movement. Your nervous system is designed to build the dynamics of one movement on the foundations of those that preceded it. Movement is a form of action, and you've seen that action is absolutely essential for improving your effective intelligence. Just knowing something is of very little value. Doing something about what you know is what effective intelligence is all about. So how does the body *do* things?

Hammering the Nail on the Head with Your Head

Let's examine a simple task: what happens when you decide to build something out of wood? Sounds like a simple action. You pick up a hammer and pound a piece of metal into a slab of wood, right? Well, look closer—it's a much more complicated affair than you might think. Here are just some of the highlights:

➤ You pick up the hammer—this involves pressure, touch, and thermal receptors; the flexing and extending of myriad muscles in your hand and arm, large and small.

➤ You set the nail in place. This again involves fine-tuned muscular control, as well as vision. You have to place the nail, judge the distances between the hammer and the head and shaft of the nail, and note the location of your fingers, which have to hold the nail in place for the first blow (and not get hit by mistake!).

➤ You calculate, anticipate, and *decide* to strike the nail, picking the trajectory of the blow so that hammer hits the nail, not your finger or the wood.

➤ You give your extensor muscles a free rein to let the hammer go and "let it rip." Then there is that moment of faith. You must trust that the laws of physics haven't changed overnight, and that the angle and force you've chosen will work to drive nail into wood, not hammer into flesh.

➤ After the action is complete, you feel the "bang" of the hammer against its target. You quickly do a check with your ears and vibration receptors and eyes to see how much the nail did go in. You also check pain receptors in the fingers to be sure that they're not hurting.

What Does It All Mean?

Flexors of the arm contract the biceps, bringing the hand up to the shoulder while the triceps are relaxed. *Extensors* of the arm straighten the arm by flexing the triceps while the biceps relax.

Complete this exercise:

Consider a movement you do with your arms and hands and break it down, modality by modality, mental process by mental process. Make the movement something small—something you do every day, like opening the door or taking the lid off of a jar. Visualize yourself doing it, or do the action in slow motion. Take note of what your nervous system is doing with each action as you plan the task, initiate the plan, and then complete the plan and assess its effectiveness.

Every Action Has an Opposite Reaction

The motor system is built on *antagonism*, literally. The flexors and extensors mentioned previously are examples of two specialized kinds of muscle groups—antagonists, which work against each other; and synergists, which work with each other. Usually, flexors are synergistic with other flexors, while they are antagonistic against extensors. So while the biceps is flexed, the triceps is extended, and vice versa.

In addition to flexion and extension, your motor system has other types of muscle interactions. Movements are almost always the result of motor programs; that is, groups of muscles working in concert. For example, even as your flexors and extensors are interacting to swing the hammer, other muscles in your legs and torso must contract to provide a stable base, so that your body doesn't swing wildly about as you hammer the nail. But what about more complex actions?

Brain Food

Synergists and antagonists aren't always opposed. A flexor on one arm can be synergistic with an extensor on the other arm. For example, let's say you touch a hot kettle in the kitchen. The arm that *is* burnt is withdrawn and the opposite arm extends so you can brace yourself.

Walking the Walk

How many steps do you take in a day? We all do a lot of walking—even the most sedentary among us. And while we're on the subject, remember that our walk does more than get us from point A to B. It often also tells people what we want when we get there. Like almost *everything* we do, motion is communication. The seductive saunter of a Blanche DuBois in *A Streetcar Named Desire* says something very different from the message sent by Gary Cooper's big, bold strides into the middle of town on his way to a showdown at *High Noon*.

You probably take it for granted, but your ability to walk is an extremely complicated undertaking. At the outset, you first anticipate where you want to go. On a less conscious level, you consider the length of stride you want to take. When you begin the walk, you let the flexors in the moving leg predominate. Meanwhile, in the stationary leg, you're letting the extensors in the stationary leg run the show—this is so you can balance yourself. And, speaking of balance, you *do* know that while you're walking, you have to be one-legged for a time, right? Well, if you don't, your body does—it seeks to keep you steady as you push off into those brief one-legged moments.

So, now you've committed yourself to a trajectory, an arc of movement in which the flexors initially dominate, and then the extensors in the relocated limb take over once your foot hits the ground. You feel the pressure on your foot and balance yourself, using information from receptors all over your body, including your gut. Is the ground solid enough to use to propel yourself up for the next step? And you're using a few other sensory clues to figure out just *what* was that soft, smelly stuff you just stepped on.

179

Mind This!

The science of movement is a discipline unto itself. Different creatures get from point A to point B in different ways. Two-legged creatures walk and run, skip, dance, shuffle, saunter, stomp, and strut. Other creatures slither, ooze, flutter, or scuttle. Do you associate different moods and emotions with these different types of gaits?

When theater or film actors are getting into a part, one of the first things they do is to imitate the walk. The general idea is that if your feet are in the right place, the performance will be on target. The kind of walk you do also influences your mind—it can actually have an effect on what you think, and it can definitely influence how you feel. If your stride is bold and confident, these qualities are reflected in your emotional state—you feel good, even great. If, on the other hand, you habitually walk with your shoulders drawn in, taking short, tentative steps, you begin to feel as depressed and dull as your walk makes you look. Ever wonder why the words "motion" and "emotion" share the same root?

Complete this exercise:

Prop a full-length mirror against the wall and walk towards it. Study your normal walk, taking note of your movements, but also noting everything you think and feel about what your nervous system is doing. Now, do the exercise again, but this time adopt a different gait. Again take note of not just your physical movement, but also of what you think and feel while moving. Do you feel natural with this new mode of walking? Awkward? Do other aspects of your appearance change—your facial expression, perhaps, or the way your arms swing? You'll find that a strong stride will automatically call up a more confident facial expression, while a depressed shuffle will be matched with a more downcast appearance. Do your emotions shift to match your physical appearance?

Creatures with more than two legs have a much wider repertoire of movement than we do. And organizing all the extra movements can be extremely complex. A horse, for example, has a walk, trot, canter/lope, and gallop, which have specific sequences in which the feet hit the ground.

Luckily, we only have two feet to worry about. But even that takes a great deal of teamwork.

Complete this exercise:

Give a speech or a talk to others while doing (a) the confident walk, and then (b) a more hesitant shuffle. In either case, ask your listeners to rate you as a speaker and to recall the material. Which walk was more conducive to coming up with new ideas on the spot and developing novel effective ways to get your points across?

Muscle movement, for walking or for anything else, has several qualities that make it effective. Movement must be smooth, it must have sufficient power, and it must be coordinated with the simultaneous action of other muscles.

Use Your Head

Remember that motion and emotion are interrelated. Different states of motion give different emotional states, and vice versa. Different emotional states make different parts of the brain available for use. The posture and gait that you adopt has a profound effect on your resourcefulness.

➤ Smoothness. Two systems are in active mode in order to make a movement smooth rather than jerky. Your basal ganglia make sure that muscles that are not actively involved with the motions at hand stay steady in tone and length. Meanwhile, your cerebellum helps smooth the actions of the moving limb by using sensory feedback it gets directly from the muscle.

➤ Power. How fast and forcefully do you want to accomplish the action? Are you pounding that nail into rough planks to cover the windows before the hurricane arrives? Or are you gently tapping it into the side of that fragile dollhouse you're building for your daughter? In either case, the orders come directly from the motor cortex of your brain, traveling down a single neuron that connects to the spinal cord (this is called the corticospinal tract). Even in matters of brawn, it's really the brain that's running the show.

➤ Coordination. Once a movement is initiated, your cerebellum gets into the act to make sure that your movements remain coordinated. You can think of it this way: your cerebral cortex and corticospinal tract make their self-involved demands, with a kind of "damn the torpedoes, full speed ahead" attitude. Your cerebellum is the diplomat, listening to all these clamoring complaints and trying to keep some sort of order on the scene. It reconciles opposing orders, keeping the antagonistic flexor and extensor muscles working together.

The Brain as Programmer

In terms of planning, eating a bowl of soup is as complicated a movement as doing brain surgery. In both activities, flexor and extensor muscles must move in coordinated action. It all comes down to this: For every action that moves a part of the body in one direction, there is another set of muscles that moves everything the other way. It's a kind of constant state of tug-of-war.

And let's not ignore the main body trunk. Whether you're singing with the Three Tenors at Carnegie Hall or playing the fiddle at the Grand Ole Opry, you've gotta stand on your own two feet, fighting gravity with every swing of your body. You're not just using throat, or arm and hand muscles. The flexors and extensors in your legs are busily interacting, too. So there is just enough give in the feet to get a rhythm going, but not so much that you end up with your rear end on the floor. All of this is under the control of your cerebral cortex—and all of it is to some degree under your direct control. *None* of it is pure reflex.

So what's the point? Well, first of all, you have to know that even at the level of basic movement, you have a great deal of control over how your motor system functions— in effect, *you* write the motor programs your body puts into use. Second, if you can write the original programs, you can change them. Finally, because there's a real link between how you move and how you think and feel, you can affect a whole lot more than just the way you walk when you rewrite your motor programs. You can affect your attitude and even your effective intelligence.

How much influence do your motor programs have on your life? Lots. You can quickly see how the way you move your body can be determined by the way you feel—when you're feeling down, it's hard to keep that confident stride going, and when you feel triumphant, you will most likely stand up tall. But the reverse is also true. And that's where this knowledge becomes useful for increasing your effective intelligence.

Complete this exercise:

Hold your body the way you would if you were extremely depressed. Hang your head down low, round out your shoulders, slump, and walk with a shuffling gait. Now try to smile, try to tell an animated story about how good you were at something, or how you triumphed in the face of adversity. Tough huh?

Right now, all you need to remember is that your physical state greatly affects your emotional and intellectual state. But there's more to the story than that. In Chapter 26, we will explore a little more closely how you can use this relationship between physiology and emotional state to change your attitudes and effectiveness every day.

The Least You Need to Know

➤ Harmonious movement is built on antagonistic and synergistic muscles.

➤ Motion and emotion are interrelated.

➤ Adopting different gaits can communicate different emotions.

➤ You can change your emotional state with movement.

➤ Complex movements are directed by motor programs, and these can be changed by practice.

Chapter 21

Communication: Your Brain's Most Powerful Cannon

What's the most *direct* way to lift a 2000 pound rock? Roll up your shirt sleeves, spit into your palms, and get lifting. What's the *smartest* way to lift a 2000 pound rock? Ask the 100 people around you with the cranes and levers for some assistance.

It sounds simple, and it is. A real Einstein is a great communicator. No man or woman is an island, and there are some things we really *do* need to do with the participation or advice of others.

So, increasing your effective intelligence clearly includes working on your communications skills. How can you make the strangers around you allies and eventually friends? By communicating wisely.

You're Always Communicating Something

Communication is what we do only when we send faxes, make phone calls, type out emails, and converse with our bosses, spouses, and friends. Right? WRONG.

We are *always* communicating to others. Some things we mean, some we don't mean, and some we don't even know we are thinking. And our broadcasts reach far more antennae than we can ever imagine.

Take one of those "nothing" moments. Suppose you just made a stellar presentation of your new computer chip design to Manheim-DeAngelo Microsystems. Mr. DeAngelo smiles and Dr. Manheim does three of his famous "very interesting" praise-nods during the presentation. You graciously accept the board's applause and you *know* that the deal is clinched. All that remains is the writing of the 7-figure check to your company.

On the break, you take the elevator down to the donut shop in the building lobby, feeling on top of the world. Your fellow elevator riders actually smile at you. You walk up to the counter clerk and place your order: "A chocolate glazed and a coffee," you say as you whip out a one-hundred dollar bill. The clerk *could* get testy—most of these little shops are less than thrilled breaking anything over a $20—but you're standing tall, feeling good, and those vibes are just *rolling* out from you to everybody around you. So the clerk smiles courteously and looks for change. While you wait you look over at the travel shop across the street thinking, "what island do I want to buy" rather than "what economy fare can I get to anywhere." When the clerk returns, asking for something smaller than a C-note, she's apologetic, not surly. And when you oblige, you hear those oh-so-rare words that seem to have disappeared from the service industry in late 20th century American culture: "Thank you. Have a good day." As you prepare to go back up to the meeting and collect your check, you catch a brief glimpse of yourself in the storefront window. You give yourself a self-congratulatory wink. "Life is good," you think as you spring up the stairs to the boardroom.

Lots happened here. First, who did you communicate with once you left the boardroom? The donut shop clerk, of course, but also everyone else whose paths you crossed on your trip down to the lobby and back up to the boardroom.

Now, *what* did you communicate? Your donut-and-coffee order, true, but also a lot more. You sent a message that you're confident in your economic future, that you've elevated your social status, and that you're very proud of yourself—all very positive messages.

But *how* did you communicate all these extra messages? Your eye line, body orientation, and tone of voice—all these contributed to the total message you were sending to everyone around you. And even *before* you had that successful meeting you made choices that are part of this current communicative act: the clothing you chose, the perfume or after shave you wear, the shine—or lack of it—on the shoes. All these contribute to what you're saying about yourself, even if you don't say a word out loud.

Ever watch great actors on the screen or emotional liars in real life? If you want to find out what they really mean, watch what they do, don't listen to what they say.

Great drama always has juxtaposition in it. The actor is frequently called upon to express a meaning that exactly contradicts the words he or she says. When Meg Ryan hugs Billy Crystal at the end of *When Harry Met Sally*, her lines of eternal affection read,

"I hate you, I hate you, I hate you". But her loving eyes say something completely different. And recall all those scenes from the TV series *Moonlighting*—Maddy Hayes (Cybil Shepherd) and David Addison (Bruce Willis) often managed to get their momentary dissatisfaction for each other across to the audience very clearly, even when their scripts called for them to just deliver the words, "Fine, fine."

Body language, tone of voice, and the look in your eye are the most effective ways you deliver messages to others about how you *really* feel. The words we use don't really matter. This is often particularly true when dealing with matters of the heart. As the song says, "If you want to know if he loves you so, it's in his kiss."

Mind This!

Although it's very true that our behavior often belies our words, there are still times when what you hear is what you'd be best advised to act upon. Classic case in point: in a dating situation, "no" means *no*. In these days of sexual harassment suits, it's best to take your partner literally at his or her word.

Complete this exercise:

Take three "nothing" one-minute interactions that you have with people in a single day. Try parsing them out—evaluating all elements of your message (manner, tone of voice, and so on). What did you *intend* to communicate? To whom? What did you in fact send out to others that you didn't intend on them finding out?

The Voice as Emotional Barometer

How we say something determines what we mean and what we convey to others about what we mean. More than one pathological liar has related, in a fit of honesty, that "I've been lying so often, I don't know when I'm telling the truth any more." Dennis Miller's pet peeve is politicians who "start believing their own bull——."

Take an example from everyday life. All medical practitioners listen to their patients. This is not just good customer relations. It's essential to the diagnostic process. What is the person's tone of voice when he/she talks about the different things that happened

Brain Food

Before we make specific pronounce-ments about linking voice to emotion, we must ask the following question: how do we want to *classify* human emotion? In China, the classical Taoist practitioner starts out with the idea that there are five basic human emotions, each associated with an organ system that is thought to have the most influence on it. Excessive chi (energy) in one such organ system causes specific changes in the related emotion, while deficient chi will have a reverse effect.

last week? What upset the patients? What inspires them? What are they afraid to talk about because it is too painful or too revealing?

People's understandings of their emotions are different, depending on the society and culture in which they live. The meanings that Western society assigns to emotions is different from those assigned in Eastern cultures, but there is one universal rule—emotions are complicated. Just as you think you're beginning to understand the emotional clues around you, you're likely to discover that what's on the surface frequently masks other, more deeply hidden emotions. Think about the general who knows he has lost the battle. He keeps barking out orders at full volume, seemingly confident. Underneath, however, he is scared—he just can't show it to the troops. Or how about the kitchen table comic, tossing out non-stop one-liners and laughing at his own jokes, but privately coping with a personal grief.

In addition to emotional content that is generally disclosed through tone and volume, voices also have rhythm and emphasis. We speak in sentences or sen-tence fragments, not just in single words. If there are three words in an utterance, one tends to be stressed over the others. If there are five or more words, one is given heavy stress, one or two words are spoken with moderate stress, and the rest of the linking words are given a steady, low-volume tone. When actors and directors break down scripts, the words of emphasis are circled, and with good reason. This gives meaning to the line, revealing what the actor really means.

Take the following "nothing" line, for example:

"My name is John Smith."

Not a whole lot of information here, but things can change radically with a small change in emphasis.

"My name is John Smith." A flat, even delivery might mean: "I have a name, a little respect here, you got a problem with that?"

"My NAME is John Smith." Stressing the second word might mean: "You are putting me in a category. I'm a person, not a number."

"My name IS John Smith." Stressing the verb might mean: "You doubt my identity, but I'm telling it to you straight here.

"My name is JOHN Smith." Stress on the first name might mean: "My brother, Joe, is the one who owes you money, so please take my check—it *is* good."

"My name is John SMITH." Stressing the last name might mean: "I am a professional, and want to keep this business transaction profession, so please use my surname, Mister Jones."

The rhythm of the spoken line is important as well. In print, we use punctuation to convey the intention behind the information. In real life, we forget that the punctuation is always at the end of every sentence delivered. For example:

(A) Even stress ("My name is John Smith.") = I inform. A declarative fact. Non-confrontational.

(B) Forceful stress at end ("My name is John Smith!") = I command. I MAKE you accept this information. This is the imperative tense.

(C) Upswing of the voice ("My name is John Smith?") = I ask your approval to continue talking and that I can keep my name/identity in your presence.

Each of these three tonal modes has an appropriate time and place. When you just want to inform, and the audience is receptive, in your flow, mode "A" will do just fine. Things move along quickly. If there is some problem getting someone's attention, the forceful "B" mode may be in order. When pitching a complex concept to a slow-thinking person—say, someone with lots of power or money to invest in a pet project of yours—you have to avoid shorting his brain circuits out with too much information. Mode "C" lets you ask him if he is ready to be fed more data.

Mind This!

Be careful not to use the *wrong* invisible punctuation at the end of a sentence. Information with "A" mode is ineffective unless the listener is on your emotional wavelength. The imperative "B" mode won't work if the listener is hostile and is a lot more powerful than you are. The "May I have your approval?" "C" inquiry is deadly if you're trying to assert your authority.

Listening to Yourself Before Opening Your Mouth

You never can hear what you really sound like. You might think you're roaring like a lion, when you're actually whimpering like a timid lamb. We all have speech mannerisms that affect our delivery: the "uhhhs" we insert between thoughts so we don't lose our turn as the one who's talking, or stammers and hesitancies when we're unsure of our argument. These can dilute the effectiveness of your verbal communication, but they *are* areas that you can correct. All it takes is practice—and the help of an impartial observer or two.

Complete this exercise:

The next time you talk with someone on the phone, take time to notice what your body feels like after delivering your volley of words. Write it down while the other person is talking. Record the conversation and play it back. How many times did you stutter? When did you use filler words such as "like," "ya know," and "uh"? What were you saying and feeling during those rocky times that you thought were smooth sailing?

We use our voice like a saber, defending territory that is ours and, when we can or have to, invading someone else's emotional space. Medical diagnosticians, police interrogators, and salespeople know that the best way to be invited into someone else's private cranial vault is by appearing to be a potential friend, not an all-powering conqueror. And we instinctively work on this assumption. When we meet someone new, we shake hands, smile, establish neutral ground, sense what the other person might want, and adjust our strategy accordingly.

One popular sales technique is to match your pace, mood, and emotional tone to those established by the customer, and then bring her or him gradually into a speed and tone that is the one *you* prefer. Are we advocating deception? No. Just acknowledging some facts of human nature.

Complete this exercise:

Record yourself talking to a group of people or doing a performance involving spoken words. Pick a situation or an acting piece that makes you express a wide range of emotions. Take note of which emotions made your voice "stronger," not "louder." With which emotion were you most convincing? What emotions would a critic call hokey, superficial, or brilliant? Rate your performance.

Each species has its own language. A rabbit pulls back its ears when it is apparently curious, but a horse with ears pulled back is really ticked off at something. When a dog rolls on its back, it's a sign of submission. A wide monkey smile often means just the opposite of "glad to see you, pal."

Animals communicate with their bodies all the time, and seem to be very good at it. Just look at how they settle disputes. For example, domestic animals seldom really hurt each other, but they are always competing for territory, food, and the affection of the humans they own. The average dog, horse, or cat argument lasts less than three seconds and seldom blows up into a brawl.

They "talk it out" first, with a mock-kick, a growl, a hiss, or hair raised on the back. Fewer than 5% of the emergency admissions to an average veterinary hospital are because of kicks, scratches, or bites between argumentative creatures great or small. Compare that stat with the number of people who come into emergency rooms every night because of interpersonal "disputes."

The Basic Vocabulary of Human Body Language

What are the two most often used concepts we convey to each other by word or action? "Yes" and "no." In the sensory modality, "yes" is: "I am receptive to what you are saying," "I really am listening," or "I am going to actively interact with you whether you want me to or not." "No" is the opposite: "I'm in my own space, I don't want to share my energy, thoughts, or emotions."

"Yes" and "no" are most often conveyed with head nods and hand gestures, but bring your cultural dictionary if you leave North America and Western Europe. Many a western businessperson, tourist, and sailor in an exotic port have learned the problems of communicating cross-culturally the hard way. For example, head nods and hand signals for "yes" and "no" are based in cultural traditions—what might mean yes on Main Street in the U.S.A. can have the opposite meaning elsewhere. But there is another set of signals for yes/no communication that is more universal—and you can pick them up from body language.

Some "yes" signals, from the bottom up:

➤ Toes splayed outward, heels close to each other

➤ Legs apart

➤ Chest thrust forward and exposed to the person being talked to

➤ Shoulders held back

➤ Head and neck "ahead of the line" (forward from the plane of the back and spinal cord, with the center of gravity below the navel)

➤ Chin up

➤ Eyes looking at eyes/face of others

➤ Leaning forward when talking or listening to someone

Some "no" signals, from the top down:

➤ Leaning back when talking or listening to someone

➤ Eyes looking away from the face or eyes of the other guy(s)

➤ Chin down

➤ Head and neck "behind the line"

➤ Shoulders hunched

➤ Chest reclined, deflected away from other party (or environment)

➤ Legs crossed or close together

➤ Toes splayed in, pointing toward each other

Complete this exercise:

Next time you're in a crowded place like a mall or airport, look at the people around you. Amazingly, people in a crowd act very much like they would if they were alone. Identify each person you see, and notice if their bodies are saying "yes" or "no." When do they switch over, and why? Now, look in a mirror. What are YOU saying? Get involved in a conversation and see how your body language changes. Now try consciously changing your body position from yes to no and vice versa. What do you feel like inside? What is the relationship of your body to your mind? Do different body positions change your state of mind?

When acting, it becomes clear that your body language does have a significant effect of your mind. "I'll find out what my character is all about once I get my feet right", actors so often say. The introverted 15-year old actress who is supposed to play an over-the-top princess on stage does a lousy, lifeless, and technically-flawed reading of the script if her body is in a "no" position in a comfy chair perfect for reclining into introversion mode. But get her on stage, feet and chest open, head "in front of the line," eyes directly on the director, all body parts in "yes" position, and she'll hear "Bravo!"

We put ourselves in "yes" and "no" body positions all the time, sometimes before we interact and sometimes as a response to what has been thrown our way. Both body positions have their place. Great performers—and great communicators—alternate between introversion and extroversion a few hundred times a day.

Complete this exercises:

Find a comfy chair, find the most "no" position you can find, and have a conversation. Record it. Then try to come up with ten new ideas to solve the world's problems. Write them down and time how long it takes. Now, put your body in a "yes" position. Have a conversation, and record it. Then try again to come up with ten ideas to solve the world's problems. Compare the quality of the two conversations and the lists of world problem solutions. You'll probably find greater dynamism in your conversation, as well as more concrete solutions, in the second position.

When the body position matches what the mind wants to do, good things happen. But when body position is contradictory to what the brain wants to feel or convey, the message seems to get stuck somewhere behind the eyes and in the back of the throat. Try it: it's tough being tough when you've pasted on a big, bright smile; and it's hard to come across as friendly if you've pre-set your jaw and taken up a belligerent body posture.

Where are You Really Coming From?

Each emotion has a unique "energy," but where does energy come from? Yes, from the brain and the mind, but the body also has a part in this. Ever wonder why when we imitate several accents, and do it convincingly, we feel the "voice" come out of a different part of our throat, and body, each time? An East Indian accent may feel effortless, coming straight from the head, while an Irish brogue seems to spring out of the chest, untangling the spine in ways you never thought possible. The fact is, different accents do use different face, throat, and neck muscles.

There is a lot of cultural conditioning that goes into how we feel our emotions, and there are few "road maps" that tell us where they originate. But we all have felt a tightness in the chest associated with grief, and a kind of pang at the level of the heart when we know that we are about to make a wrong decision or already have committed to something we know to be a wrong choice.

Aggressive, "villain-like" emotions may be felt in front of the windpipe, throat, or spine. Passive, "victim-like" emotions are sensed as coming from behind the throat. And some actors sense female characters coming from the top half of the spine; male roles coming from the lower half.

Great actors and effective real-life Einsteins need to be able to connect to all emotions. Feeling and expressing them is essential for communication, and communication is essential for effective intelligence. How can you check in with where they come from before the show begins?

An exercise recommended by teachers at the Actors' Film Factory in Vancouver is to close your eyes, lean forward, touch the ground, then come up—slowly. Feel the energy come up from the bottom of the spine upward, letting yourself feel the energy centers (sometimes called chakras) in front of and behind the spine. Now, when YOU are ready (usually after 20 seconds to a minute), open your eyes. Take a deep breath from the diaphragm, connecting to the chi point about two inches below the navel. This is a great exercise, even out of an Actors' Studio. Try it just before you tackle your next big challenging task.

Brain Food

NFL football is a battle of morals and wills as much as strategy. A team that is down by two touchdowns and prepared for sure defeat can be energized by one defensive lineman pulling off a quarterback sack. The whole momentum of the game is so susceptible to that one big play made by one player in one moment of confident defiance. This shift in momentum is a form of communication. This man leads by *example*.

193

Effective Intelligence Is Contagious

Because effective intelligence is based on communication and people are always communicating, one way to increase your own skills is to make sure you surround yourself with the right people. Ever notice that you feel smarter around smart people and duller around dull ones?

The Least You Need to Know

➤ The rhythm, tone, and quality of voice often say more than what the words mean.

➤ Your body language tells the world what you mean, whether you know it or not.

➤ The developed mind can feel emotions coming out of specific areas of the body.

➤ Good communication between body, mind, and emotion makes for great communication with the world and development of Effective Intelligence.

➤ Effective Intelligence can be expressed in many ways and is contagious.

Chapter 22

The Automatic Nervous System: Thinking without the Brain

In This Chapter

➤ The war for control of your heart

➤ Windows on the brain

➤ More about body language

➤ The wonders of biofeedback

When we think of communication, most of us think of verbal or written communication. The more sophisticated among us think also of body language, movements, and postures that can be mastered and ultimately changed at will. But not all body language is under our conscious control. Go south of the cerebral cortex and you find a whole network of neuronal circuits that influence heart rate, blood pressure, breathing, pupil size, sweating, and a myriad of other things.

All of these functions have meaning. Before we talk about the communications carried by autonomic functions, let's learn a little more about the system.

The Sympathetic Nervous System: The Yang Master

All schools of medicine that have lasted beyond the first snake-oil salesmen or mad scientist have built into their framework one concept—balance. Oriental medicine is always concerned with the "yin" and "yang" of a disease.

What Does It All Mean?

Chinese medical practitioners often speak of yin and yang, two opposing views of the universe. *Yin* is a concept representing those functions that "maintain the household." *Yang* represents the more aggressive concept of "fight or flight."

In the Oriental medical tradition, illness means imbalance. But there are reflections of this same concern with balance in the precursors to Western medical thought. Hippocrates went on at length about how a well balanced life is a healthy one, and even "modern" Western medicine shows some awareness of that sense of balance: for every "up" disease, there is a "down" counterpart. For instance, too much thyroid hormone—hyperthyroidism—has an opposite number in the disease hall of fame, hypothyroidism, a condition where the sufferer has too little.

But what keeps the physical and physiological world in balance while the brain is busy doing other things? Enter the *autonomic* nervous system; a bipartisan neurological system in your body's biological government.

The Sympathetic Nervous System (SNS) is perhaps the best known branch of your autonomic nervous system—its what we refer to when we talk about the "fight or flight" response to stimuli. Its "center" is in the brain stem and in certain places of the hypothalamus, particularly the posterior region of that structure. From there, it projects messages through relay stations in the spinal cord and nearby ganglia (collections of nerve cell bodies). These ganglia are important: they carry impulses to the nerves that innervate most every organ and tissue in your body.

The SNS is activated by key arousal areas in the brain, such as the locus coeruleus, the amygdala, and the hypothalamus. Once stimulated, it releases noradrenalin and (in some cases) acetylcholine from its nerve terminals in the body. The SNS also stimulates the adrenal gland to release adrenalin and noradrenalin into the blood.

What's the reason for all this chemical activity? Well, think about it. What do we need to do in "fight or flight" situations? We need to be able to move quickly, keep our oxygen supply maximized so that we can think fast, and stay aware. We're reacting to disruption in our environment and we need to be on our toes. The SNS activates special nerve receptors in the heart (called beta-1 receptors) that act to elevate the rate and efficiency of cardiac output, up to four times the normal levels. Other receptors, called alpha receptors, are also activated. These cause your blood pressure to increase and shift blood from reservoirs in the veins into active capillaries. During this response, your pupils dilate, letting more light into the retina. Blood vessels in your skin are constricted, diverting the life-giving red stuff to areas where it's needed most—your muscles and your brain. In the muscles, beta 2 and cholinergic receptors are activated, opening up blood vessels. Very possibly, blood flow to specific areas of the nervous system might be enhanced according to the needs at the moment.

The SNS also stimulates your sweat glands, enabling you to vent off excess body heat as your body goes into hyperdrive while it deals with the crisis. Your hair stands on end. And, in some cases, the SNS may make you cry by stimulating the lachrymal glands behind the eye. And while all *this* is going on, beta cell activation also breaks down fat in adipose tissue, letting even someone with low blood sugar (perhaps from starvation) get an emergency boost of fuel to handle the situation.

But these days, it seems as if we're always in stress. And it's true. The SNS is always active, keeping us on battlefield alert.

Mind This!

Drugs that block the actions of the sympathetic nervous system in stress situations (agents that block alpha or beta receptors) can cause problems in "resting" individuals. These problems can include life-threatening decreases in blood pressure, pupillary constriction, closing of the airways in the lungs, lowered cardiac output, and a range of other problems.

The Parasympathetic Nervous System: The Yin Master

Having an SNS working at maximal speed all the time is like driving on a mountain road with the accelerator floored. Yes, the car may get from Point A to Point B faster, but it's more likely that it will crash—very, very soon. So the SNS needs something to keep it under control. What keeps the "yang" of the SNS in check? It's the "yin" counterpart—the Parasympathetic Nervous System (PSN).

The PNS has its source in the brain stem and it gets its message out to the body through the vagus nerve, which innervates many of the same organs that the SNS does. It has another network through which to send messages as well—this one originates from the lower portion of the spinal cord. It communicates with your body by releasing a chemical called acetylcholine. This chemical acts on a particular group of neural receptors, called muscarinic receptors, which are different than the kinds of receptors on skeletal muscles that are involved with most "voluntary" movement. If you want a quick and easy way to think about the PNS, you can seldom go wrong if you say that whatever the SNS does, the PNS does the opposite. The PNS and SNS essentially fight each other for control of the body with more ferocity and wit than the Republicans and Democrats ever did in any election year.

At the level of the brain, the PNS and SNS centers inhibit each other's activity by means of something called interneuronal networks. But the battle is also fought out at the level of your body's organs—there the war for nervous system supremacy is taken to the physiological streets, and its fought by both overt and covert strategies.

It's a "push me, pull you" situation. The SNS stimulates heart rate and strength, increasing the pressure with which the ventricles pump out blood for each beat. But the PNS decreases heart rate. The SNS dilates the pupils, but the PNS closes the shutter of the ocular camera by pupil constriction. The SNS may divert blood from the intestinal tract so that it goes to the muscles where it's needed for action, but the PNS increases the blood flow to the intestinal tract when food is around, causing a shunting of blood to digestion. The SNS would like to shut off blood flow to the skin during emergencies, but in those more quiet moments when everything is fine, the PNS overrides it. We then experience the "oops, I thought something scary was going on, but now I know all is well and ooooh am I embarrassed" blush in the face.

The Window on the Brain

"I see it in your eyes", goes the expression that has trapped so many who have tried to tell white, black, or gray lies. When people lie, their eyes shift, turning their focus away from the listener. Then there is the blank stare, a "freezing" of the eyes to hide what's behind them, a trick the more practiced fibbers are so good at (particularly toddlers and politicians).

The SNS and PNS tell those around us how well we really do have it all together or how badly we are faking it. Terror in the heart or anger in the spirit will cause your pupils to dilate, no matter what you are trying to fake. Blood pressure rises, sweat starts to pour, heart rate elevates, and hair stands on end when the SNS is given control of the wheel. Lie detector tests are based on these biological signals.

But if your inner brain is saying "intimate" or "mellow," and you're trying to act tough or aloof, the red blush in your face will be visible to the people around you, no matter what kind of "hood" hat you have on backwards or how many of George Carlin's forbidden words you utter.

Complete this exercise:

Observe footage of someone talking after you know what they really meant. This might be an old news clip of a political figure who was caught red-handed with the goods after making a denial speech seven months before. Compare the denial to footage of that same individual when he was discussing some topic with which he or she felt comfortable. To really focus in on the body-language cues, view these clips with the sound turned off. Take note of what changes you see in the eyes and face color, and try to identify what the state of arousal of the person was from the eyes and face only.

Being Ruler of the Yin and Yang Autonomic Masters

Effective intelligence is about guiding actions to meet our individualized goals. To change what is on the outside, you also have to change the inside, which means that one way or another, we must become masters of our own bodies before we exert effects on anyone else. This doesn't mean that we have to be able to make our hearts stop beating before we can pump up the world around us. Or does it?

Highly-disciplined people can use their heart rate as a biofeedback mechanism. When heart rates get too high, the wise Einstein calms down, takes a deep breath, and re-equilibrates before taking action. This is not always possible, but "taking your moment" could require only two seconds. Physiologically, the deep breath produces changes in the vagal nerve to the heart, lowering the rate.

> **Brain Food**
>
> Many colloquialisms are based on autonomic events. "You make my heart race," communicates excitement. "He opened my eyes" is a line that could find its way into any country song about a new love that enters your life or a flame who breaks your heart by leaving. Having a "gut feeling" probably has to do with autonomically regulated blood flow to the gut and is a form of self-communication.

We've all heard stories about yogis in Tibet or maybe even meditative masters in Cleveland who can make their blood pressure go down, radically slow their breathing, and shut all their body systems down to almost clinical death. They then open their eyes to give you a playful "I'm still alive, thank you for being concerned about me" laugh. These stories are true. Meditation and associated yogic techniques are now widely prescribed as a way to control hypertension, asthma, and a whole range of autonomic-imbalance disorders, even depression.

These techniques are not just for mystics. Think about the poker player who's holding a pair of deuces and has a fortune on the table, bluffing his way against a guy with a Royal Flush. And consider the legal reality that lie detector tests are often not valid for use in a court of law, even if someone scores "honest" with flying colors after all the "did you do it" questions have been asked. There's just too much possibility for manipulation of even "involuntary" body responses to trust the test results. Remember the last time you were somehow able to save the day in a crisis at work or at home—no doubt you were feeling real panic on the inside, but it's equally likely that to everyone around you seemed cool, calm, and in control.

The "hows" of biofeedback are complex, and we clearly don't know much more than what is in textbooks and lab reports. But we do know some things to be biological fact, leading to some interesting speculations. For example, deep inspiration will activate the sensory fibers in the vagus nerve through receptors in your lungs. This inhibits the inspiratory center so that the expiratory center takes over. Then, when the lungs are deflated, pressure and chemical sensors in the blood vessels stimulate inspiration again. We can still control the rate and depth of breathing by altering our states of awareness and mental acuity.

Complete this exercise:

Monitor your heart rate and respiration under the following conditions:

> Panic mode
>
> Contented
>
> Before and after exercise
>
> Before, after, and during meditation.

Note how the different emotional and physical states result in different heart and breathing rates.

This brings us back around to congruency between body language and words. People often say things that they do not mean or that they do not feel in their hearts. They may intellectually express a point of view, but their body language, both through the motor system and their autonomic system, says the exact opposite. Pay attention to these signals. Learn to read them in others and even in yourself. They are the prime way that the non-verbal "subconscious mind" has to communicate.

If you are about to make a decision, and your gut tells you otherwise, stop. Consider the opposite view. Keep working through the problem until it feels right. There is no greater power than a strong congruent decision.

The Least You Need to Know

➤ The sympathetic and parasympathetic nervous systems are always warring with each other for control of our bodies.

➤ These systems can tell the world, and us, what we are feeling.

➤ We can use and control these systems.

➤ There is no greater power than a strong, congruent decision, endorsed by both mind and body.

Maybe You Want to Rephrase that?

Unless you're a Trappist monk who took a vow of silence, or you like to test the strength of duct tape by having the guys in the lab put it over your mouth, you talk. We all do. We're a very talkative species. Many of us choose our words casually and carelessly. But we do so at our own peril! The words that you habitually choose affect how you communicate—not only with others but also with yourself. And they have a big impact on what you experience. Think of it this way: Words are the software that run the hardware of the brain. Do you want your hard drive to crash?

Effective intelligence depends upon effective communication. To be a genius, you don't need to be glib, but you *do* need to know how to adjust your words to your environment and the people in it. Why? Doing so is a strategic plus in your quest to define and achieve your goals.

Talk Is *Never* Cheap

People with an impoverished vocabulary live impoverished lives. Think about it: People with rich vocabularies have a multi-hued pallet of colors with which to paint their experience, not only for others but for themselves as well. Try relating a lecture about biochemistry of lipids with only knowledge of street slang. Can't be done. Or, turning it around, try motivating a crowd at a political rally using scientific terms more suited for a textbook on physical chemistry.

Simply by changing your habitual vocabulary—the words you consistently use to describe the emotions of your life—you can instantaneously change how you think, how you feel, and how you live. It's about more than just putting on a Dixie accent when crossing from Kentucky into Tennessee, or picking up an idiom or two from a mobster flick before that trip to Atlantic City, New Jousey, pally.

It is about observing, controlling, and channeling the emotion behind the words. After all, that's what people (including you and me) listen to: the emotional content, not the words themselves. Why? Because all words have strong associations. We associate different mental images and levels of emotion with the words we use and the words we hear. In other words, the words we attach to our experience become our experience.

Complete this exercise:

Make a list of all the words you know that describe emotion. Then for each emotion, make a list of all the different ways of expressing it, sorted by emotional intensity. Start with a simple emotion, say disliking someone. On the optimistic end, you could "not have an affinity for" that person. You could be "displeased with" him or her. Upping the emotional ante will get you "disturbed," "angry," "miffed," "peeved," "pissed off," or "*really* pissed off." The greater your vocabulary resources, the more colorful, and the more effective, your expressiveness will be.

Brain Food

Is it possible that by adopting someone else's habitual vocabulary, you begin to adopt their emotional patterns as well? It appears to be true. (This phenomenon, called modeling, will be discussed in greater detail in Chapter 27). The idea is that by adopting certain habits of successful people, you can create similar internal representations, enter similar states, and obtain similar results. But simply using somebody else's words isn't enough; you must also adopt the volume, intensity, and tonality of these words.

Lots of Words, Lots of Emotions, Endless Communication Possibilities

For most of us, our habitual vocabulary is extremely limited. Linguists tell us that the average person's working vocabulary consists of between 2,500 to 11,000 words, but the English language contains at least 500,000 words. Over 3,000 words in the English language describe emotions. Of these, 1,000 or so are positively descriptive, and about 2,000 are negative. How many words do you have in your vocabulary to describe emotions? The more words you have, the more nuances of experience you can express and communicate.

If you want to change your life, you need to consciously select the words you habitually use and you need to constantly strive to expand your choices. Most stand-up comics will tell you that the secret to a successful performance—and a career that pays off in dollars and TV deals rather than donuts and beer—is the versatile use of language. Seinfeld never uses the "f" word in his act, but you fully understand how peeved he is with a thing, person, or place. And Dennis Miller, who would refer to a Slurpy as a plastic-containing-happy-colored beverage rather than "a soft drink," shows a different kind of versatility: he knows the comedic power of quirky descriptions.

Word Up!

Have you ever found yourself overwhelmed by a verbal opponent, and then spent weeks thinking of all the things you *should* have said? Do you know the sense of frustration that comes from being unable to get your point across in an argument? Do you know the feeling—it's almost self-pity—that comes from feeling as if nobody understands you? We all get these feelings, but we don't have to live with them. And step one is finding the words.

Mind This!

Your state of mind is the greatest determinant of behavior, and words are the most powerful way to create internal representations that change your state of mind. The words you say to other people have a similar effect. Be careful. Examine your use of words. If you habitually use a pattern of words that disempower you, then change them!

But it's not just in public that words count. When we're not talking to other people, we are talking to ourselves, even when our mouths are not moving. One of the conventions used in novels is the interior monolog: it's a stylistic device that lets the reader inside the heads of the characters, exposing their thoughts and feelings. Take the following passage from *Of Lions and Lambs* (M.J. Politis and Bart Mozer, Longrider Productions, in press), featuring a cynical, emotionally-intense, highly intelligent, and extremely frustrated middle-aged stand-up comedienne, as she prepares to go on stage.

"Earth is a strange planet to do time on," Atti 'the Hun' Nichololoias thought as she lit up her third pack of smokes on what would be a five pack night.

"Remember the rules," she muttered under her breath as she buzzed through her joke cards for the last time.

"Rule number one—know your audience," she recalled to herself in a silent voice drowned by the groans and moans of a crowd already past the fourth beer, whisky and/or vodka. "Maybe I should have taken the first spot, before their poor, tired souls were drowned with cheap no-name booze. But no one in this crowd is brave enough to loosen up without pharmaco-logical help. Maybe no one in ANY crowd is brave enough to be loose without being hammered."

Use Your Head

In any communicative event, your object is to bond with your audi-ence. Self-doubt is often a poor way to start off. If you begin with the assumption that you can't relate to your listeners, you set the stage for them to reject your message. Try to find some point of identification at the outset. It will make all the difference.

A brief example, but an illustrative one. Atti is nervous, she is sure of her fire and the soundness of her comedic insights, but she does not know if they will relate to this crowd. Before even going out onto the stage and getting their real reactions, she is imagining what they will do, based on what she thinks they are all about. For her act to work and to collect a paycheck at the end of the night, she has to establish communication with the crowd. But what is that crowd? It is something she feels angry at, pity for, and then compassion for. And because she is working very hard at finding the real answer about the way things are and the way they should be, she comes up with a theory about human nature: "Maybe no one in ANY crowd is brave enough to be loose (open-spirited) without being hammered."

Is Atti right in her theory about the audience, and people in general? Is she wrong? All of that is irrelevant—this is an internal monolog, in which she's just working through the thoughts and feelings that she's experiencing just before she has to go out and perform. What *is* relevant is the state that her words put her in. Her words, whether spoken aloud or just mulled-over in her mind, have an impact on her effectiveness. Has she chosen to craft her internal conversation in such a way that it will put her in the most resourceful state?

Suiting Words to Deeds

At this point, you might be saying, "This is just semantics, isn't it? How much can choosing different words affect how I perform in my life?" Well, the answer is "a lot!" Just changing your choice of words is not going to accomplish much. But by changing words, you also change your internal representations. Now *that* gives you a powerful tool—it lets you break old emotional patterns. And if your old emotional patterns were ineffective or even self-defeating, changing them can truly change your life.

Table 23.1 Shifting words—Shifting Moods

Original words (negative)	Replace with these words (positive/empowering)
I feeling angry	I feel challenged
I hate X	I prefer Y
I'm not learning fast enough	Look how much I've already learned
I'm overwhelmed	I'm in demand
I'm nervous	I'm energized

Complete this exercise:

Come up with three words that you habitually use to denote negative feelings in your life, and then write a list of empowering or positive alternatives.

One way to move beyond the limits of your habitual speech is through the use—and examination—of metaphor. Metaphors are a kind of shorthand we use to internally represent things, situations, even our whole lives, in a single summary thought.

Our metaphors of life, what we might call our *global* metaphors, can be very powerful. It's one thing to say "life is like a battle" (which is a simile, or simple comparison), but it's a very different thing to say "life *is* a battle." If life *is* a battle, then all subsequent internal representations about life will have a battlefield quality. We'll think in terms of winners and losers, of attacking and defending, of conquest or submission, and of enemies and allies.

Even when we use them in everyday situations, metaphors generate extremely vivid images. It is this very ability to paint vivid *images* that makes them powerful. If you're hanging at the end of your rope or walking through the fire, you're facing some difficult challenges indeed. In fact, you've got a pretty good excuse to just quit the rat race, or at least blow your stack, right? At the very least, metaphors establish the framework in which you must act.

What Does It All Mean?

A *metaphor* is a figure of speech in which one thing is likened to another thing by being spoken of as if it *were* that other. "Life is a battle" is a metaphor. A simile makes comparisons, but no direct association: "Life is *like* a battle." Similes allow the brain more wiggle room than metaphors do.

Complete this exercise:

Take the following global metaphors for life and develop mental images for all of them. What rules of behavior would they dictate? What would be the best and worst outcomes you could expect from a life lived according to their terms? What skills are required to succeed in the world you've created around this metaphor? What kind of person must you be to succeed?

Life is

a battle

a dance

a party

a dream

a job

a calling

Now try to *visualize* what implications these metaphorical worlds would have for concepts like love, career success, vacationing, making friends, dealing with others, and so on.

Last, enter some situations and conversations as if you *believed* in one of these metaphors. See what effect it has on how you approach the events of your life—and pay attention to the reactions you get from others, as well.

You'll quickly learn the power of the metaphors you choose to use in going about your life. Once you recognize their power, you're in a position to actively take charge. If a habitual metaphor has been working against your best interests you can change it. For example, if thinking that "life is a battle" has you relating to the world confrontationally, maybe that's causing trouble when you want to make friends. See what happens if you switch to a new metaphor.

The Least You Need to Know

➤ Words are the software that run the hardware of the brain.

➤ Impoverished vocabulary leads to an impoverished emotional life.

➤ Watch what you say to yourself.

➤ Create new empowering global metaphors.

Part 5

Head, Heart, and Mind: Emotions and Effective Intelligence

For truly effective intelligence, you'll need to learn how to use everything you've got. Part 5 gives you a tour of your emotions and how they contribute to—or inhibit—your success in achieving your goals. You might be surprised at just how much of your emotional response to the world is a function of your brain's wiring, but once you learn how the emotions really work, you're ready to enlist them in your quest for improving your effective intelligence.

The chapters in this section will provide you with a map of the emotional you, and show you just where your emotions come from. You'll then learn ways to manipulate your emotional state so that you can keep your reactions from sabotaging your goals. You'll discover ways to use your emotions to ease you into "the Zone"—a mindset in which everything you do is optimized. Once you learn the secrets of "the Zone" you'll find that your effective intelligence has improved immeasurably.

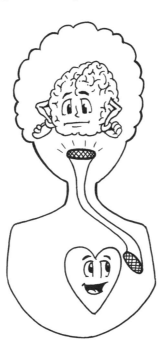

Chapter 24

Emotions: Turning the Intensity Up or Down

> ### In This Chapter
>
> ➤ Channeling anger's energy
>
> ➤ Learning to read emotion and act on what it has to say
>
> ➤ Bringing your life to life through emotion
>
> ➤ The importance of empathy

The ancient Greeks got a lot of things right—architecture, the first model of Western democracy, great cheese and olives, the birth of modern drama, and new experiments such as freedom.

The Greeks valued freedom of the human spirit from the shackles of irrational emotion (passion) above all other kinds of freedom. But that's probably the hardest kind of freedom to secure. How can you avoid being passion's slave? Well, you can withdraw from the world and enter a monastery, but that seems a little drastic. No, there's a better way—one that doesn't require that you wander off to a mountain top. That way is something the Greeks called *sophrosyne*. Loosely translated, it means the tempered balance of wisdom, care, and intelligence in living one's life.

Anyone familiar with Greek drama and the vibrant writings of Homer and Aristophanes knows that the Greeks were no shrinking violets. The characters are physically and emotionally vital. Heroes who won the battle and got the girl, or walked off with the basket of cheese and olives at the end of the drama were emotionally intelligent. They knew how to channel their emotional energy to get what they wanted.

Advantageous Anger

Anger! Sounds like bad stuff, doesn't it? You might think that really smart people never get hot under the collar, but that's not exactly true. Without obstacles and conflict, challenge is not possible. Without challenge, you never have the opportunity to improve your effective intelligence. Your life is static—safe, maybe, but about as vibrant as a rock.

Brain Food

Every emotion carries a message. Anger usually means that a rule or standard that you have for your life has been violated by someone else. But this can be easily misinterpreted. Did the person realize that this was an important rule for you? Maybe we should discuss it? Let me see this from his perspective? What can I learn from this? The message may cause you to re-evaluate how you communicate your important standards to others.

Let's get rid of the stereotype that geniuses are always cool, calm, and collected. Do you really think that Albert Einstein never got passionate about anything? If that's what you think, you'd be wrong—this is the man who said "Great spirits have always encountered violent opposition from mediocre minds." Einstein had a powerful social conscience. He reacted with true anger against his fellow academics when they didn't stand up against the Nazis in 1933 and the McCarthy witch hunts in 1953. And Einstein was quite willing to express his anger at his fellow scientists when they refused to open their minds to new ideas and tried to keep alive a style of education that treated rote memorization as more important than true learning.

Anger fuels the fire of human emotions like few other feelings do. As long as we want things we can't have, we will be susceptible to anger. Because of that, anger can be galvanizing. But beware! Anger can also easily derail our best attempts to achieve our goals, and can blind us to the good in the world around us. So the question is, how do you tame the tiger of anger, making it work for—and not against—you?

Taming Anger's Tiger by the Tail

Energy cannot be created nor destroyed. It can only be transformed. That's a basic law of physics. And it's just as true for emotional energy as well as any other kind. Anger once felt cannot be ignored. But it can be *used*. If you mine your anger for its energy and use it as fuel in your drive to achieve your goals, it becomes a constructive component of effective intelligence.

In cases of clinical depression, the brain's neurotransmitters, such as norepinephrine and serotonin, are altered, so it's difficult to think your way out of whatever emotional hole you're in, even if you want to. For now, suffice it to say that depression can clearly destroy your will. When you're in the throes of depression, you don't really care about setting goals and you certainly are not interested in taking action to accomplish them.

But even the demon of depression can be used to open yourself up to creative states. Edgar Allan Poe wrote his best work when he was depressed. And Beethoven was depressed about his deafness. He found a way to react to that depression, however—one that led him to rail against his fate. By converting his depression to anger, he found the energy to compose his masterful 7th and 9th symphonies. He channeled his depression and his anger into the creation of some of the great masterpieces of all time.

Use Your Head

Channeling anger is not the same thing as *internalizing* it. Internalizing anger—swallowing your angry thoughts so that you don't have to face them—leads to self-pity and depression. Both of these are crippling emotions, so avoid them as much as possible.

Mind This!

You always retain some conscious control over the biochemistry and physiology of your brain. Through visualization techniques, you can shift your focus onto a happier time, and use the positive emotions of your vision to overcome your depressive state. These momentary changes in mood require changes in the brain's biochemistry, and to make the mood shift permanent takes time and practice. Antidepressant medications can give you a start. But medications only go so far. It is still up to you to take charge of your emotions and make your life better.

Manipulating Angry Memories

But to make anger or other negative emotions work for you takes effort. Simply venting your anger indiscriminately doesn't accomplish much. Sure, it might feel good just to "let it out." And maybe you can use it to generate some energy. But the cathartic effect of venting is short-lived, unless it's followed by effective, intelligently-directed, assertive action.

The best way to deal with anger is to deal with the problem, situation, or person that caused it. Sometimes, the problem is immediately identifiable: Your boyfriend or girlfriend dumped you, or your boss yelled at you in front of your co-workers. But some of our anger is older: You still haven't gotten over your big brother's bullying when you were a child, or you're harboring resentment because your parents didn't support your desire to go to college. Whether the cause of the anger is immediate or rooted far in the past, there are ways to deal with it creatively and constructively.

How do you do this? First, take your focus off of the situation, person, or thing that "causes" your anger. That's not something within your control—if it were, you wouldn't have allowed it to make you angry in the first place. Put the focus on *you*. Take a look at how you may have contributed to the situation. Maybe there are things you could do to change the way it worked out.

The past is past. Reliving the hurts and injustices that happened in the past is futile, but that's just what we often do. Rather than reliving your bad times over and over, use your head—literally. We humans have a wonderful but underutilized ability to manipulate our memories. We can, in effect, go back in time. When we call up old memories, we can edit them, choose different endings, different characters, or different lines; and then reincorporate them. Or we can choose to let them go. But this is a difficult thing to learn to do. For some, it's important to find a therapist or other professional who can help them make a start. However you go about it, it's important to learn to break the destructive cycle.

Use Your Head

Taking responsibility is a good way to transform your anger into a creative force. But there's a difference between taking responsibility and taking on an inappropriate load of guilt. Make certain that when you honestly assess the ways in which you might have contributed to your problem you don't assign yourself the *blame* for it. Taking responsibility is only useful when you learn something and then take action to make the outcome different next time.

Lightening Up with Laughter

What is laughter? This most important and valued emotion of them all is also the most poorly understood. No one has successfully identified the "humor" center of the cerebral cortex. But when it comes to increasing your effective intelligence, laughter is one of the most powerful tools in your emotional repertoire.

Humor is subjective. We all laugh, but we all laugh at different things. Men, in general, tend to like slapstick; women, according to comedian Paula Poundstone, don't get off quite so much on a pie in the face or a slip on a banana peel. But whatever your personal favorite brand of humor, you *do* need to laugh at least once a day.

Laughter opens your mind to a wider range of possibilities and more expansive perspectives. And it has therapeutic uses, too. If you take something you're afraid of and make it funny, it loses its power over you. That's the principle behind the "black humor" that was featured in the TV series *M.A.S.H.*—Hawkeye and Trapper's irreverence was a way to deal with the horrors of the war around them.

And you can make the humor come from almost anywhere, including yourself. In fact, one very good way to keep a positive outlook is to learn to take yourself less seriously. It's hard to keep a righteous sense of anger going if you can let yourself admit that you, too, have silly moments.

The Wonderful World of Wonder

In the book *The World as I See It*, Albert Einstein identified the emotion of wonderment as the single most important one in the human repertoire, at least when it comes to enhancing our ability to learn. It is, unfortunately, the one quality that our schools seem least interested in passing along to its students.

Einstein wrote his book nearly half a century ago, and we've had any number of studies done on improving our schools since then. But even without the benefit of all those later studies, Einstein had it right: If you aren't *emotionally* interested in what you're trying to learn, the information you're being taught goes in one ear and out the other. Maybe you can spit it back for an exam, but you certainly won't retain it long enough to make it part of your life.

What's true in the school setting is also true in everyday life: Everyone needs to find a reason to care about learning something before they can effectively learn it. This principle is something that you can learn to use in your quest to increase your effective intelligence.

Brain Food

In a recent study, people were given a book of matches, a candle, and some tacks; and were told to attach the candles to a corkboard so that the candles would burn, but not drip any wax. One group was shown a funny movie beforehand, another watched an instructional film, and a third did physical exercise. The group that did the best was the one that viewed the funny movie. The other two groups had far less success.

Communications Skills 101: Making Your Listeners Care

When we talk, most of the time we're trying to communicate specific information about our environment to somebody else. Some examples: "The blue books are behind the green cabinet." "The car is a foreign model and needs metric tools." "I'll meet you in five minutes at the dingy diner, across from the gym where all the hunks are working out."

If your listener has a vested interest in the subject of your remark (she needs to get a blue book, he's trying to do some repairs on his BMW), you'll have no trouble getting him or her to listen. But, in many situations, it's up to *you* to provide your listeners with a reason to pay attention. You need to provide a reason for them to *care*. One way to do this is to work on *how* you say what you want them to hear. That means developing your skills at using colorful, evocative language.

For example, you may want to make an observation about a guy, let's call him Fred, who is obsessed with all-natural food products. If you call him a "granola head" you accomplish several things at once. First, you're getting your listener's attention with a quick, pithy, descriptive phrase. Second, you're drawing attention to Fred's food preferences. And, in the same two-word phrase, you're making it clear just what *you* think of such an obsession.

Complete this exercise:

Take a common generic term for a specific and familiar person, place, or thing. Your next-door neighbor, for example, the park in the center of your town, or even something as basic as the pen on your desk. Now embellish this term with as many "colorful" phrases as you can, connected to the many different opinions you have about that person, place, or thing.

Getting the Message

All of your emotions are trying to tell you something. But the actual experience of the emotion can be so strong, so overwhelming, that you don't get the specific message. And that can mean that you never learn to deal with the sources of your emotions. But there is an art to understanding these internal forms of communication. You can teach yourself to ask the important questions: What are my emotions trying to tell me? What can I do about it?

Dealing with emotions is all about asking the right questions—*and* choosing the right answers. Getting it wrong can have dire consequences. If, for example, you're angry about being caught in a mistake, you have to ask yourself, "Where is that anger coming from?" If you don't identify the source (a fear of looking foolish, perhaps) you can't overcome it—which means you'll never be open to learning how to avoid that mistake in the future.

Here are some of the messages commonly associated with certain everyday emotions:

Fear. This can take many forms, with many different levels of intensity, from concern to terror. If your common reaction to a particular person or situation is fear, this may mean that you know that you are unprepared to deal with it. But, fear being what it is, along with the message comes the automatic response of avoidance—we often run from what we fear. Your first objective, then, is to try to bring your fear under control. It helps to know that most of the time, our fears are basically unfounded—the world won't come to an end if you find yourself in a difficult situation and you don't know how to handle it. Franklin D. Roosevelt really had it right: "We have nothing to fear but fear itself."

That done, you need to try to figure out what it is about the person or situation that you need to prepare for. If you always dread the weekly departmental meeting, maybe it would be a good idea to spend the night before the meeting reviewing your files, so you're ready with an answer when the boss asks where things stand.

Frustration. This one's really insidious—especially for all us achievers. The more we try to do, the more we risk frustration. Why? Because all frustration means is that you don't get the result you want—but if you never try to do anything, your efforts can't ever be frustrated. So how do you cope with frustration? Take a good look at how you're going about achieving your goals. Maybe there's a better way.

Frustration can actually be useful—it can prod you into trying new approaches to problems that you might not have thought of before. But you've got to clear away your frustration before you can take effective action. If one particular task is frustrating you, step away from it for awhile. Do something else while you let your subconscious mind work out a new way to get the job done. Another way to break through frustration is to visualize the problem as belonging to someone else. Sometimes, when you remove the personal factor, the solution to a task becomes clear.

Use Your Head

If you find yourself intimidated by that rude clerk at the local grocery store, maybe that's because you don't know what to say when he (or she) makes an unpleasant remark. You *could* try practicing some snappy "comebacks," but you're probably better off recognizing that the clerk is obviously an unhappy person—and that a kind word or compliment from you could be enough to change his or her attitude.

Disappointment. This is another very frequently encountered emotion for those of us who set ourselves high aspirations and challenging goals. It can be very destructive—if we let it. Often, when we are disappointed, we will pull back and give up.

Disappointment is the realization that a goal or set of goals will probably not be met. It is frequently accompanied by a sense of sadness and loss. It should be a time for major reassessment. Is this a temporary setback, or does it truly mean that the goal is unattainable? Honest assessment is important here. If your disappointment is due to a temporary setback, maybe all you need is to find a new, more effective way of achieving your goal. Only if you realize that your original goal is truly unattainable should you pull back and reconsider your options.

For example, let's say that you're trying out for a part in the local theater company's annual production. You audition, but the part goes to somebody else. This is a temporary setback, and there are steps you can take to achieve your goal—next year. You can join an acting workshop. You can study the script more thoroughly next time. And so on.

Now let's say that you always dreamed of winning the Boston Marathon. You train and train, but every year you come in close to dead last. You also happen to have a chronic case of arthritis in the knees. Well, maybe it's time to recognize that you're not likely to ever come in first in the race. That doesn't mean you need to quit participating. You just need to get your expectations more in line with your reality.

Guilt. Where would 90% of all the stand-up comics be in the world without the primary emotion that drove the Borscht Belt, guilt? In the audience! But, seriously, folks, when not mastered, guilt is a very damaging emotion, and one that we should do our best to avoid. Guilt is a form of disappointment, disappointment in our own behavior. It usually means that we did not live up to one of the standards that we have set for ourselves. The best response is to immediately decide which standard that was and to take steps to discover just *why* we failed to live up to it, so that we won't fail to do so in the future.

But sometimes, guilt is foisted upon us by others, and we are taken on a "guilt trip." This usually means that we have violated a standard set for us by someone else, that they were disappointed in us. In such a situation, the first thing you should do is ask yourself if the standard according to which you are being judged is a reasonable one. If it is, fine—take steps to do better next time. But often, other people try to impose on us standards that are inappropriate, or self-serving. Those are judgments to avoid. They'll only make you feel bad about yourself.

Complete this exercise:

We've got you started with the emotions discussed in this chapter. Now it's your turn. Make a list of other emotions that you experience and dissect them for their message. What can you learn from them? How can you use them creatively so that you can more effectively attain your goals?

Next, make a list of the emotions you have experienced in the last few days. Which ones do you want to spend time in? Which were disruptive and unpleasant? Explore ways to orient your life so that you spend more time in the former and less in the latter.

A Prerequisite for Effective Social Interaction: Empathy

The heartfelt advice from the talent agent on Rodeo Drive goes, "Sincerity is the most powerful tool you got (kid), and if you can fake that...." But in the real world, caring can't be faked. At least, not for very long. People usually know when you're putting them on. And once you become known for not really caring, you'll find it hard to get other people to care about *you*. To be sincere, however, you have to be in touch with your feelings.

The "feeling" part of your brain is called the amygdala, and most researchers would agree that a functional connection between the amygdala and the other parts of your central nervous system is essential to generate the personal quality known as empathy. Severing connections between the amygdala and the cerebral cortex in monkeys produces creatures that are unable to relate emotionally to other primates in the band. These animals are unable to pick up even the simplest form of monkey body language.

In humans and in monkeys, empathy is a mental skill, an ability to see into others' heads and to hear what is echoing in their troubled hearts. The person skilled in empathy knows what the other person is feeling, from the inside. But where does this ability come from?

You can take note of someone's sweaty brow, dilated pupils, and quivering lips and say, logically, "This person is afraid." Empathy goes far beyond this, however. With empathy, you don't just *recognize* the other person's fear—you feel it with him or her. You understand *why* he or she is terrified and how badly fear is gripping their souls. If you can empathize with the person, you can better determine ways to ease the frightened person's fear.

And empathy does not mean only that you can feel another person's pain—you can empathically share in pleasure as well. But chances are that if you can't feel the pain behind a person's groan, you can't feel the happiness behind her smiles, either. Joy is rare enough and very easily shared. Why deprive yourself of a free ration of happiness?

No Color Without Emotions

What happens when emotions are missing? When the feeling and thinking parts of the brain are disconnected? The term used for this clinical condition is "alexithymic." Most of us aren't that bad, but many of us have difficulty expressing ourselves emotionally. Let's work on this.

Complete this exercise:

Take the driest piece of writing you can find about a person, object, or event with which you are familiar. Now, rework the words and phrases so that they

➤ are more musical (*sound* more interesting, tonally, with a poetic rhythm)

➤ use more humor, metaphor and innuendo

➤ generally pack more emotional punch

You'll find that people remember and internalize messages more readily when they are presented with emotional punch.

The Least You Need to Know

➤ Internalized anger becomes depression, so channel that energy into a positive direction instead.

➤ Medication may be necessary to treat your depression, but it is still your responsibility to make positive things happen in your life.

➤ Laughter is the best medicine.

➤ Messages are more meaningful with an emotional punch.

➤ Empathy is a prerequisite to effective social interaction.

Chapter 25

Heart and Head: How the Brain Makes You Laugh or Cry

It's 1996. The last pitch of the game clinches the World Championship for the New York Yankees. The catcher, arms raised, fists clenched in triumph, runs towards the mound. The neurobiology of these movements is extremely complex, involving coordination of thousands of neurons, most of which oppose each other's actions. The neurobiology of the feeling behind the movement is even more complicated.

Amygdala—Grand Central Station for the Emotional Express

As you learned in the last chapter, the part of your central nervous system that is most involved with telling you how you feel is probably that part of your cortex called the amygdala. The cerebral cortex enables you to see the mate of your dreams. The hippocampus lets you remember, years later, what he or she looked like back in the days when you first began to date. But the amygdala tells you how we feel about that companion, hopefully for better, but also for worse.

The amygdala is a small collection of neuronal cell bodies and synapses located in the *limbic system* (also known as the seat of emotions). It sits in the middle of the brain, just below the center of the parietal cortex and just in front of the temporal cortex. It's divided into two areas, the corticomedial region, which is connected to your olfactory system, and the basolateral area, which links up to neural centers on all sides. Animals have the greatest number of connections to the nose; human brains like their emotion to be more even-handedly distributed. For this reason, the basolateral area, with its many connections, is very highly developed.

What Does It All Mean?

The *amygdala* is a part of the limbic system—that part of your brain that is specifically concerned with emotions and motivations. The imaginative faculty is somehow linked to the amygdala, while the faculty of remembrance is the province of another part of the limbic system, called the hippocampus.

Brain Food

What happens when the amygdala is missing? (The syndrome is called Kluver-Bucy syndrome). Primates become social misfits, showing little interest in the band. They also become less fearful, but at the same time, they become less aggressive. They become zombie-like, and even appear to be blind on occasion.

The amygdala is extremely well "connected." When it is damaged by probes, scalpels, or disease, or if it is stimulated in the laboratory, major emotional mood swings occur.

With all its connections to the rest of your nervous system, the amygdala is well-positioned to act as your Emotional Control Central. It takes all incoming signals from your motor cortex, your primary sensory cortex, the rest of the association cortex, and from the parietal and occipital lobes of your brain. In other words, from pretty much every source there is.

And your central nervous system puts in its two cents worth of information, too—even your hypothalamus pipes up with info on hormonal changes in the blood. With all this data coming in, does the amygdala sit back and just listen? Heck no! It cops an attitude and talks back!

First of all, it's always got orders to give to your thalamus—that gateway of all except olfactory sensory information to the cortex. And it's got things to tell the septum (which controls the brain's electrical wave formation—what you see in an EEG) and your hippocampus (where your feelings, once felt, are stored).

Artificial stimulation of the amygdala done in the lab produces big-time changes in body, mind, and spirit. The emotions produced range from rage to fear to feelings of intense pain or pleasure. It also causes changes in heart rate, a release of pituitary hormones (especially those connected with reproduction), "goose bumps," pupil dilation, and chewing movements of the tongue and mouth. Many of these can be recognized as components of various emotional responses.

The Prefrontal Cortex: Not for Lobotomy Only

In the early 19th century, a New England laborer named Phineas Gage had an accident in which a railroad spike went through his head. He survived and was given the day off afterward. Before that accident, he was a model citizen. Afterward, however, he became a social misfit who said and did whatever came into his head. If you crossed Howard Stern with John Cleese, and then transported him back in time to Victorian Massachusetts, you'd have the new Phineas Gage. He had been lobotomized by a railroad spike.

Remember *One Flew Over the Cuckoo's Nest*? Set in a psychiatric hospital, the book had a lot to say about a once common type of mental treatment—the prefrontal lobotomy. In this infamous operation, the frontal portion of the patient's motor cortex is removed. This part of the brain tells us the "why" and the "how" about moving our appendages.

When Wrong Emotional Reflexes Become Learned Facts

We associate stimuli with response. Usually, this helps us. The message "Hand on hot stove" calls forth the reflex response "withdraw hand." "Person making threatening gestures with a weapon" calls forth a "fight or flight" response. But what happens when we learn the wrong lessons? We've all heard about the classic cases of Vietnam vets suffering flashbacks that are triggered by simple, everyday sounds. That's an example of a potentially dangerous automatic association of stimulus with response. That phenomenon has since been identified and given a name—Post-Traumatic Stress Disorder (PTSD). It's not limited to war veterans, by the way. PTSD has been recognized in victims of sexual abuse and other traumas as well.

Use Your Head

Warfare, imprisonment, and other interpersonal acts of criminal cruelty or hardship set up reflexes that can be retained long after the condition or events have ended. This has come to be called Post-Traumatic Stress Disorder (PTSD), which gained its broadest recognition in the post-Vietnam War years. It's not something to suffer alone! Big-time therapy is usually called for to help a sufferer overcome it.

The Problems of Passivity

Some people just never seem to be willing or able to take charge of their own lives. This special kind of passivity is called *learned helplessness*, and it's what happens when your neural circuitry is conditioned to "know" that you are at the mercy of the world around you, and that any action you may take is futile. Victimhood is perceived as inevitable so the temptation to surrender overshadows the biological instinct to survive. The sufferer is frozen—a sitting duck in a world full of vultures.

A dramatic animal model of learned helplessness can be created in rats. If you put a rat into a tank of water that has a clear escape route, the rodent will swim its way to safety. But now take this rat and repeatedly subject it to maze games that it can never win (you shut the door on the reward at the end of the maze every time the rat gets close to winning it), and something pretty dramatic happens. After a few sessions running the frustrating maze, that same rat will no longer handle the water tank experiment the way it used to. Instead of making the effort to swim to safety, the rodent will simply freeze, fall to the bottom of the tank, and drown.

Learned helplessness and PTSD have been linked to profound changes in the amygdala. Alterations in brain chemistry that are most frequently cited involve changes in the neurotransmitter norepinephrine, which is released from neurons based in the brain's "arousal" center. There are certain receptors in the normal brain that inhibit the release of norepinephrine—but people with PTSD have fewer of these than the general population. End result—excess norepinephrine is released. Instead of arousal, you get panic. Instead of red-alert responsiveness, you get blind terror.

Hormones and Emotion: A Match Made In Heaven?

Another factor that is frequently forgotten is that the brain is really very isolated from the body. That handful of gray matter we call the brain floats in its own little lake of cerebral spinal fluid, and is encased by Mother Nature's crash helmet, the skull. In addition to all this physical isolation, there's also the blood-brain barrier—a physical and chemical barrier that keeps hormones, bacteria, and proteins from getting into your brain tissue. But even in the face of all this isolation, your nervous system constantly communicates with your endocrine glands and even your immune system in a complex two-way dialogue.

How does this communication work? Let's say that your cerebral cortex notices something that needs to be handled with a squirt of hormones. It sends appropriate signals to the amygdala, which passes the message along to the hypothalamus. The hypothalamus then ships a package of chemicals to the master gland, the pituitary, and the pituitary gland then releases hormones that activate any or all of the following:

➤ The thyroid gland, which ups the octane on all body systems.

➤ The adrenals, which increase cortisone release and can alter the proportion of norepinephrine to epinephrine.

➤ Reproductive organs, which pump out testosterone and estrogen into the circulatory system.

The system works in reverse also. Hormones have select abilities to activate the cerebral cortex directly. And they *do* affect how you feel and how you think, sometimes profoundly. But you don't have to just sit there passively and take it—you can take steps to minimize the negative effects and maximize the positive effects of hormones.

Stress Can Make You Sick

A healthy immune system means a healthy endocrine system, which, in turn, means balanced and appropriate cross-talk between the hormones and the mind. And recent studies have begun to indicate that your neurons can connect directly to cells in your immune system. Your emotional states will profoundly affect the balance between the parasympathetic branch of your autonomic nervous system—the one that handles situations when all is well—and the sympathetic branch that specializes in coping with circumstances that call for the fight-or-flight response.

With stress, however, the delicate balance between the parasympathetic and sympathetic nervous systems is thrown off. The adrenal gland, a very big part of the sympathetic nervous system, releases noradrenaline, adrenaline, and cortisol. Cortisol subsequently depresses the formation of antibodies. In addition, white blood cells that normally fight infection don't do their job properly anymore. Certain white blood cells that normally assist your body in fighting infection start slacking off on the job. Result: People under stress get sick more often.

The point here is that your brain is hardwired in such a way that almost every system is affected by emotion. Emotional states can instantly change the chemical and electrical makeup of the brain. And this has very real implications for you in your quest to increase your effective intelligence. Controlling your state of mind is perhaps the single most important skill to develop if you want to take more direct control of the emotions that affect your brain. To learn how to take charge, read on.

The Least You Need to Know

➤ The amygdala is the main "feeling" center of the brain and is connected to everything.

➤ The prefrontal lobe rides herd over emotions.

➤ The brain can be conditioned to run from things that mean no harm.

➤ The nervous system talks with the hormonal system and immune system a lot.

➤ Changes in emotional state instantly change the chemical and electrical makeup of the entire brain.

Chapter 26

In the Zone

In This Chapter

➤ The importance of being in the Zone

➤ How to change your state

➤ Different states allow us access to different parts of the brain

➤ How to model successful people

Everybody's using the phrase today: "Being in the Zone." You hear it being talked about by musicians, actors, scientists, athletes, and politicians. But what does it mean? Experiencing "the Zone" requires no doctoral degrees, no time spent in the Himalayas, and no membership in any new self-help seminar or wacky cult. Some people call it by other names. They say they're "on a roll," or "in the groove." And it's what they mean when people say, "When you're hot, you're hot."

"Locked in" is what surfers call the situation when board and rider manage to find themselves in the very heart of the wave—inserted into the place where the surfer can access all of the power of this mountain of water but not be crushed by it. That image makes a good metaphor for the state of mind, body, and spirit in which everything inside is balanced and even the environment outside of you seems to be moving according to *your* personal timetable. It's that condition where it seems like everything is going your way—and it's the place where effective intelligence thrives.

Most importantly, it is a state that you can actually learn to achieve at will. In this chapter, you'll learn a little more about this state and some ways to get yourself there.

The Importance of State

In neurological circles, you don't hear many people talking about "the Zone." Scientists tend instead to use the far less colorful term "state." But whether you use a term like "the Zone" or "state," you're still talking about the same thing: having all your resources operating at full capacity and at lightning speed. When you're in "the Zone," you have no sense of time or anything at all except the sense of being optimally effective. In fact, you feel as if you have all the time in the world—exactly enough time to do whatever needs to be done.

Wouldn't it be great if you could snap right into "the Zone" any time you wanted to? If you could go straight from being the metaphorical surfer paddling along on the sea to suddenly being "locked in" at the curl of the mother of all waves?

A dream? Only if you don't *let* it become a reality. The Zone" can be occupied at any time, and you can stay there indefinitely, rent-free, once you understand the mechanics of getting there. Your brain won't mind—the Zone is a place it likes to go to, a lot. And in this chapter, you'll learn how to get there whenever you choose.

Complete this exercise:

You've experienced "the Zone" before—probably by accident. Think back to a time when everything seemed to be going right—a day when you made every green light on your commute into work; that report that gave you trouble the day before just seemed to write itself; and you always managed to think of exactly the right witty remark to make in conversation with your co-workers. That was a day in the Zone. Reconstruct in your memory the elements of such a day. Make that memory as clear, as complete, and as detailed as you can. Commit that memory to paper and keep it with you. Read it often to remind yourself of the sense of being so totally connected to everything in your environment and so very capable of making things work out according to your own plans.

The Zone: A State of Mind, Brain, and Biology

The biochemical environment of your brain profoundly affects its overall function. The cartoon character Popeye went from geek to god-like with a pipe full of spinach. For the rest of us, the superjuice is a little more biochemically complicated than a can of spinach. But there's good news: We can tap into the superfuel that powers us into the Zone any time we want. And it doesn't take pills, powders, needles, chants, or crystals to get it.

Getting into the Zone is a function of neurobiological changes that also affect the functioning of the brain as a whole. Widespread chemical and electrical changes have a powerful effect on the entire tapestry of all the systems that feed into your cortex.

Change the chemical and electrical mix, and you change your "state," altering your level of resourcefulness and effectiveness. When you're in the Zone, it's because the biochemical and electrical climate of your brain is such that it fosters peak performance when you need it.

The Zone is the direct opposite of a state of depression—not just in how it *feels*, subjectively, but in the chemical and electrical condition of your brain. In major depression, a decrease in serotonin results in a characteristic change in the brain's chemical makeup. Certain parts of your brain are now maximally active—a different set of areas seen in other states—and this directly affects your ability to access certain parts of your brain. In effect, you are cut off from many of your normal brain resources.

Brain Food

Different states have different tapestries of active brain centers. In other words, the composition of your mental toolbox changes. You may need a psychological steak knife when you only have access to a drawer full of butter knives.

We've been aware of these physical manifestations of resourcefulness (or lack of same) for some time, and we often use them in training for particular tasks. For example, back in Chapter 7, you read about a soldier charged with the task of monitoring a radar screen for hours on end, waiting for a blip that might never appear. To accomplish his task, he had to prepare himself to concentrate exclusively, but completely attentively, on the screen. This concentration is played out in his brain by actual biochemical and electrical changes. A structure called the *anterior cingulate gyrus* normally has the job of handling multiple simultaneous sensory inputs. This needed to be turned *down* while the soldier did his job—effectively rendering him insensate to extraneous stimuli. A perfect solution for the task at hand, but not a very resourceful state for normal life.

Mind This!

One of our most dramatic state changes occurs during the "flight-or-fight" reaction when we believe that our life is threatened. Reaction times shorten and your strength increases. People have been known to lift cars single-handedly during one of these states.

Use Your Head

Most of our states happen without any conscious direction on our part. We see something, respond to it, and go into a particular state of mind. The difference between those who succeed in life and those who do not is that the first group has more effective control over its state of mind.

Brain Food

You have a recipe for each state. You know how to make yourself depressed. You start by pushing your shoulders forward, hanging your head, adopting a shuffling gait, relaxing your facial muscles. In other words, adopt the physiology of depression. Now start thinking depressing thoughts. Tell yourself you're worthless, etc. Now try to smile. Difficult.

What worked for the soldier can be made to work, in reverse, by those of us who want to increase our Effective intelligence. By learning to arouse ourselves emotionally, we ratchet up the levels of norepinephrine released into our systems. This increase in norepinephrine turns up the octane on circuits throughout the brain.

But how to stimulate such a state of arousal? One simple method is to learn to control how you breathe. Deep breathing from the diaphragm brings more oxygen-rich blood to the brain—blood that serves to open up more and more of the brain's resources for your personal, conscious use.

Creating a State of "Zone"

Effective intelligence begins by achieving an optimal state—getting yourself into the Zone. And controlled breathing is one practical means of getting yourself there. But there are others—read on.

Beyond the purely mechanical aspects of alertness and arousal, the biggest determinants of your state are the quality of your internal representations and the efficiency of your physiological functions. These are not independent of one another, by any means. For example, if you are in a physiologic state of great muscular tension, if you are extremely tired, or if you are experiencing pain or low blood sugar, your physical condition will play itself out in your mental representations. Negative feelings will tend to be magnified. By the same token, certain postures and movements seem to promote positive internal representations: It's hard *not* to feel good when you stand up straight, put your shoulders back, breathe deeply, and smile.

Complete this exercise:

One very effective way to change your state quickly is through music. Put some of your favorite music on the CD player. Now respond to it in any way you wish: Dance, sing, play the air guitar, or conduct an invisible orchestra until you're feeling wonderful. When you're feeling your strongest and your happiest with this music, make some unusual physical gesture that involves a large muscle movement: a broad swing of your arm, for example, or the classic pumped fist. If you repeat the movement approximately 10 or 20 times while you're feeling wonderful and listening to the music, you will anchor that movement to that state of mind. In effect, you will be able to recall the state of mind simply by repeating the movement—with or without music playing in the background.

Act Like You Know What You Are Doing, and Sooner or Later You *Will*

Another illustration of the power of physiology and state is a technique known as modeling. For this technique, you first need to identify who you want to be. The concept of modeling says that if you adopt the specific beliefs, internal representations, associations, and actions of a mentor or role model, you can more rapidly learn to become like that person.

How do we actively use modeling? Let's look at a common situation: The transition from the status of student to the status of professional, which can be very disconcerting. Most people are very insecure at this point and their insecurity is likely to be reflected in the way they carry themselves. How then do you make the transition?

Modeling provides the answer to this problem. Find a mentor, colleague, or other person who has the bearing and the attitudes that you wish to acquire. Then, it's simple: Model your behavior on the behavior of this person. Adopt his or her posture, stride, or even some mannerisms. You can even create a mentor from your own imagination.

Complete this exercise:

Think of a time when you were in a powerful state, when you were unstoppable. Now adopt the physical bearing you associate with that condition. Stand up straight, puff your chest out, and pull your shoulders back. Hold your head high. Take deep breaths. Close your eyes and imagine and feel what you would *feel* if you were unstoppable. See what you would *see* if you were unstoppable. Hear what you would *hear* if you were unstoppable. Imagination counts as practice if you do it properly.

The point is, if you want to become something, behave as if you already *are* that something. The behavior gives rise to the state: If you hold yourself and behave as if you are confident, you will soon *become* confident. The message that determines your emotional state is sent to your brain by your *body*. By taking control of the body's message, you take control of the kind of emotional state that your brain will adopt.

The Least You Need to Know

➤ Being in the Zone is a biological phenomenon.

➤ Resourceful states allow us access to the most resourceful parts of our brain.

➤ You can control the state you are in.

➤ The two biggest determinants of state are the quality of your internal representations and your physiology.

➤ You can make rapid progress in altering your state by modeling your behavior after the example set by other people.

Part 6
Behave Yourself

In these final chapters, it's time to coordinate everything you've learned up to now. You've learned to improve your powers of information-gathering, you've learned to take charge of how your brain processes that information, and you've learned how to coordinate the knowledge you've gained from all sources into a truly impressive package called effective intelligence. Now's the time to learn how to creatively use that intelligence, and these final chapters are devoted to that end.

Most important of all is to learn exactly how you can increase the clarity of your conscious thought and harness it to the speed and creativity of your unconscious. Believe it or not, this is a learnable skill. It all has to do with breaking out of preconceived notions and pigeon-hole thinking, and these chapters will help you learn how to do just that. Once you learn to forge new associations between concepts and information, you can join the geniuses of effective intelligence, and you'll find your ability to successfully use your brain power to accomplish your goals has vastly increased. And that, after all, is the true meaning of the word "intelligence!"

Chapter 27

Consciousness: Is the Emperor Wearing any Clothes?

If reality were to take on perception, the big R would undoubtedly open the spar of the century with "You can't handle the truth." Hard science would back up reality's claims. Our conscious brains are not comfortable with raw data. As you have learned in this book, we create our own internal worlds, customizing the data to make it more useful in serving our goals. We can handle the truth, but we prefer to manhandle it, bending it to our liking. Ultimately, perception *becomes* reality.

It's a biological fact that the actual locations of the conscious and unconscious parts of your mind have not been physically identified: No one can give you a road map to show just where each one operates in your brain. Moreover, the degree to which you are consciously aware of and processing sensory information is unique to you: It varies from one individual to the next. How consciously aware you are very much affects the development and maintenance of that wonderment we call intelligence. But it is by no means the only factor involved. The scientific findings in the last decade show us, very clearly, that the conscious mind and the unconscious mind are *partners* in producing *our* reality.

What You See Is *Not* What's There: An Old Problem

Brain Food

In the early days of photography, anthropological expeditions to the far corners of the world where cameras were as yet unknown turned up an odd fact: You have to learn to recognize two-dimensional images. When local people were shown photographs of themselves they expressed no interest—because they couldn't recognize their three-dimensional reality in the two-dimensional representation.

Nothing exists in nature without a purpose, with the possible exception of the hungry mosquito on a hot summer's day. So we have to assume that both the conscious and the unconscious mind exist for a reason. What might that reason be? How do the conscious and unconscious mind work together. And how do both of them work with reality to provide us with a fully developed perception of the world around us?

Emanuel Kant made the important distinction 300 years ago, when he wrote about "Das Ding an sich" (things as they are) and "Das Ding fur uns" (things as we know them). They are not the same things. Your sensory equipment picks up signals from the world of "things as they are," but you *process* that information so you can perceive things as you know them to be. And that processing is affected by more than just objectively received sensory signals: Your conscious perception is also influenced by your past experiences. That's just the way your brain works: Everything you perceive must be related to something else in order to make sense.

A Category for Everything, and Everything in Its Category

Your brain *needs* to categorize the information it receives. When it cannot find a familiar category for an experience, it will try to force one upon it: The alternative is often to flee in terror. Witness the experience of a San bushman who was taken on a drive through the plains of the American West. When he saw bison grazing in the distance, he asked, "What kind of insects are those?" His life, spent in the close confines of the forest, gave him no experience by which to judge the vast open perspective of "big sky country." And when the vehicle in which he was riding sped closer to the herd, he was terrified by the magical transformation of those "insects" into huge, shaggy beasts.

Now You See It, Now You Don't

The Gestalt psychologists knew that we could be fooled by what we see, and felt the best way to explore this was through optical illusions. Their experiments showed that your processing systems can be misled by illusion, and that there are some parts of the visual picture that never even reach your brain!

Complete this exercise:

Where you look is what becomes closest to you, perceptually speaking. The object in focus "jumps out" to greet you. Look at this classical Necker cube. Seem flat on first glance? Now look at the line at the top margin. See any square popping out at you? Look at the lower margin line now and notice how it seems to move out from the page to emerge higher, upstaging all the other squares.

Attention also molds the quality of the perceptual landscape. We can only be attentive to or conscious of one primary thing at any time.

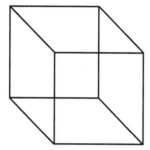

Figure 27.1: The Necker Cube

In addition to the effects of your brain filling in gaps and interpreting your point of focus as closest to you, your mind has all sorts of other tricks with which to customize the sensory data it collects. But, my fellow Einsteins, do not despair. This is not the time to look into the Whole Earth Catalogue and get your brain transplanted into the latest multimodality-sensing unit from Texas Instruments. "Faults" in our nervous systems are like flaws in people, wondrous things that can be converted into useful tools if applied toward innovative ends, once we gain a better understanding of how the "defective" machinery sets its own rules.

Of Two Minds

As if the field of sensory perception weren't complicated enough, it's also now known that we have not one but *two* conscious minds. Neurosurgeon Roger Sperry discovered in the 1960s that the two hemispheres of the brain were good at different things. The left hemisphere was linguistic, analytical, and rational. The right hemisphere is more spatial, holistic, and intuitive. There is some overlap in the functions of the two hemispheres, but the distinction between the left and right brain generally holds true.

When the two parts of the brain do not communicate, it is possible to "talk" to one side of the brain without talking to the other. As we mentioned previously, one patient was asked what he wanted to be when he grew up. The left brain said "a draftsman," and the right brain wanted to be a race car driver! The sides often disagree, and people seem to be in the best moods when the two sides are in accord.

Brain Food

Studies of left brain/right brain function were carried out using "split-brain" patients. These people had severe seizures that would spread from one side of the brain to the other. Surgeons found that by severing the fibers that connected the two sides of the brain, the spread of the seizures could be stopped.

This gives us further inoòght as to how the brain constantly strives to understand reality. In one experiment, a split-brain patient was told to look at a chicken claw with his left brain and a snow scene with his right brain. Each side of the brain was given an additional set of pictures and the patient was asked to pick the one that best matched the scenes. The right brain picked a shovel to match the snow scene; the left brain picked a chicken to match the claw. Remember, neither side knows what the other is doing.

Next, the left brain was asked why it picked the cards. It said "because the claw belongs to a chicken and you need a shovel to clean out the chicken house!" The point: The left brain did not know *why* the shovel was picked because it couldn't see the snow scene. But it *did* know that the shovel had been picked, so it quickly came up with a rationalization for the selection. It *had* to make up a reason in order for things to make sense. It lied to itself for the sake of continuity.

There's an old saying—don't let one hand know what the other is doing. The left and right hemispheres of your brain seem to agree. But when they *do* find out, the left side will surely invent a good cover story!

Definitions of Cerebral Cyberspace

This "cover story" is necessary because new experience is understandable only if it relates to other experiences that you've already had. Each new experience is compared with the ones that have gone before, and it is categorized with the earlier ones that seem to help make it make sense. But by definition, each new experience is unique in some way. Your brain is constantly making comparisons between perceptions and categorizing the result. Sometimes, these syntheses end up in an old familiar category; sometimes, the brain ends up creating a new one.

Mind This!

In many ways, brilliance comes from the ability to see the similarities and differences between things and events, and to then synthesize new approaches or solutions. In many cases, people from outside particular fields of study make the greatest strides forward because they are not limited by formal training and are able to free-associate.

The Role of the Unconscious

The "job" of the unconscious mind is to take information in, sort it out, and prioritize it. The unconscious mind makes the chaos of unprocessed, raw sensory information relatable and handleable. It is the underpaid, overworked Assistant Director on a film set—handling all the details, running all the errands, and generally making life smooth for the director (the conscious mind).

The unconscious mind also "primes" the circuitry of the brain so that once a conscious decision is made, all systems are prepared to go. But the unconscious mind goes beyond this. It often changes the script, the tone of delivery, or the actors. In other words, it adds its own two cents' worth into the interpretation of the data it processes, and does it without letting the conscious mind know what it's doing. It gets away with this because it's much faster than the conscious mind, and it gets first crack at the sensory data, anyway. Sometimes, the unconscious mind will use its faster processing time to take over the whole show.

The capability of the unconscious mind to rapidly assimilate and memorize information is often used by actors in something called the "Italian rehearsal." Here, lines are rehearsed quickly, again

Brain Food

Anyone who has been in a bad car accident has experienced the sensation of "time slowing down." People describe this weird feeling where a few seconds seems like minutes and everything appears as if it is in slow motion. You feel like a bystander as your body goes through the motions. In these situations, the body dances to the tune of the faster subconscious mind.

and again. It keeps going, faster and faster, until the assistant director yells "All quiet on the set!" By the time the director shouts "Action," actors who barely knew their lines and reactions ten minutes before often show perfect execution.

Complete this exercise:

You'll need the cooperation of a friend for this one. Read two pages in a newspaper, very quickly (make sure your helper has a copy, too). Scan; don't outline or try to memorize anything. Now, close the newspaper. After a few minutes, go back and read it again, this time for comprehension, using all your multimodality tricks (saying the words while reading them, underlining key words, highlighting with colored markers, etc.). Finally, read a third article, using the comprehension aids without preliminary scanning. Now, go to sleep and in the morning, call in your friend and have him check your recall of the articles you read. (If it's the same person who's been helping you with all the other exercises, make him breakfast—he deserves it for all the trouble he's gone through for you.) See if there's a difference in how well you recall the information in the three articles. Which approach to reading gave you the best recall?

The Conscious Mind Might Be Smarter, but the Unconscious Mind Is Faster—Who Wins?

Let's consider things synaptically. The longest delay in the transmission of nerve signals usually occurs at the synapse. The more synaptic stops the train has to make, the longer it takes the sensory message to get to final processing station for conversion into some kind of action. As a rule, it takes a greater number of synapses and more processing to bring something to consciousness than it does to accomplish the task at the subconscious level. Consider the eye and its connection to the brain.

The journey from retinal ganglion cell to your secondary association cortex—where the image is finally put together consciously—requires five stops. But the journey from retinal ganglion cell to the brain centers that move the eyes, open or close the iris (altering amount of light that comes in), and change the shape of the lens (changing focal length) requires only *two* synapses. If you had to think about accommodating the pupil and iris to a change in the amount of light, it would take much longer. It is much more efficient to simply let the subconscious take care of it.

So, at least in the case of the visual system, adjustment to the signal at the level of the eye can happen long before the original image is actually seen in your brain. A matter of simple synaptic delays.

But this is not just a numbers game. There seems to be a greater delay in information processing than can be accounted for by the increased number of stops. Lets look at what happens when you are touched. The amount of time it takes a signal traveling along the nervous system to get from the skin to the sensory cortex is 0.02 seconds. The amount of time it takes for you to be aware that you've been touched is about 25 times longer, at 0.50 seconds. The conscious mind is one-half second late in knowing what is happening.

But wait! Does this mean that there's a half-second delay between the time you tap a key on your computer and the time that you register the feeling of the tap? Yes, it does. You'd think you would notice this delayed reaction, wouldn't you? But you don't—and the reason you don't is because of the creative abilities of your mind to alter your perceptions. In effect, your brain fills in the time lag for you, so that you perceive the action and the sensation as happening simultaneously.

How do we know this? Psychological researcher Benjamin Libet measured the time it took for a touch applied to your finger to evoke an electrical response in your brain. It took 0.02 seconds. However, patients were not aware of the stimulus for 0.5 seconds. The action was set up and reacted to before "consciously" thinking about it.

In a whole other area of life, football great Joe Montana has said that he is not conscious while he is playing. Does he mean he is sleeping? No, what he means is that the speed and accuracy required in professional football does not allow time enough for things to become conscious and for decisions to be consciously made. His subconscious takes in the rapidly changing environment, calculates the next move, and executes, all without consulting the conscious mind.

So, we *think* we see things as they happen, but we don't. In fact, you could say that your brain fools you into thinking that you are living in the present when you actually live in the past—the past of at least a half second ago.

There you go! Deja vu all over again.

The Least You Need to Know

➤ Things are not always as they seem to be.

➤ The different sides of the brain have different abilities and different points of view.

➤ Many things you do are done subconsciously—the conscious mind is informed on a need to know basis

➤ We live our conscious lives about one-half second behind the physical world.

Chapter 28

The Unconscious Mind: Who Is Running this Show, Anyway?

In This Chapter

➤ Subliminal messages

➤ Blind men who can see

➤ Decisions can be made subconsciously

➤ How the conscious mind and the subconscious brain can work together to attain maximum effective intelligence

The brain can be thought of as possessing qualities of "fire" and qualities of "form." The conscious mind often deals in form, preferring structure to impulsiveness, slow deliberation to reckless speed. The unconscious mind is often quite the opposite. Most of us seek a balance between the "yes" brain and the "think about it first" mind. But how do these two forces inside us share power?

Is a "natural" quarterback, who says that he plays instead of thinks, better than a thinker who calculates the possibilities consciously before throwing the ball? "Instinct" players and "thinking" players may have different lag-times for awareness, but they still get the ball out before they get sacked. We need both kinds of players, on and off the field. How then, can we make them co-exist in a way that serves us?

The Unconscious Takes It All In

There are messages that talk to the subconscious—and the subconscious alone. We've all heard about the subliminal messages inserted into movies in the 50s and 60s, telling us to buy a certain brand of cola, eat this kind of chocolate, or marry this kind of spouse. Many of us have been kept awake by the language records played by our roommates at college who figure they can go to sleep knowing two words of German and wake up with the ability to understand a Wagnerian opera libretto.

Brain Food

When we see something quickly enough to see it but not analyze it, we not only retain a memory of it, but we usually also associate an attitude with it. In one experiment, people were told brief stories about women with various attributes, the "good" stories being about women with long hair and the "bad" ones about women with short hair. When asked to recall the nature of each woman after the flashcard presentation, the women with long hair were identified as angelic, and those with short hair were called less-than-virtuous.

Subliminal messages are real. Flashing information to subjects at rapid speed (something that also increases arousal level) does go into the memory banks, and in some interesting ways. Very brief subliminal exposure of normal subjects to any item makes that person "like" it, even if *it* is nothing but an impersonal figure.

You know by now that much more is taken in than becomes conscious. In fact, it has been proposed that the main job of the brain is to delete information. That is, to make sure the conscious mind is not overwhelmed.

"OK, OK," you say, "I'll buy the fact that the unconscious mind controls the information that the conscious mind can see. But the conscious mind is the only one that can make decisions based on that information, right?"

Not necessarily.

The Visionaries Who Could Not See

In the 1970s, doctors began taking a closer look at patients who were *cortically blind* on one side.

The experiments went like this. A subject, Joe, was unable to see anything in the left half of his visual field. In other words, he could see the world to the right of his nose, but everything to the left of his nose was black. It would stand to reason, then, that if you placed an object in his left visual field, he wouldn't know it was there.

Mind This!

When a person is cortically blind it means that the visual cortex is damaged. Light is picked up by the eyes and sent to the brain in the normal way, but the brain is not capable of putting together the final picture. As a result, vision does not reach consciousness and the person is functionally blind.

Well, Joe and many other subjects all confirmed that they could not see the object, yet when they were asked whether it was there or not, they all guessed correctly. Not only that, but they could point to it, grab it, and describe its orientation. How could they do this if they couldn't see it?

The answer: They couldn't see it consciously. But the rest of the brain knew it was there. Information about the object was still going through the eyes to other parts of the brain. The only thing wrong with these people is that the conscious picture could not be made. The rest of the brain knew and just went about the business of answering the examiners' questions.

Similarly, people can "guess" the difference in tiny weights placed on their fingertips. They could not consciously tell the difference between the two weights (one was slightly heavier than the other), but they were asked to guess anyway. As it turns out, they guessed correctly most of the time, much more often than that expected by chance. Again, the rest of the brain, the unconscious, could tell, but the difference was not great enough for the conscious mind to be informed.

So, now we know that not only can the subconscious brain take in information and be influenced by subliminal stimuli that the conscious is unaware of, but it can also follow commands and answer questions. But can it make more sophisticated decisions without the help of the conscious mind?

Decisions, Decisions, Decisions

Yes. Let's go back to the story of the car accident from the last chapter and add to it. Suppose you are driving down a street and suddenly a child appears from behind a car. You can't stop in time. You have to make a decision. You can hit the child, veer to the left, and hit an oncoming car head-on, or you can veer to the right and go onto someone's lawn. All this analysis, decision-making, and action has to take place in one second.

And all of this takes place subconsciously. Again, time seems to slow down as the conscious mind watches you veer to the right. The truth is that it simply takes longer to decide on an action than it takes to react unconsciously to a stimulus.

This shows that we can react to something that we are never conscious of. More than that, we can make decisions that never reach consciousness.

In fact, a number of skills we use in everyday life are not conscious when we use them. Through training and practice, we often develop automatic processes that we perform best when we are unaware of them. Our conscious minds control the learning of these skills, but not their performance.

Brain Food

There are even more common illustrations of the role of the unconscious in making complex decisions. Have you ever been driving alone and then suddenly realized that you made a series of turns taking you to your old school or old apartment? Often, you have no conscious recollection of getting to where you are. Who was driving?

We all have had this experience when learning a new task. At first we are awkward, slow, and confused. Then, suddenly one day, something happens and we can perform the task. We really sense no conscious change; we are just suddenly able to do it! Our subconscious has taken over, and often we do best with this new task when we stop thinking about it and let it go on automatically, while the conscious mind turns its attention to something else.

Therefore, it is clear that we not conscious of very much of the information we take in with our sense organs. In fact, people are only conscious of a very small part of the complex thought process behind their actions, and often even unaware of the actions themselves. People are primarily unconscious beings. This explains the feeling we all get of being more than ourselves; of fighting off urges that seem to come from nowhere. We have met the enemy, and often it is us.

Advanced Decision Making

Our conscious minds always want to control the situation, which sometimes leads to discord. But when the two minds act in concert, magic can happen. Perhaps the best illustration of this is in artistic performance. In acting, the conscious mind utters the words but allows the unconscious mind the freedom to express itself non-verbally. When the verbal and body language match, we have the makings of a convincing performance. But when the conscious mind does not trust the body, when we try to control the whole performance consciously, we have a show riddled with awkwardness and hesitation.

Brain Food

All of us have had situations when we were "in the zone." Things were just zooming along famously, but we're not sure where all this talent was coming from. Think back and you'll discover that these situations probably did not involve a great deal of conscious thought. You just "let yourself go" and enjoyed the experience. Answers just seemed to spring up from nowhere. This is the unconscious at its best.

Perhaps this is even easier to see in musical performance. In music, we often hear of musicians wanting to be "one with their instrument," letting their fingers do the talking. They sit there with eyes closed, swaying with the rhythm, the conscious mind just going along for the ride. The virtuoso performers manage this feat. The merely "technically correct" do not.

Performers learn to trust their unconscious through training. At first, training is directed by the conscious mind, but surprises then begin to happen as the motor programs begin to develop. Things start to happen automatically. Soon, the conscious mind learns to trust that these things can be handled unconsciously and turns its attention to other things.

But the conscious and unconscious minds do not always think alike. For example, suppose you have decided to lose weight or to be more punctual. You've thought these things out carefully, made lists of the positive and negative aspects of each decision, and agreed with yourself that this was the proper course.

The next day, you find yourself late for work because you stopped to have a second piece of pie. Why? The problem lies in the relationship between the conscious mind and the unconscious brain. They have two very different "personalities." The unconscious brain is unpredictable, disorderly, willful, and quick. The conscious mind strives for order; it possesses the power of language, and can make agreements with other conscious minds and with itself. But the unconscious mind often has difficulties abiding by these agreements. It "sees" a different reality, certainly one based on more data, and may develop different goals. Often, it would rather have the pie.

All of us have experienced this battle between what we know consciously we ought to do and what our bodies want us to do. Nevertheless, the whole fabric of society, the notion of personal responsibility, is based on the fact that the conscious mind is responsible for the behavior of both itself and the unconscious mind—for the behavior of the whole person.

So, if so much of our life is unconscious, and actions can be initiated and implemented without involving consciousness, where does that leave free will? Do we not have control of our actions?

Free Will

We all know that although we may feel a nearly irresistible urge to eat that cake or hit our boss over the head with a hammer, we can choose to resist it. It is our conscious brain that does the choosing. Yes, although man's life is lived more in the unconscious world than the conscious, ultimately it is his conscious mind that makes him human. The ability to choose, to veto certain urges, and to nurture and direct others is what makes us capable of responsible action. Our life is determined by the workings of our entire brain.

Even with these differences, we can train the conscious and unconscious minds and perhaps we can teach them to be more alike. Imagine a conscious mind that works faster and that is open to all possibilities. Envision an unconscious mind that doesn't make you the slave to any urge that pops into your head.

Complete this exercise:

List ten activities that you consider important. After doing that, rate your success at each activity on a scale of 1 to 10. Are the unsuccessful endeavors more often associated with more impulsiveness? In those you do not do as well, do you ram on ahead at full speed with too little thinking? Does your demand for logical thought sometimes slow some of these activities down or make them less effective? Can you change the mode by which you conduct these functions?

Effective Intelligence

So, effective intelligence demands that we strike a balance between the conscious and non-conscious world. Effective intelligence pervades every well-played piece of music. But is it because the notes are written according to correct structure or because simple notes are played with a range of intense emotions? The answer is obvious. The complexity of a Beethoven symphony or a Bach Brandenburg concerto is a work of art. But have these works played by a lifeless orchestra that brings no emotion into the endeavor and you empty the house out real fast. On the other end of the spectrum, try listening to a blues guitarist who knows only three chords or a singer who puts 100% emotion into notes that are way off-key. Again, a no-go.

The trial-and-error of effective intelligence uses the entire brain. Most data collection and processing is done by the unconscious mind. Perceptions are created and analyses of these perceptions in light of past experiences are done consciously. Goals are developed and orders issued that direct the workings of the unconscious mind again as we talk back to the world both verbally and non-verbally. The cycle is continuously repeated by this unruly team as we inch closer and closer to attaining our goals and realize the magic that is human existence.

The Least You Need to Know

➤ Subliminal messages can be taken in without conscious awareness.

➤ Your subconscious brain can make its own decisions.

➤ The conscious mind has ultimate control.

➤ The conscious mind and subconscious brain must work together to maximize your effective intelligence.

Chapter 29

Just Follow These Simple Rules

In This Chapter

➤ A review of effective intelligence

➤ A look at passion

➤ Personal changes that come with becoming more intelligent

In this book, we explored the range of ways available to us to increase our effective intelligence. We talked about how intelligence is about more than just book-learning or solving logic puzzles, and how it has a very practical application as well. The goal was to show that we can all be Einsteins: in the kitchen, the tool shop, the operating room, the bedroom, the boardroom, the stage, the podium, and out on the open range (for you cowboys out there, reading this on the back of your favorite horse).

Even sitting in your favorite chair, reading this book, has been an exercise in increasing your effective intelligence—not just because you may have learned a few new things, but because you have been using the neurological equipment of your brain. Every time you give those synapses of yours a workout, you're increasing your brainpower. Like our friend Andy Aplysia, you're even adding to and improving upon the wiring you've already got.

But before we come to the parting of our ways, each to travel our own road up Mount Intelligentsia, one brief review is in order.

Intelligence: "To Apprehend the Presented Facts to Guide Action Toward a Desired Goal"

We began this book with the following definition of the word "intelligence": "The apprehension of presented facts in such a way as to guide action towards a desired goal." Most people accept the first part of that definition: In the general view, intelligence is all about *knowing* things. Knowing the answers to the questions on a test. Knowing what's in all the heavy books on the shelves of a university library. But that's only part of the story.

"To apprehend the presented facts..." True intelligence means not only *knowing*, but also *knowing how*. Having a whole slew of factoids rattling around in your brain is useless if you don't have any way to put them to effective use. But that's where this book comes in. Its aim is to give you methods that allow you to improve your abilities in both parts of the definition: apprehension and action.

Understanding the Hardware

You literally change your brain when you learn. Axons sprout, new synapses form, connections get more complex, and there is even a selective discontinuation of circuits you *don't* need so that you can build those you *do*. If you take charge of the way you learn, you have some control over the kinds of new connections, capabilities, and systems you develop in your brain. You can literally streamline your learning process so that it more effectively contributes toward achieving your goals.

Your neural systems gather information from the environment around you—from books, from visual images, from sensations of heat and cold, smell, and sound. All these systems can be sharpened at the *physical* level: You can train yourself to see more, to attend more closely to the sounds around you, to *apprehend* greater detail in the world you live in. And that serves to increase the amount of information available to your brain.

Rewriting the Software

But it's not just building and reinforcing your neurological hardware that can improve your effectiveness in apprehending the world around you. There's the "software" to work on, as well. That means understanding the way in which your brain *interprets* the sensory data that you learn. You now know that your brain customizes the input it receives—filling in a gap here, making associations there, all in order to make sense of the information it takes in.

Even here, where your unconscious mind takes charge, there are techniques that let you take some control over the process. Knowing the way your brain imposes a sense of order on your sensory world means you can *work with* the process instead of just letting it happen. When you realize that your past experiences provide the framework

248

for your current interpretation of sensory data, you can take steps to understand that past experience, deal with it, and make sure that it's not getting in the way of developing full effective intelligence. If old patterns of association are forcing your perceptions of the world into non-constructive directions, you can work to change them.

The first part of the definition of intelligence, then, the part that has to do with apprehension, allows you many opportunities to increase your effective brainpower. But still, that's not the whole story.

"...to guide action..." Knowledge alone—apprehension alone—is not enough to constitute effective intelligence. You need to be able to *do* something with what you know. How many times have you remarked upon a "brilliant" person—with lots of book learning and advanced degrees—who doesn't seem to have a clue about how to get along in the real world? That person has accumulated a great deal of information, but has made no effort to take charge of what he or she knows in order to use it effectively.

Your brain has a natural need to impose order on the universe that it apprehends, and it tends to use what it knows in order to get things done. It is not, by nature, a passive organ. So if you don't tell it where you want to get from here, it will make plans on its own. Left to its own devices, your brain's plans are likely to be heavily influenced by your unconscious mind and its concerns—especially because it is so much quicker on the uptake than your conscious mind—but your unconscious mind's plans may not be the same as your conscious ones. In fact, they might even be contradictory to what you consciously want to achieve.

Guidance is an active term—it implies that something is taking charge of how things turn out. You have a choice: You can leave your unconscious in charge or you can learn to exercise more direct control. By learning how your brain defines the world in its own terms, you can begin to set the terms that it recognizes. Improving your intelligence is an *active* process.

Mind This!

The way to do this is to train yourself to attend more closely to the world around you, to constantly reorient your attention when confronted by obstacles, to practice effective decision-making, to act on those decisions, and to evaluate—and re-evaluate—the results of those decisions. In other words, use the triad of effective intelligence.

"...toward a desired goal..." Information gathering and processing is something that largely occurs in the brain. But when you start taking on the task of *acting* on that information, you move into a whole-body experience. Your brain has two main mechanisms through which it puts its decisions into action: speech and movement. These, too, are areas in which you can take positive steps to improve your effectiveness. In fact, if you don't, you're like that "brilliant" fellow we referred to before, the one who knows a lot but can't do anything with that knowledge.

It is through action that you, like all of us, move the external world. Through action you can stir things up, make your mark, and provide your brain with the experience and feedback it needs to make decisions—and to make the *next* set of decisions even better. Any action—well-planned or simply a reflex—provides you with *some* experience and feedback. And it's almost always better than taking no action at all. So any time you've set yourself a goal, but aren't sure just how to begin to make it happen, begin by *doing something.*

But random action isn't particularly effective. For effective action, as for effective intelligence, you want to remember that guidance is important. Your brain specializes in *directed action.* Directed toward what? Directed toward goals. And *you* get to choose the goal! You're the one who ultimately calls the shots when it comes to choosing where you want to go in life: a corner office at the company, a career in stand-up, a higher score on the Mensa test—anything you can conceive of, you can make plans to achieve.

Brain Food

Becoming more intelligent is the act of becoming more effective at reaching your goals. As you reach goal after goal, you will begin to expand your choices in life. You'll begin to consider a greater variety of possibilities. Your self-image will change and the boundaries of your world will expand. Chances are, this process will lead you down roads you didn't even know existed.

And there are techniques that will improve your ability to enlist your brain in the process of directing your actions towards your goals. These techniques focus on developing your powers of imagination. That makes sense, when you think about it: Goals exist in the future—if they were in your present, you wouldn't have to work to achieve them. So the best brain hardware in the world, coupled with the most highly developed processing software, can't perceive goals the way they can perceive "I'm cold," or "That smells funny."

You enlist your brain's cooperation in striving for your goals by learning what are generally known as "visualization" techniques. You make your brain perceive your as-yet-unattained goals by *imagining* them. Because your brain is no stranger to manipulating its inputs from reality, and because it doesn't differentiate between a "real" thought and an imagined concept, it will happily work with you as long as you provide it with a vividly visualized goal. The best way to improve your skills in this area? Daydream. And do it often.

Choose Your Passion!

Whatever you choose to do in life, effective intelligence dictates that you define it clearly. But that's *still* not enough. You need also to be passionate about it. Although our brains are marvelous mechanisms for thinking and doing, they tend to avoid change. It's that old law of inertia from Physics 101. To counteract the tendency to avoid the unsettling feelings that go with change, nothing beats passion. And even here, you have room to improve your effectiveness.

Complete this exercise:

Write down at least ten things you want to do or experience before you die. Be as specific as possible: Don't just write "take a trip," for example, but rather write "spend a month traveling by freighter on the Arctic Ocean during the Northern Lights display." Prioritize the list and post it on every wall of your house and office, on your bathroom mirror where you'll see it every morning, and on the ceiling above the chair where you tend to flop down and lean back to contemplate what you're going to do with your life. Over time, the items on the list will become a part of your daily consciousness. You'll find that even in your sleep, your mind is working away at how it might go about making those goals a reality.

It's a fact: Without goals, you're like a boat without a rudder. You tend to just drift along, passively experiencing daily life with nothing to look forward to. And don't worry that, once you set a goal, you're locked into it—goals change, all the time, as we go through life gathering more and more experiences. That's not to say that you should change your goals as often as you change your shirt—shifting from goal to goal to goal all the time means never making any constructive progress to achieving any one of them. What you're aiming for here is flexibility, yes, but consistency as well.

Now you're ready to crank up your effective intelligence. Find that something that really stirs you—travel, education, a career-making change—anything that really turns you on. Then begin taking actions that consistently move you toward that goal. Reread this book and apply its principles. You'll be humming along in no time. But there is one other thing to keep in mind: Even your capacity for passion can be made more effective.

Who Do You Need to Become to Feed Your Passion?

The wonderful thing about effective intelligence is that it not only helps you realize your goals, it also makes positive changes in who you are and who you can be, every step of the way. Day by day, month by month, as you progress on your journey, you change. "Without science, spirituality is blind. Without spirituality, science is lame," warned Einstein. But he wasn't just talking about going to church on Sunday. Einstein was talking about the two worlds: science and art. Or "head and heart." The world of our emotions is as important to our effective intelligence as the world of sensory input—you need a healthy emotional life to keep your passions alive.

Mind This!

Take your list of goals and, for each one, describe the type of person you must become to achieve that goal. Develop a list of traits and qualities you must have in order to get there. These goals are every bit as important as the list of things you want to do or experience— maybe even more so. Working to develop these traits and qualities will bring you closer to achieving your goals, and will bring untold richness both to you and to those around you.

Visualize yourself as a more effective, responsible, and loving person. Believe it or not, these are attributes that will go a long way to helping you achieve even the most pragmatic of goals. And don't let the idea of constant growth and change put you off— you'll find out that it's a wonderful way to live, and one that will send you straight to the top of whatever goals or achievements you hope to attain. Finally, don't believe that old saying "It's lonely at the top." You'll soon find out that there is one heck of a party going on up there. A place at the table is still open for you. See you there!!!

The Least You Need to Know

➤ Effective intelligence is a natural process and one that you can improve with practice.

➤ The brain is always striving to become more intelligent.

➤ You must be passionate about your goals.

➤ Effective intelligence means growth; growth means change; know who you need to become to get where you want to go.

➤ Don't forget to use the triad of effective intelligence: Make decisions, act on them, and evaluate the results for future decisions.

Glossary

Action Potential: Wave of depolarization that spreads down an axon, usually in one direction only.

Afferent: Term referring to nerve fibers that send sensory information from the body/environment into the central nervous system.

Autonomic Nervous System: Efferent system dealing with "involuntary" functions, divided into the sympathetic and parasympathetic nervous systems.

Axon: The shaft of a neuron that extends from the cell body outward to where a neurotransmitter is released or to where signals from the environment are being detected.

Axonal Regeneration: Process by which an axon grows from the traumatized area after it has been cut or crushed.

Axonal Sprouting: Process by which axons that are not cut or crushed extend extra branches outward to fill in connection points left vacant by axons that have degenerated.

Blood-Brain Barrier: A structural and functional barrier between blood in capillaries and brain tissue that prevents many materials in the blood from getting to brain tissue, and vice versa.

Central Nervous System: The brain, spinal cord, and optic nerve.

Cerebrospinal Fluid (CSF): Shock-absorbing fluid that surrounds the brain and spinal cord, keeping them from caving in and crashing into the skull and/or vertebrae.

Dendrites: Branches extending off the neuronal soma that receive electrical input from axons originating from other axons.

Depolarization: Process whereby a biological membrane becomes less polarized electrically, usually leading to neurotransmitter release or more action potentials.

Efferent: Term referring to nerve fibers that send motor impulses from the central nervous system out to the body, usually to a skeletal muscle.

Excitatory Neurotransmitter: A neurotransmitter that causes depolarization at the other side of the synapse, where it is released.

Ganglia: Collection of adjacent neuronal cell bodies in the peripheral nervous system.

Glial Cells: Cells in the central nervous system, other than neurons, which have specific functions. For instance, astrocytes maintain the blood-brain barrier, elaborate space-filling scars after injury, and take up excess neurotransmitter and potassium. Oligodendrocytes make myelin, needed for rapid conduction in CNS tracts.

Gray Matter: Parts of the central nervous system not occupied by myelin or myelinated fibers.

Hormone: Substance that is released in one location in the body and has to be transported by the circulatory system (bloodstream) to the place where it has a biological effect.

Hyperpolarization: Process whereby a biological membrane becomes more polarized electrically, usually leading to less neurotransmitter release or fewer action potentials.

Inhibitory Neurotransmitter: Neurotransmitter that causes hyperpolarization of the membrane at the other side of the synapse.

Interneurons: Small neurons that lie between sensory and motor fibers, particularly in the spinal cord, brainstem, and cerebral cortex.

Motor: Refers to fibers or processing centers that send impulses from the central nervous system outward to the body, where physical changes are implemented.

Myelin: Multiple whirl of membranes from Schwann cells or oligodendrocytes that insulate axons and make them conduct action potentials faster.

Nerve: A bundle of axons in the peripheral nervous system.

Neuropathy: A disease in which the functional and structural integrity of axons in the central or peripheral nervous system is deleteriously affected.

Neurotransmitter: A substance released from an axon terminal following activation by an action potential. The release has a biological effect on the cell on the other side of the synapse.

Nucleus: Collection of adjacent neuronal cell bodies in the central nervous system.

Parasympathetic Nervous System: The "keep the home front going and calm" branch of the autonomic nervous system.

Peripheral Nervous System: Any nervous system tissue outside the brain, spinal cord, and optic nerve.

Receptor: A specific receptor molecule (usually a protein) on a biological membrane, which binds to a specific signaling molecule (neurotransmitter and/or hormone). This union produces a biological effect on the cell where the binding happens.

Schwann Cells: "Glial" cells in the peripheral nervous system that surround axons, make myelin, and promote axonal elongation after nerve injury.

Sensory: Refers to a fiber or processing area that takes in information from the environment and sends it toward the cerebral cortex.

Soma: The cell body of the neuron, the location where protein synthesis and genetic expression happens.

Somatic Nervous System: The "voluntary" nervous system, connected to skeletal muscles.

Synapse: Small space between an axon and a dendrite, or some other kind of target tissue.

Sympathetic Nervous System: The "arousal" branch of the autonomic nervous system.

Tract: Bundle of axons in the central nervous system.

Vesicle: Small "bag" inside the axon and/or axon terminal that may contain neurotransmitters.

White Matter: Areas of the central nervous system that contain myelinated fibers.

Index